LES COLLECTIONS PRIVÉES

Approches historiques et juridiques

Collection Droit du patrimoine culturel et naturel
dirigée par Marie Cornu et Jérôme Fromageau

Cette collection, initiée par le Centre de recherche « Droit du patrimoine culturel et naturel » a pour but de développer et enrichir la réflexion sur les objets et modes de protection dans le domaine du patrimoine culturel et naturel. Les questions que soulèvent la conservation, la circulation, la valorisation du patrimoine sollicitent, en effet, ces deux disciplines. Le contexte d'un monument historique, son environnement, le paysage dans lequel il s'inscrit sont souvent essentiels à sa mise en valeur. Le droit de la culture et le droit de l'environnement développent cependant des concepts propres. Ils ne sont pas toujours en accord sur les méthodes et les moyens de protection, d'où l'intérêt de la confrontation et de la comparaison des ressources tirées de ces deux dispositifs.

C'est pourquoi la réflexion doit se renouveler sur les concepts fondamentaux du patrimoine, sur la délimitation des éléments qui méritent protection. Dans la compréhension des différents mécanismes et l'ouverture vers de nouveaux modèles, le droit comparé est essentiel, ainsi que le droit international.

Derniers ouvrages parus

Perrine MARX, *La place de la création contemporaine dans la fabrique urbaine. État des lieux juridique de l'initiative artistique dans la ville*, 2021.

Mylène LE ROUX (sous la direction de), *La reconversion du patrimoine public monumental. L'exemple du Grand Hôtel-Dieu de Lyon*, 2020.

Guillaume LAMBERT, *Blanchiment et marché de l'art. Le droit et la pratique*, 2020.

Solène GRANDJEAN, *La forêt et le droit. La définition de la forêt en droit français*, 2020.

Agathe LAGAUCHE, *Les musées de France à l'heure de la métropolisation*, 2019.

Nathalie BETTIO, Pierre-Alain COLLOT (sous la direction de), *Le financement privé du patrimoine culturel*, 2018.

Inès LAMOURI, *Les ensembles décoratifs en droit. Enjeux juridiques de la protection patrimoniale des meubles et des immeubles formant une cohérence d'ensemble,* 2018.

Géraldine GOFFAUX CALLEBAUT (sous la direction de), *Éthique et patrimoine culturel. Regards croisés*, 2016.

Sophie MONNIER, Karen FIORENTINO (sous la direction de), *Les archives hospitalières. Regards croisés*, 2016.

MARIE-CHRISTINE PIATTI, ALEXANDRE QUIQUEREZ (sous la direction de), *L'accès aux biens culturels. Quel(s) défi(s) pour le droit ?,* 2016.

MARIE CORNU, JEROME FROMAGEAU, YANN POTIN (sous la direction de), *Les archives et la genèse des lois*, 2016.

Sous la direction de
Marie Cornu et Jérôme Fromageau

LES COLLECTIONS PRIVÉES

Approches historiques et juridiques

L'Harmattan

Cet ouvrage est issu du colloque organisé par UNIDROIT, l'ISCHAL, l'Institut des sciences sociales du politique (CNRS, ENS de Paris-Saclay, Université Paris-Nanterre) et le cabinet BonelliErede
Avec le soutien de l'Università Degli Studi di Milano, du centre de droit de l'art de Genève et des Instituts IDEP et IEDP de l'Université Paris-Saclay
16-17 mars 2017
Rome

5-7, rue de l'École-Polytechnique, 75005 Paris

www.editions-harmattan.fr

ISBN : 978-2-343-23330-7
EAN : 9782343233307

Avant-propos

Jérôme FROMAGEAU
Président de l'ISCHAL

Les contributions réunies dans cet ouvrage ont été présentées lors de deux journées d'études consacrées aux approches historique et juridique des collections privées organisées les 16 et 17 mars 2019 à Rome, sur une l'initiative conjointe d'UNIDROIT, de l'ISCHAL (Société Internationale pour la recherche en droit du patrimoine culturel et droit de l'art), avec le soutien de l'Institut des Sciences du politique (École Normale Supérieure de Paris-Saclay, CNRS, Université Paris-Nanterre), de l'Università Degli Studi di Milano, du cabinet BonelliErede de Milan et des Instituts IDEP (Institut Droit Éthique Patrimoine) et IEDP (Institut d'Études de Droit Public) de l'Université Paris-Saclay.

Il convient de remercier tout particulièrement, d'une part, le Professeur Jorge Sánchez Cordero qui est à l'origine de ces journées, et, d'autre part, Marina Schneider qui, avec son équipe a fait plus que nous accueillir, contribuant ainsi à la réussite de cette manifestation dans ces lieux chargés d'histoire. En effet, la Villa Aldobrandini, qui héberge UNIDROIT depuis 1929, fut à la fin du XVIe et au début du XVIIe siècles, la demeure d'un grand collectionneur, le cardinal Pietro Aldobrandi, cardinal camerlingue, fin diplomate. Et comme il s'agit ici d'un colloque consacré aux collections privées rappelons que Pietro Aldobrandi fut un des plus grands collectionneurs européens du tout début XVIIe siècle. En effet, c'est ici, dans ce vénérable édifice somptueusement décoré, qu'il constitua sa très riche collection d'œuvres d'art. Ce grand mécène y exposait en alternance une centaine de tapisseries historiées dont les célèbres séries de Saint-Paul et de l'Histoire de Troie mais aussi des antiquités de la Rome républicaine et impériale, de nombreux tableaux et sculptures des principaux artistes italiens dont Giovani Bellini, Correggio, Giorgione, Leonardo, Mantegna, le Tintoret, le Titien, Véronèse… autant de chefs-d'œuvre qui sont aujourd'hui, pour la plupart, exposés dans les grands musées d'Europe et d'Amérique du nord.

La grande diversité des législations relatives aux collections d'art privées explique pour beaucoup les difficultés qu'il convient de surmonter pour en proposer une synthèse comparative aussi limpide que possible, exercice d'autant plus difficile qu'il n'y a pas de règles communes concernant ces collections. Par le passé comme aujourd'hui, celles-ci peuvent être considérées comme l'antichambre des musées. Et les mécanismes acquisitifs sont finalement assez semblables, les objectifs de conservation et de transmission obéissent à des logiques voisines. Comparer le collectionnisme privé et le collectionnisme public c'est, d'une certaine façon, faire une histoire de leurs rapprochements et éloignements. En effet, les collections privées s'ouvrent très souvent au public sous une forme muséale, les objets sont mis à disposition des institutions publiques par le biais de prêts à plus ou moins long terme, de dépôts, voire, de manière définitive, sont transmis par des dons et legs. Les collections publiques dépendent toujours plus étroitement du dynamisme du secteur privé pour pouvoir continuer à assumer leurs missions, ce qui explique finalement le caractère ténu de la distinction entre collectionnismes public et privé.

SOMMAIRE

Avant-propos, Jérôme Fromageau 5
Sommaire 7

CONSTITUTION DES COLLECTIONS PRIVÉES

Sous la présidence de Jorge Sánchez Cordero

The private art collections. The challenges, Jorge Sánchez Cordero 11
Les collections privées en France au XVIIIe siècle : une approche méthodologique, Patrick Michel 35
Collectionnisme public et privé en comparaison, Antoinette Maget Dominicé 61
La collection source de savoir : les figures du collectionneur « scientifique » en histoire naturelle, Michel Van Praët 77
National laws on private collections: problems and solution, Elina N. Moustaira 93

LA PROTECTION PUBLIQUE DES COLLECTIONS PRIVÉES

Sous la présidence de Marina Schneider

La notion de collection en droit français, Mathilde Roellinger 109
The notion of private collection and its protection from an Italian perspective, Manlio Frigo 119
La protection publique des collections privées, Marie Cornu 127

MISES EN VALEUR ET ACCESSIBILITÉ DES COLLECTIONS

Sous la présidence de Manlio Frigo

L'accessibilité publique des collections privées, Marc-André Renold 143
Interactions entre collections privées et secteur privé. Approche de droit français, Géraldine Goffaux Callebaut 161
Enrichissement des collections publiques avec transfert de propriété (dons et legs), Apolline Sans 173
Les archives privées, Stéphane Duroy 187

Acquérir, documenter, intéresser, publier : les missions du conservateur à la Fondation Gandur pour l'Art, Jean-Claude Gandur & Isabelle Tassignon 203
La fiscalité française favorise-t-elle l'accès aux collections privées ?, Armelle Verjat,.. 215

I

Constitution des collections privées

Sous la présidence de Jorge Sánchez Cordero

The private art collections
The challenges

Jorge Sánchez CORDERO
PhD Université Panthéon-Assas
Director of the Mexican Center of Uniform Law
Vice President of the International Academy of Comparative Law
Member of the Governing Council of UNIDROIT)

I. Introduction

Collecting is a practice inherent to our human nature. In their seminal work, John Elsner and Roger Cardinal[1] mentioned the biblical character Noah to be the first 'collector'[2]. This first human collection "turned to be the first bastion against the deluge of time"[3]. But Noah, obeying a divine mandate, was able to assemble in the legendary Ark all of God's creatures because they had been previously classified, as a collection so to say, by Adan. The symbiosis of classification and collections became incontrovertible; the taxonomy makes collections a feasible concept and the brisk nature of humans collecting has been a catalyst of classification. In Elsner´s and Cardinal´s words:
"Classification is the mirror of collective humanity's thoughts and perceptions, then collecting is its material embodiment...the history of collecting is thus the narrative of how human beings have striven to accommodate, to appropriate and to extend the taxonomies and systems of knowledge they have inherited."[4]

It is nevertheless difficult to trace the origin of the notion of collections. It is perhaps precisely in the religious realm that the first recognizable traces of collecting can be found. The great canonical collections with their architectural heritage, *deus ex machina*, witnessed the power of the Church, who imposed the exultation of the faith[5]. Moreover, the

[1] Genesis, 6.19-20.
[2] Elsner, John and Roger Cardinal, Editors, *The Cultures of Collecting,* Reaktion Books, London, Reprinted 1997, p. 1.
[3] *Ibidem, op. cit., supra,* note 2, p. 1.
[4] *Ibidem, op. cit., supra,* note 2, p. 1.
[5] *Ibidem, op. cit., supra,* note 2, p. 4.

religious rhetoric dictated the aesthetic canon and created the fundamentals of Western art. In this context, it can be acknowledged that one of the first Christian collections belonged to the Duke of Berry; the nucleus of this collection was religious relics. Another aristocrat, the Duke of Urbin, was known to assemble one of the most important collections of Christian books[6].

As the art of collecting spread through Europe, the painting of portraits quickly became commonplace in the elite societies. At the end of the XV century, everybody in Europe knew the great names of the painters hired by prominent people in their societies to paint mostly portraits, which enriched the different art collections. The Medici's proclivity to foster and collect art is frequently cited as something unprecedented in this field.

Decades later, at the decadence of Florence, the imperial city of Augsburg in Bavaria, Germany, blossomed as a famous art center, this largely attributed to the bankers and brothers Antoine and Ulrich Fugger, following the Medici family tradition[7]. The Habsburg collection was one of the oldest and most prestigious European collections. It started in the XIII century and ended with the collapse of the Austro-Hungarian Empire after the Great War at the outset of the XX century. It included not only art works, but documents, symbols, insignia and regalia, among other cultural objects[8].

It is precisely in this age where new features entered into the art markets and started to pose new queries in the scaffolding of collections. Were these new features suitable to be collectable? It was the encountering of two worlds -the European and the Indies- introduced new and appealing features into the European art market. These novelties attracted European collectors. Francesco I as Grand Duke of Tuscany displayed his collection for the public in the newly built Uffizi Palace in Florence in 1570. The Florentine Mannerist Ludovico Buti, at the request of Ferdinand I de Medici, painted in 1588 the ceiling in the Uffizi's

---

[6] Rheims, Maurice, *Les Collectionneurs. De la curiosité, de la beauté, du goût, de la mode et de la spéculation,* présenté par Michel Tournier, Éditions Ramsay, 1981, Paris, p. 35.

[7] *Ibid., op. cit., supra,* note 6, p. 52.

[8] Dacosta Kaufmann, Thomas, *From treasury to Museum: The Collection of the Austrian Habsburgs. In* Elsner, John and Roger Cardinal, *op. cit., supra,* note 2, p. 137.

Armory with allegories of indigenous noblemen, surrounded by tropical and exotic birds; other frescoes illustrated the conquest of Mexico and battles between Pagans and Christians[9]. He even constructed a natural history museum as a center of teaching and research[10].
The interest of the Indies diminished very rapidly, mostly governed by theological debates. The Conquistadors were determined by aesthetic canons inherited from medieval perceptions and they dismissed all materials or artefacts not valued in Europe. The Spaniard's mind-set was commended by these medieval categories impregnated by religious ideology, such as divine revelation and the discourse of the origins. Paganism was the leading category of classification and any cultural practices and features were relevant only as evidence of Paganism's existence. Through these lenses the Conquistadors translated indigenous symbolic values of artefacts into European chrematistic values[11]. In 1577, a Spanish Royal Decree prohibited the clergy to make any further compilations of indigenous customs and made the export of cultural features a strictly prohibited practice. Under this rule, few items travelled to Europe, and those that did went mostly to Italy through clandestine channels.
In sum, the cultural material coming from the New World never constituted a collection in technical terms. Under Castilian legislation - the corpus juris with the Siete Partidas of Alfonso X The Wise, enforced in the Indies- all the new lands and indigenous monuments belonged to the Spanish Crown, which lacked a policy of collecting and preserving the antiquities[12]. The features coming as booty or gifts were diffused all over Europe with an unpredictable future; the British Museum, through auctions and bequests, was one of the major receptacles of these items. These arguments constituted the fundamentals of Eurocentrism in the art market.
In the XVII century, it was in the Netherlands where the most conspicuous collectors could be found. At the end of the XVIII century, between 1790 and 1830, the wars and revolutions discouraged the building of private collections[13]. Krsystof Pomian[14] cited that the

[9] Shelton, Anthony Alan, *Renaissance Collections and the New World. In* Elsner, John and Roger Cardinal, *op. cit., supra,* note 2, p. 189.
[10] *Ibid., op. cit. In* Elsner, John and Roger Cardinal, *op. cit., supra,* note 2, p. 188.
[11] *Ibid., op. cit. In* Elsner, John and Roger Cardinal, *op. cit., supra,* note 2, p. 199.
[12] *Ibid., op. cit. In* Elsner, John and Roger Cardinal, *op. cit.*, p. 199.
[13] Rheims, Maurice, *op. cit., supra,* note 6, p. 39.
[14] Pomian, Krzystof, *Collectionneurs, amateurs, curieux : Paris-Venise, XVI*^e^*-XVIII*^e^

Dutchman Hubertus Goltzius had listed 968 collections to be found in the Netherlands, Germany, Austria, Switzerland, France and Italy; another collector, the Frenchman Pierre Borel, knew of 63 collections in France and 70 in Venice[15].

The French collectors suggested a whole new approach to collecting and classification. They suggested an encyclopedic approach towards art collections, one for deepening knowledge and aiding the search for the nature of the universe. This new approach spread throughout Europe, with Italy being a repository of these ideas. In this context, Cosimo I de Medici founded the Accademia del Cimento, where Mexican plants were cultivated and their use in medicine encouraged.

It is in this age that, with this new approach and following, the Medici´s tradition started the interest in collecting the cultural objects of the New World. It is worth mentioning that the appendix penned by Lorenzo Pignorini in the Vincenzo Cartari's book Lo vero e nove imagini degli dei delli antichi[16], published in 1615, became very popular. This book encouraged a comparative approach between Mexican, Japanese and Chinese mythology.

Still in Italy, guided by this encyclopedic approach, the illustrious Aldrovandi collection in the University of Bologna was exploited for scientific purposes. The results are found in the Museum metallicum catalogue[17]. In this realm, the interaction of private and public collection was also recognizable. Aldrovandi donated his collection to the Senate of Bologna in 1603 and in the sixteenth century, two of the sixteen leading galleries of pictures in Milan belonged to the government. This attitude was attributed "to the expression of the worthiness of an individual life. Private biography was thereby magnified and projected through public exhibition."[18]

As stated by Antoinette Maget, with the Enlightenment continued the tradition of collecting, but the exchange of knowledge was substantially modified and new institutions emerged across all of Europe[19].

---

siècles, Paris, Gallimard, 1987, p. 30.

[15] *Ibidem, op. cit., supra,* note 14, p. 31.

[16] Cited in Shelton, Anthony Alan, *Renaissance Collections and the New World, op. cit., supra,* note 9. *In* Elsner, John and Roger Cardinal, *op. cit.,* p. 184.

[17] Shelton, Anthony Alan, *Renaissance Collections and the New World*, *op. cit., supra*, note 9. *In* Elsner, John and Roger Cardinal, *op. cit.*, p. 186.

[18] *Ibid., op. cit. In* Elsner, John and Roger Cardinal, *op. cit., supra*, note 2, p. 186.

[19] Maget, Antoinette, *Collectionnisme Public et Conscience Patrimoniale,* collection *Droit du Patrimoine culturel et naturel,* L'Harmattan, Paris, 2008, p. 21.

Emanuelle Teasauro, one of the distinguished museographers of the XVII century, expressed it in his words: "all natural objects contained their own particular allusion to specific ideas…if nature speaks through such metaphors then the encyclopedic collection, which is the sum of all possible metaphors, logically becomes the great metaphor of the world."

During the XIX century, private collectors were preeminent people in their respective countries. However, art collecting spread to all stretches of society. Just to mention the most prominent collectors, in the XIX century two French experts, Charles Blanc and Théophile Gautier, brought in a new élan in the fostering of collections. New collectors, such as the Austrian Frederic Spitzer or the Turkish Isaac de Camondo, both Parisian residents, became, among others, new field players in the art market in France[20]. But it is certainly the Rothschild family who was one of the most prominent collectors all over Europe. Cultural heritage at the end of the XIX still remained as an aristocratic matter. During the XX century, a deep rooted process of democratization could be witnessed and the public access to private art collections was and should not be an exception.

In the XX century, after the likes of Hans Heinrich von Thyssen-Bornemisza, Norton Winfred Simon, Armand Hammer, Alfred Barnes and David David-Weill, some other important names that arose were Peggy Guggenheim, Charles Saatchi, Henri Nannen and those of the German husband and wife Peter and Irene Ludwig. In addition to private collectors, other new players emerged, mostly financial agencies, such as JP Morgan Chase and Deutsche Bank, just to mention some.

For others collectors, the social prestige was the driving force behind collecting; this was the case of Henry Clay Frick, J. Paul Getty and Charles Saatchi; but many others who were much more humble, and who remained in the shadows, were also important collectors, such as Joan Soane, Charles Willson Peale, Kurt Schwitters and even Sigmund Freud[21].

In our time, the interrelation of collections and collectors poses a lot of queries and legal challenges. As well stated by the distinguished scholar Elina Moustaira[22], private art collections are the daughters of our time.

---

[20] Rheims, Maurice, *op. cit., supra,* note 6, p. 39.

[21] Elsner, John and Roger Cardinal, *op. cit., supra,* note 2, p. 6.

[22] Moustaira, Elina, *Art Collections, Private and Public: A comparative Legal Study,*

It is safe to say that they reflect a changing mentality about the significance of the collections of art that move to and from different cultural alternatives, and that they serve as confirmation that they currently move in relation to economic choices.
The dawn of the XXI century can be summarized as follows:
« Témoin de son temps et artisan de la consolidation de certaines des valeurs de la société, le droit participe et renforce la modification des relations en matière de patrimoine culturel…On observe ainsi une accélération dans la production de normes, ce qui permet à l'aube du XXIe siècle de recourir à des solutions inédites. Celles-ci tirent parti des progrès réalisés et suscitent de nouvelles interrogations… les enjeux et les évolutions du collectionnisme public demeurant donc à la croisée des chemins de l'histoire, de la culture et du droit »[23].
To state the obvious, each society has an interest in preserving works of art, in learning from them and in making them accessible to scholars for study, as well as to the public for education and enjoyment[24]. These elements all generate public interest[25].
A superficial analysis of domestic legislations proved to be so diverse that it makes finding common ground very difficult and hinders any attempt to systemize them in a broader perspective. Moreover, a comparative study of different legal systems proves that there in not a specific legally recognized regime for private collections and less so for contemporary art[26]. Some provisions, although they exist, are completely dispersed.
The international arena is less encouraging; meagre international efforts to foster and protect cultural private collections can be recognized. One of the first serious endeavors is the UNIDROIT Convention on Stolen or Illegally Exported Cultural objects, approved in the diplomatic conference held in June 1995 in Rome (UNIDROIT Convention). Since its inception, a great deal of ink has flowed into well-structured analyses. The verdict of time has proven favorable to this Convention[27]

Springer, Cham Heidelberg New York Dorrecht London, 2015, p. 47.
[23] Maget, Antoinette, *op. cit., supra,* note 19, p. 571.
[24] Fischer, Cornelia, *Partner oder Kontrahenten. Eine rechtliche Untersuchung der Zummenarbeit öffentlicher Museen und privater Kunstsammler*, Nomos Verlagsgesellschaft, Baden Baden, Germany, 2012, p. 24.
[25] Merryman, John Henry, *The Public interest in Cultural Property*, 77 Cal. L. Rev. 339 (1989), p. 346.
[26] Moustaira, Elina, *op. cit., supra,* note 22, p. 8.
[27] http://www.unidroit.org/instruments/cultural-property/1995-convention. Last accessed October 14th 2017.

and the new international cultural order has been strengthened with an instrument of great use[28]. Using this universal tool's mechanism, the international community is better prepared to overcome the new challenges that it faces because of social unrest and controversial religious movements present at the beginning of the 21st century. This turmoil has put in jeopardy an important part of humanity's cultural heritage. Hence, the UNIDROIT Convention is a privileged device that enriches the International Cultural new order. One of its great features is the opening of a new cultural space (**Section I**), where the development of provisions of private art collections are still pending.
The endeavor should now be to begin from one of its most creative aspects and try to develop, after thorough analysis, the legal issues that are arising (**Section II**). This is the outset of this search, which is currently rich in questioning and enquiry, but lacking in answers.

Section I. The Private Cultural Space

One of these proposals is based on the findings that most of the legal literature has agreed upon. These are that in contrast to the Convention on the Means of Prohibiting and Preventing the Illicit Import, Export and Transfer of Ownership of Cultural Property approved at the UNESCO in Paris in November 1970 (UNESCO 1970 Convention), that the UNIDROIT Convention confers to private collectors the active legal right to claim, within international jurisdictions, the return of stolen cultural objects. The cultural effect is predictable: a breaking of the cultural hegemony that the UNESCO 1970 Convention conferred on national states by granting them the power to determine which objects, due to their cultural importance, should be protected. Through these means, the UNIDROIT Convention opened a space of cultural freedom that should be developed. One of the greatest challenges consists of determining how to root this cultural freedom in a social realm.

A. The Challenges of its Framing

Trying to frame the boundaries of this theme has proven to be a Herculean task, mainly due to the multiple edges that arise and the

[28] For the time being 40 countries have ratified the UNIDROIT Convention; among others practically all the Latin American countries.

important tangential points that occur with other legal domains such as museums, auctions, and copyright legislations, among other.

Private collections are constantly increasing and their cultural and economic importance is forever becoming greater. This is especially the case if one considers that public resources are now scarcer than ever before and, predictably, that they will become more so in the coming decades. Private collections are continuing to gain a huge share of the market without encountering any battles along the way[29].

The main concerns center on the laws and obligations that are specific to the collector: the care and preservation of their collection[30] ; the borrowing of their objects for exhibitions; and the taxation for possession or sale of their collections, amongst others. Two of them, nevertheless, seem to be fundamental: to determine who is entitled to claim an action as a collector is an indispensable task and another, as a consequence of the prior, is to delimit the contours of the cultural collection.

In the art of collectors there exist some very clear differences. There are those collectors who value the aesthetics of the work, whose decision is fundamentally based on their aesthetic joy. In their collections, quality prevails over quantity, or, as stated by Jean Baudrillard, the extract of the collection is qualitative, whereas its material organization is quantitative[31]. At the other extreme, there are the collectors who view art as a commercial investment. Their criteria are based on speculation or on using art as a refuge during financial turmoil.

There are other diverse, recognizable motives, such as snobbery and passion as well. The Russian empress, Catherine II, was renowned for her feverish collecting of art, which became the axis of the Hermitage Museum[32].

Distinguished jurists have postulated that both the economic and cultural values are social constructions and that between them exists a clear link in which the collector is considered as one of the major players in the art market[33]. The collectors figure as one of the most relevant economic agents in their paradigm and they determine to a great degree the viability and sustainability of artistic production.

---

[29] Moustaira, Elina, *op. cit., supra*, note 22, p. 47.
[30] *Ibid., op. cit., supra,* note 22, p. 21.
[31] Baudrillard, Jean, *The system of collecting. In* Elsner, John and Roger Cardinal, *op. cit., supra,* note 2, p. 10.
[32] Rheims, Maurice, *op. cit., supra,* note 6, p. 67.
[33] Merryman, John Henry, *op. cit., supra*, note 25, p. 346.

To elucidate who is a collector in this context, it is foremost necessary to ascertain the basic difference between private and public collections. The motivation for the creation of private collections varies considerably: philanthropy, social status, relationships with prestigious museums institutions, or bequests, among others[34].
The anecdote of the bequest of French Doctor Maurice Girardin (1884-1951) is quite eloquent. With this bequest, Girardin, who was an unknown collector, became famous under the name of Gérardin. By these means Paris City Hall inherited in 1951 more than 500 masterpieces[35].
Some collectors even feel that they are no more than the fortunate, but if only provisional, trustees of certain works of art, having no right to deprive others who appreciate beautiful objects as much as the collectors do themselves[36]. This creates a clear convergence between both notions: private collections tend to have an institutional character, as does the *museumisation* and public access of these collections. A museum's trustees try to capture the attention of collectors by giving the names of the donors, testators or patrons of art, to the exhibition halls. By doing so they enriched the museum's assets.
Collections have turned into an important financial asset, as well as a source of the hoarding of art as an expression of identity. In this context, Maurice Rheims[37] has analyzed the art market and its skyrocketing prices, mostly in European and American Art. He also focused on the variations and mobility of taste and fashion, as well as on painting an accurate picture of the collector's psychology. Even more so, however, his analysis went far beyond art amateurs and fans[38]. The initial difficulties are rooted in the very notion of the collector[39].
From another perspective, the private collections of cultural objects have been, and still are, greatly controversial, oscillating between two extremes. One of these is considered a fundamental axis in the constitution of cultural heritage, especially in the countries where the commercial art market flourishes. The other is the countries of origin that maintain that it is precisely the collectors who are the catalysts for the destruction of their cultural heritage. These two postures appear to

[34] Moustaira, Elina, *op. cit., supra,* note 22, p. 48.
[35] Rheims, Maurice, *op. cit., supra,* note 6, p. 80.
[36] Merryman, John Henry, *op. cit., supra,* note 25, p. 346.
[37] Rheims, Maurice, *op. cit., supra,* note 6, p. 289 to 442.
[38] *Ibidem, op. cit., supra,* note 6, p. 43 to 83.
[39] Moustaira, Elina, *op. cit., supra,* note 22, p. 7.

be totally irreconcilable. The debate must, however, be considered within different cultures. Only by analyzing each different context can the different arguments and their meanings be understood.
The collector assures an important social function; he turns into a trustee of the artist's genius. As stated by Rheims, without Paul Gacher, Vincent van Gogh would have not been able to continuing painting[40].
The function of the collectors is also to carry out an aesthetic valuation, derived from a process of social construction in each market. Despite this, the legitimacy of this valuation is of ongoing controversy[41].
The notion of cultural collections poses many challenges as well. It is in the international field where some elements can be found. Article I of the UNESCO 1970 Convention refers to rare collections and specimens of fauna, flora, minerals and anatomy, and to objects of paleontological interest. It also refers to rare manuscripts and incunabula, old books, documents and publications of special interest, such as historical, artistic, scientific and literary, singly or in collections. That is to say that the gathering of individual pieces should create a cohesive element which consequently generates unity[42].
It is perhaps French law which provides with better analysis so to have a better perspective of this notion. French legislation states that the convergence of different elements in a set gives coherence to the unit and the distinguishable value of the whole in comparison with the value of the individual. These two elements determine the existence of a collection. Moreover, value and coherence should be appreciated for their interest in history, of art history, of civilizations, of sciences and of techniques[43].

B. Private and Public Collections

It is perhaps Sir Hans Sloane that was the forefather of the modern museum, as he left in his will his whole collection to the British Empire; this was the starting point of the British Museum. As stated by Wolgang Ernst, the formation of British Museum was not a fissure, but rather a continuation of the private galleries and the public museum[44]. On

---

[40] Rheims, Maurice, *supra*, note 7, p. 82.
[41] Moustaira, Elina, *op. cit., supra,* note 22, p. 7.
[42] Maget, Antoinette, *op. cit., supra,* note 19, p. 332.
[43]https://www.legifrance.gouv.fr/affichTexte.do?cidTexte=JORFTEXT000000592102&categorieLien=id. Last accessed October 14th 2017.
[44] Maget, Antoinette, *op. cit., supra,* note 19, p. 26.

January 15th, 1759 the public discovered for the first time the British Museum, finding no difference between it and private galleries. It was a delicate metamorphosis of the private space into a public space[45].
France followed another path[46]. The foundation of the Louvre Museum, heir of the Napoleon Museum, under the talented leadership of Dominique Vivant Denon, can be considered as a rupture with the Ancien Regime. The sources of its collections vary enormously from aristocracy, private collections taken in the revolutionary movement, to the war tributes from during the Napoleon campaigns, among others. In Germany, different approaches also prevailed; the State intervention in creating the Museumsinsel in Berlin is clear, following what has been baptized as the Friedrich Willhelm III model, whereas the Munich Museums can be qualified as private museums[47].
At the cusp of the XX century, the features of European museums are clear: the British Museum obeys to a universal compilation, while the Louvre Museum is expansionist and displays domination of artistic and professional training[48]. Other European museums followed similar archetypes such as the Kunsthistorisches Museum in Vienna and the State Hermitage Museum in Saint Petersburg.
It is safe to say that public museums respond to national regulations, which are exclusive of essential private collections. Private museums, in this analysis, qualify as private collections. It must be pointed out as well that in the last decades a clear transition from private museums to public ones can be observed. This movement has had the principal effect of metamorphosing a system of ownership that passes private property into public ownership[49].
The legislation of public museums mostly concerned management and labor relations; the regulations of maintenance acquisitions, deaccessioning of art, and other important issues are still pending[50]. The interference by different driving social forces in the management of the museums remains as a highly controversial issue that poses challenges mostly related to the freedom fundamentals in different perspectives.
The issues of maintenance and acquisitions have been suggested as highly important by the International Council of Museums (ICOM) and

---

45 *Ibid., op. cit., supra,* note 19, p. 33.
46 *Ibid., op. cit., supra,* note 19, p. 37.
47 *Ibid., op. cit., supra,* note 19, p. 53.
48 *Ibid., op. cit., supra,* note 19, p. 51.
49 Moustaira, Elina, *op. cit., supra,* note 22, p. 7
50 Maget, Antoinette, *op. cit., supra,* note 19, p. 422.

have so far been tackled by means of ethic codes, which are considered in the legal practice as soft law and as such non-binding[51]. This initiative has induced museums or museum's associations to draft their own code of ethics.

Section II. The State and the Private Cultural Collections

One of the most polemic issues is to develop a legal relation between the State and the private collections.

A. The Legal Issues

The displaying of private collections is a practice that started a long time ago. In fact, museums have seen the benefits of private collections. In this way, the German, Wilhelm von Bode, at the time director of the Museums of Berlin, had the initiative to form the Kaiser Friedrich Museum Association, which significantly enriched the collections of these museums[52]. Also in Germany, due to the grave economic crisis after the First World War, the interaction between public museums and private collectors blossomed into an interesting partnership.
In the second part of the 20th century, a debate arose about the notion of freedom. This was of great importance to public museums and determined their link with the collectors. In this respect, it is noteworthy that after the Second World War Germany elaborated a new constitution, which ensured and further fostered the freedom of art[53].
It is also in this era that the link between public museums and private collections intensified. They became firmly involved in the debate of freedom and the sovereignty of the state to determine the course of exhibitions and as a consequence the orientation of education. The link, however, is extremely complex. The conditions that the private collectors aimed to impose on the public museums were the duration of lending contracts, the maintenance of the collections, and the costs of transportation, amongst other features. One of the most famous cases is that of the collection of the foundation of the German energy

[51] ICOM Code of Ethics for Museums. *In* http://icom.museum/fileadmin/user_upload/pdf/Codes/code_ethics2013_eng.pdf. Last accessed October 14th, 2017
[52] Fischer, Cornelia, *op. cit., supra,* note 24, p. 29.
[53] https://www.bundestag.de/grundgesetz. Last accessed Oct. 14th 2017

consortium, E.on, displayed in the Museum of Düsseldorf, Germany. It was for a great time considered as a paradigmatic case in the cooperation between a city hall and the industry. At the end of the relationship, the Museum Director did not hesitate in denouncing the grave interferences of this foundation in the artistic management of the museum[54]. Worse still, it demonstrated the search for power on the part of the private collectors, who with it would not only determine the aesthetic considerations, but also what could be considered as art.

In this complex relationship between the private collectors and the museums, the latter became more vulnerable when they did exhibit extensive collections. This was the case of Helga and Walter Lauff's collection, which had been lent the Kaiser Wilhelm Museum in Krefeld, Germany. It was a collection of close to five hundred works of art[55]. The dependency of the museums on these large collections was apparent.

Other considerations that are deemed relevant should be taken into account. The function of the state in the exhibition of private collections in public museums must be limited to avoid any kind of censure[56].

The arrangement of munificence also encourages this approach; this legal mechanism has had different legal expressions. In this context, it is worth mentioning the case of Sir Dennis Mahon (1910-2011), who through his charitable fund[57] in the United Kingdom agreed to share his collection with six British museums. These were The National Gallery of Scotland, in Edinburgh; The National Gallery of London; The Ashmolean Museum in Oxford; The Fitzwilliam Museum in Cambridge; The Birmingham Art Gallery; and the Newsam House Temple in Leeds[58]. The importance of this bequest was that Sir Mahon obliged the museums to give free access to the exhibits while also guaranteeing that none of his collected works could be sold. This disposition puts the issue of deaccessioning art in museums firmly in the spotlight.

The Mahon case is relevant, not only for prohibiting the sale of any of the objects in his collection, but also for the passing of the Charitable

---

[54] Fischer, Cornelia, *op. cit., supra,* note 3, p. 29.

[55] Fischer, Cornelia, *op. cit., supra,* note 24, p. 32.

[56] Moustaira, Elina, *op. cit., supra,* note 22, p. 50.

[57]https://www.nationalgalleries.org/media/_file/press_releases/Sir_Denis_Mahon_collection_press_release.pdf. Last accessed oct. 14th 2017.

[58] Moustaira, Elina, *op. cit., supra,* note 22, p. 53.

Act of 2006[59]. The act prohibits the institutions from removing access to these cultural objects, thus national collections and university collections were classified as charitable institutions[60].
Between 1895 and 1955, one of the most significant exoduses of the XX century took place. Paintings, sculptures, libraries and even entire buildings were rehomed to the United States[61]. In the United States several cases became cause célèbre, such as those in Philadelphia pertaining to the collections of John G. Johnson, Peter Arrell Browne Widener and Albert Coombs Barnes. Johnson was a successful lawyer who built one of the most important collections in the United States. He bequeathed his collection to the City of Philadelphia, but imposed a condition that new building be erected to house his collection. After an intricate legal process his trustees agreed to transfer the Johnson Collection to the Philadelphian Museum of Art[62].
The Widener collection, which included paintings of Rembrandt, Edouard Monet and Renoir, was bequeathed to the National Gallery in Washington D.C. one of the few public museums in American soil.
The Barnes Collection is renowned for being an exquisite and comprehensive collection of paintings and sculptures. Barnes was a reputable collector and he was respected in the intellectual circles of his country. He mingled with artists and leading thinker of his time; the Italian painter De Chirico made a portrait of Barnes and even Matisse accepted an invitation and painted a mural above the three principal windows of his gallery. The collection forms perhaps one of the most important art collections in the United States, only to cite the Cezanne's paintings that numbered more than the paintings in all of the Parisian museums put together[63]. Barnes ensured that after his death the collection should be closed and no painting should ever be loaned or sold. He stated that his collection be mostly used for the purpose of education. After a long legal battle this collection is now housed in a splendid museum in Philadelphia for the benefit of the public and society as a whole[64].

---

[59] http://www.legislation.gov.uk/ukpga/2006/50/contents. Last accessed Oct. 14th., 2017
[60] Moustaira, Elina, *op. cit., supra,* note 22, p. 90.
[61] Lukacs, John, *Philaldelphia Patricians and Philistines 1900-1950*, Farrar, Straus, Ciroux, New York, 1981, p. 260.
[62] *Ibidem, op. cit., supra,* note 61, p. 261.
[63] *Ibidem, op. cit., supra,* note 61, p. 273.
[64] Anderson, John, *Art held Hostage. The Battle over the Barnes Collection*, W.W.

B. Private Collections to Public Collections

Different legislations favor the transition of private collections to museums through diverse contractual means such as donations, long-term loans, or bequests. Another of the relevant aspects is, therefore, without a doubt the conservation of objects that make up a private collection. Apart from the moral right[65] in the field of copyright law, which helps to protect the work of the artists, it is not easy to identify any regulations relating to the obligation of owners to maintain the integrity and quality of the objects they own[66].

Hence, the real difficulty is to exercise the right of ownership. One of the more intense debates surrounds Diego Rivera's mural in the Rockefeller Center. In 1932, Diego Rivera, who was already a prolific Mexican artist, was hired to paint the mural on the RCA Building of the Rockefeller Center, right in the middle of Manhattan. His Marxist ideals were well known; hence it came as a shock when the Rockefeller turned to him to produce a mural in one of the most emblematic buildings of Capitalism. Its title is extremely long "*Man at the crossroad looking with uncertainty but with hope and high vision to the choosing of a course leading to a new and better future*". One version of his work is now exhibited in the Palacio de Bellas Artes, in downtown Mexico City, under the title "*Controlling Man of the Universe*".

The surprise was even greater due to Rivera having satirized John D. Rockefeller, alongside Henry Ford and J. P. Morgan, in the mural "The Orgy/The Dinner of the Rich", which is located in the head offices of the Public Education Ministry (SEP) in Mexico City. Not only this, the philanthropist Abby Aldrich Rockefeller, wife of John D. Rockefeller Jr., had organized an exhibition in the New York Museum of Modern Art (MoMa) in which the main exhibit was the painting Frozen Assets, which represented allusive scenes of the Great Depression in the United States. Nelson, who was the son of Abby, had done little less. Previously he had become entangled in an argument with left-wing artists after an exhibition was produced which scandalized the MoMa's patrons and who thus threatened to remove their support[67].

Norton and Company, New York, London, United States of America, 2013, p. 85.

[65] Moustaira, Elina, *op. cit., supra,* note 22, p. 21.

[66] *Ibid., op. cit., supra,* note 2, p. 22.

[67] Sax, Joseph, *L. Playing darts with a Rembrandt: Public and Private Rights in Cultural Treasures*, University of Michigan Press, Ann Arbor, 1999, United States of America, p. 14.

Under Rockefeller's direct supervision, Rivera continued with his work on the mural, which clearly depicted a worker's march in Moscow, gas masks, and venereal germs harassing ladies of high society. The anecdote is well known: the portrait of Lenin was what caused the greatest grief. The press began to question John D. Rockefeller Jr. because they considered he was attempting to propel communist propaganda. His son Nelson reacted and wrote a letter to Diego: he requested he remove the picture of the leader of the Russian revolution and that he changed it for a person who was http://chng.it/66jPymHh5gAs was expected, Rivera rejected the request and in May 1933 he wrote to the Rockefellers and informed them he was rather the mural was totally destroyed than edited. Nelson offered to remove the mural and donate it to the MoMa, claiming that the Rockefellers would employ the same technique with which they had removed the frescoes of Antonio Pollaiuoloa (Antonio di Jacopo Benci) and the villa of Publius Fannius Synistor in Boscoreale, close to Pompey. The MoMa rejected the offer of the mural, Rockefeller's intention failed and Nelson ended up paying the Mexican muralist an agreed amount of money. Rivera used the money to reconstruct a new version of the work on portable panels, which were then donated to the New Workers School in Manhattan, in an attempt to preserve the rights of the artists and the public interest[68].

Rivera commented ironically that the simple image of Vladimir Illich Lenin could put at risk millionaires' residences and the city's banks and stock markets. One night in February 1934, in a surreptitious matter and without prior warning, the mural was destroyed on the orders of Rockefeller. The explanation for the destruction was offensive to one's intelligence. It was argued that the destruction of the work was due to the needs for work on the building's structure. The resulting scandal grew to the point that protests ensued.

Rivera classed this event, and rightly so, as cultural vandalism. However, for this assertion to be well founded, it is fundamental to focus on the point that the destruction of the mural went against the interests of the community, which exists to safeguard human genius against the interests of the elite powers and their political and religious agendas.

The specific differences consisted in considering the work of art as simple merchandise. The arguments of John D. Rockefeller Jr, were

---

[68] *Ibid., op. cit., supra,* note 67, p. 13.

pathetic, privileging the interests of the elite over those of the community. Treating the mural as a piece of property and ignoring the talent of Rivera was complete nonsense.

The substantial arguments against cultural vandalism and in favor of the preservation of public cultural interest legitimize the protection of heritage in the matter. The genius of the artist must be above the interests of the elite who are in power, postulating that it has a modern and secular content. In this way, the work of art is valuable because it responds to the interests of the community and it is these that should be privileged above ownership.

Rivera continued despite being harassed. His famous mural in the Art Institute of Detroit also caused a great malaise, especially amongst Catholic students, who decried for a boycott of the work so it would be removed. One of the panels of the mural called The Vaccination, shows an infant being held by a nurse while being inoculated by a doctor. At the base of the scene are several stable animals, which formed the basis for an argument by an ecclesiastic name Higgins, who suggested the art work mocked the Holy Family. In this case, the community's interests prevailed over those of the group[69].

The conclusion here is clear: the fate of Rivera's work takes on a singular importance even for those who are indifferent to or even hostile to the political message it conveys. Not only this, the works of Rivera were some the greatest catalyzers of the United States Federal Art Program of American Art (PWAP), which was quickly replaced by the Federal Art Project (FAP) inserted in the New Deal of Franklin D. Roosevelt during the Great Depression[70].

One of the most important parts of the PWAP was precisely that part related to murals, which composed artists like Stuart Davis, Jackson Pollock and Arshile Gorky. To give an indication of the social depth of this program, the result is surprising. The area created more than 100,000 paintings and murals and close to 18,000 sculptures[71].

There are more queries about the absolute exercising of ownership in cultural heritage. It could be suggested that in this aspect the differences between the common law and the civil law systems may re-emerge.

[69] *Ibid., op. cit., supra,* note 67, p. 14.
[70] *Ibid., op. cit., supra,* note 67, p. 15.
[71] *Ibid., op. cit., supra,* note 67, p. 16.

These differences are merely superficial[72]; the attitude of the collectors in the countries with a tradition of common law, in general, considers that they are custodians of works of art, whose obligation is clear – to preserve them for the benefit of future generations[73]. In this way, California[74] and Massachusetts[75], in the United States, are two good examples. Both have clear provisions in their legislation that oblige the owners to preserve the cultural objects in their collections for the benefit of the public.

Some scholars have suggested that the best way to proceed is exploring the notion of stewardship and that of cultural custody[76]. The model should be that of the responsible collector who does not destroy nor conceal his treasures, this under the model of trusteeship. Collectors have long embraced the idea that owners of cultural treasures are only temporary custodians. They realize that the conservation of objects that make up private collections requires a high level of expertise, that which could well be provided by public museums. This could additionally ensure an important synergy between private and public collections in institutions that house cultural objects for previous generations[77].

This analysis avoids the discussion of droit moral being regulated in copyright legislation. It is worth mentioning that the difference in this aspect between common law and civil law systems is more conceptual than pragmatic, especially if one considers the voices and opinions of

---

[72] Moustaira, Elina, *op. cit., supra*, note 22, p. 22.

[73] *Ibid., op. cit., supra,* note 22, p. 22.

[74] The Californian Legislature declared and found in Section 989 of its Civil Code in Section 989 that there is a public interest in preserving the integrity of cultural and artistic creations. *In* http://leginfo.ca.gov/cgi-bin/displaycode?section=civ&group=00001-01000&file=980-989. Last accessed October 14th, 2017.

[75] Section 85S Chapter 231 of the General Laws states that the general court hereby finds and declares that the physical alteration or destruction of fine art, which is an expression of the artist's personality, is detrimental to the artist's reputation, and artists therefore have an interest in protecting their works of fine art against such alteration or destruction; and that there is also a public interest in preserving the integrity of cultural and artistic creations. *In* https://malegislature.gov/Laws/GeneralLaws/PartIII/TitleII/Chapter231/Section85S. Last accessed Oct. 14th., 2015.

[76] Sax, Joseph L., *op. cit., supra,* note 67, p. 60.

[77] Merryman, John Henry, *supra,* note 25, p. 345.

leading scholars on the matter. The same reasoning is also valid for Resale Royalties, Resale Rights or Droit de Suite.
Although in the countries of destination these elements are not easily recognizable, no less certain is the fact they present serious problems, especially with the bequests that prohibit the deaccessioning of the objects housed there. This is the case in the Barnes Collection in the United States and the collection of Sir Dennis Mahon in the United Kingdom.
The epitome of the bequests to the State is the Soane collection: by an Act of Parliament it was donated to the British Empire. The trustees were forbidden to alter the collection as preserved by Sir John Soane. The Act impeded the dispersion of the collection and insisted that it be preserved and entirely unchanged. This act is one of the first State attempts to convert private collections into public ones; it is a clear passage from the intimacy of a private collection to the openness of public ones, where a collection essentially becomes a museum. Soane attached to his will a Description of the House and Museum on the North side of Lincoln's Inn Fields drafted by himself both in English and French as a guide[78]. The Soane Museum itself remained largely true to his wish.

The interrelation between private collections and public museums is always governed by private law, as is the case with German law[79]. The links between the museums and the collectors must continue to be under private law[80]. These relationships have demonstrated enormous versatility[81]. It is sufficient to mention only a few cases that have transcended national borders, such as the Thyseen Bornemisza collection in Madrid[82] or the equally interesting Bayeler Museum, in Basel, created by the Swiss artist Ernst Beyeler.
Ernst Beyeler obtained a favorable judgement of the European Court of Human Rights, adjudicating that Italy violated Beyeler's right to

---

78 Belsen, John, *The House and Museum of Sir John Soane. In* Elsner, John and Roger Cardinal, *op. cit., supra*, note 2, p. 157.
79 Moustaira, Elina, *op. cit., supra,* note 22, p. 50.
80 Moustaira, Elina, *op. cit., supra,* note 22, p. 49.
81 Fischer, Cornelia, *op. cit., supra,* note 24, p. 39.
82 Boletín Oficial del Estado No. 224, III Section, P. 72006; véase también http://www.boe.es/diario_boe/txt.php?id=BOE-A-1993-15901. Last accessed oct. 14th 2015.

peaceful enjoyment of his possessions while using Italy's pre-emption right over the Van Gogh painting Portrait of a Young Peasant[83].
In its adjudication the court recognized the legitimate interest for a State to take measures designed to facilitate, in the most effective way, wide public access to them, in the general interest of universal culture, regardless of the illicit provenance of collections.
This argument weakens the claim of the source countries to these collections because of these countries' inability to assure the works' exhibition in a universal manner. Thus a strong argument occurs in favor of the countries of destination, as stated by Antoinette Maget[84].
The end of the colonial age and the consequent emergence of new States had a decisive repercussion in the notion of cultural heritage domineered during the XIX century by European aesthetic canons. The fervor in the building and defense of their cultural heritage became common place in these new states. The metamorphosis process was hastened in the second half of the XX century; new approaches were developed such as multiculturalism, cultural heritage of humanity, national heritage and a new perception of cultural sovereignty that influenced, if not dominated the cultural debate. A new cultural consciousness appeared and the first strides to impede the illicit trafficking of cultural objects were taken. In 1970, the UNESCO 1970 Convention was approved, cementing the new cultural international order[85]. Now the brand-new Council of Europe Convention on Offences Relating to Cultural Property, adopted on May 3rd, 2017, aims to prevent and combat illicit trafficking and destruction of cultural property.
Among other cultural objects of cultural relevance, one of the most highly valued is archaeological cultural objects, this due to their specificity, where their dimension, nature and their function in history are essential elements[86]. Archaeologists have postulated the importance of the integrity of the objects, the context of which is vital to decipher their history. Once the object is seized from its context, the amputated site and even the object diminish in value. In fact, it is a loss for universal human knowledge.

---

[83]https://www.ilsa.org/jessup/jessup17/Batch%201/Judgment%20of%20the%20ECHR-%20Beyeler%20v.%20Italy%20-2000.pdf. Last accessed oct. 14th 2017.
[84] Maget, Antoinette, *op. cit., supra,* note 19, p. 503.
[85] *Ibid., op. cit., supra,* note 19, p. 295.
[86] *Ibid., op. cit., supra*, note 19, p. 326.

The domestic legislations in this field are numerous and it is difficult to recognize any common ground. Even the UNESCO 1970 Convention obliges the countries of origin to draft an inventory, a requirement that challenges common sense due to the fact that many of them are undiscovered, as is the Mexican case. This has induced UNESCO to draft model provisions on State ownership of undiscovered cultural objects[87].

It is hence no surprise that one of the touchiest issues relates to the collection of archaeological goods. The legislation of the countries of origin is highly restrictive of the exportation of cultural objects, especially archaeological ones. To this effect, the mechanisms they have created in their legislations are those of inalienability, imprescriptibility and indefeasibility (res extra commercium). In our age, the private collections which assemble archaeological objects are under high scrutiny and face great challenges.

The latest international legislation has a considerable influence in the domestic realm. The resolutions 2199 and 2253 of February 2015[88], taken by the Security Council of the United Nations, mandate that the countries, particularly the countries of destination, take measures to forbid illicit trafficking of cultural property, which has been the second source of financing for international terrorism.

C. Public Access

One of the most controversial issues in our time is public access to private collections. A consensus exists that it was in the Renaissance that the first collections started, especially because of the nobleness and absolutist sovereignty. The accumulation of artwork quickly transformed into to a suitable means of demonstrating power. In every aristocratic residence deserving of a noble name it was considered essential to have an art collection[89]. The aristocracy therefore assumed a function of patronage, and this link between nobleness and the artist has survived for a long time.

However, the French Revolution of 1789 greatly altered the

---

[87]http://www.unesco.org/fileadmin/MULTIMEDIA/HQ/CLT/pdf/UNESCO-UNIDROIT_Model_Provisions_en.pdf. Last accessed Oct. 14th 2017.

[88] http://www.un.org/en/sc/ctc/docs/2015/N1504028_EN.pdf. Last accessed Oct. 14th 2017.

[89] Fischer, Cornelia, *op. cit. supra,* note 24, p. 23.

significance of art and culture. The postulation of individual freedom led to a liberal conception of the State. A great number of the royal palaces, amongst them the Louvre, were converted into public art museums. It is in this era in where royal heritage, nobleness and clergy were given a new significance[90]. The October Revolution of 1917 in Russia followed the same path[91]. The growing weakness of the aristocracy and the clergy allowed many individuals to gain direct benefits and form collections of great importance. Included in these are the Wallraf, Hübsch, Lysversberg and Boisserée collections[92]. Even the narrative of the visual arts mutated; it went from depicting aristocratic themes and portraits to ones informing about human progress.

Another of the many consequences was the new social function of the museums and their conception in the organization of the state. This was the outset for the assuming of cultural responsibility on the part of the State, not only in France but also in a large part of Europe. In Europe arose the notion of the Cultural State.

The creation of the British Museum in 1753 and the Louvre was followed by many others. In Munich, between 1816 and 1830 they constructed the Glyptothek, and in Berlin, between 1824 and 1828, they constructed the Ancient Museum, as well as the New Museum (1843-1855). The common ground shared in the different conceptions of the museums was the educational function served by exhibiting art works and relevant cultural objects, something that continues to this day. In our age, the museum has assumed other important notions such as the redrafting of and a new understanding of its original tasks. As stated by Antoinette Maget, the museum is in the midst of the new function of culture and of pioneering a new model[93]. The multidisciplinary associated with interdisciplinary constitutes a challenge to the traditional educational objective of a museum.

The access of the public to private collections is on the current cultural agenda[94]. Public museums offer a highly significant space to private collections. The social perception of the connection of private and

---

[90] Fischer, Cornelia, *op. cit. supra,* note 24, p. 23.

[91] Polovstoff, Alexandre, *Les trésors d'art en Russie sous le régime bolcheviste,* J. Povolozky & Cie Éditeurs, Société Française d'Imprimerie et de librairie, Paris, p. 19.

[92] Fischer, Cornelia, *op. cit., supra,* note 24, p. 24.

[93] Maget, Antoinette, *op. cit., supra*, note 19, p. 474.

[94] Moustaira, Elina, *op. cit., supra*, note 22, p. 7.

public collections varies enormously[95]. On the one hand, it assures public access to private collections, something that helps to overcome some inconsistencies in the legislation in where it is determined if some of the privately owned objects form part of the national heritage and simultaneously whether their exportation is impeded[96]. There is, nonetheless, some reluctance: although the exhibiting of private collections in public museums allows for the possibility of public access to art works that had previously been out of their reach, exposure to contemporary art could influence the art market, with substantial economic benefits for the collectors[97].
In this form, the collection belonging to the German Hans Grothe, exhibited in the Duisburg Museum, is relevant. Sometime after the exhibition, he sold various works with a considerable profit. This collection ended up being sold to Sylvia and Ulrich Ströher[98]. Displayed in the Bonn Art Museum, it was removed because the museum could not comply with the requirements of the new owners. The case of the German Lauffs family is also a clear example of a direct benefit of artworks now possessing the predicate *exhibitionally correct*. The profits made from the sale in Sotheby's auction house and in galleries were substantial.
This calls into the question the patronage of the private art collectors and sets the museums in direct competition with art galleries and auction houses[99], with the specific difference that they benefit from the museum's authority.
Notwithstanding these arguments, there are also other reasons to promote the exhibition of private collections, one particular reason being the introduction of new artists who were unknown to museums and society. On many occasions, private collections also specialize in topics that are outside of the focus of the museums.

II. Conclusions

A cultural system is a social construction in which different protagonists converge on a paradigm, one that consists of a series of principles and

---

[95] *Ibid., op. cit., supra,* note 22, p. 49.
[96] *Ibid., op. cit., supra,* note 22, p. 51.
[97] *Ibid., op. cit., supra,* note 22, p. 49.
[98] Fischer, Cornelia, *op. cit., supra,* note 24, p. 28.
[99] *Ibid., op. cit., supra,* note 24, p. 196.

attitudes that shape the form in which the protagonists think and act. Two contrary paradigms are easily distinguishable, and in this case the intervention of the state proves decisive. One of these paradigms finds its roots in collective and individual responsibility. Here social structure is horizontal and power is dispersed amongst the different advocates. In the other paradigm, power is irremediably hierarchical and concentrated within the government. It is fully dependent on public funds. These paradigms, however, seldom exist in a completely pure form. Most of them can be characterized either as publicly oriented with private variations or as fundamentally private with public variations[100]. In these cultural systems is important to find common ground in order to elaborate uniform rules that would give certainty to private art collections[101].

One of the other controversies is the debate about the freedom of art that the State must guarantee and foster. The private link between public and private actors of law must be inserted in the constellation of this freedom[102]. The predicate exhibitionally correct is an important ingredient that must be considered in the links between public museums and private collections, dominated by private law, but which are highly complex[103].

---

[100] Moustaira, Elina, *op. cit.*, note 22, p. 16.
[101] Merryman, John Henry, *op. cit.*, *supra*, note 25, p. 345.
[102] Bundestag´s Conclusions, dec. 15th. 2005. BT-Drucks. 16/96.
[103] Fischer, Cornelia, *op. cit., supra,* note 24, p. 199.

Les collections privées en France au XVIIIe siècle : une approche méthodologique

Patrick MICHEL
Professeur à l'Université de Lille et à l'École du Louvre

« Maintes fois je me suis trouvé tenté du désir de la collection, et, sans avoir entièrement succombé à cette tentation, je dois dire cependant que j'ai assez approché de mes lèvres, la coupe de ses enivrements pour en connaître les voluptés, pour être initié à ses plus secrets mystères »
(Horace de Vieil-Castel, *Les collectionneurs*, 1853)

En 2006 Christoph Vogtherr évoquant les recherches récentes sur l'art français du XVIIIe siècle et les nouvelles approches du domaine, constatait que : « L'histoire du collectionnisme constitue une grande découverte et un changement crucial des paradigmes dans l'histoire de l'art »[1]. Lorsque l'on considère l'espace de la collection comme un champ d'études, il convient en préliminaire d'en étudier la géographie, d'en cerner les contours, d'en observer les territoires, d'en dégager les acteurs. Notre ambition dans le cadre de ce colloque sera de proposer les clefs d'une lecture méthodologique du champ d'investigation, en prenant principalement pour exemple le XVIIIe siècle français, sachant qu'il est possible de l'appliquer tout autant à des études portant sur le XIXe siècle, voire dans certains cas même au XXe siècle.

À la suite des articles pionniers de Krisztof Pomian, et des ouvrages d'Antoine Schnapper[2], qui posaient les jalons de nouvelles approches et de nouvelles méthodes, le « collectionnisme » est devenu depuis une trentaine d'années un champ de recherches à part entière qui a fait l'objet de très nombreuses publications. Le plus souvent celles-ci ont privilégié dans leur approche les aspects de l'histoire sociale et

---

[1] Ch. Vogtherr, « Collectionneurs et marchands : littérature récente sur le collectionnisme français du XVIIIe siècle », *Perspective,* 2006-2, p. 347.

[2] K. Pomian, *Collectionneurs, amateurs et curieux. Paris-Venise : XVIe-XVIIIe siècle,* Paris, 1987, et A. Schnapper, *Le géant, la licorne et la tulipe. Collections et collectionneurs dans la France du XVIIe siècle. I. Histoire et histoire naturelle,* Paris, 1988, et A. Schnapper, *Curieux du Grand siècle. Collections et collectionneurs dans la France du XVIIe siècle. II. Œuvres d'art,* Paris, Flammarion, 1994.

culturelle. On a abordé également l'histoire de la pratique de la collection au travers de ses aspects économiques, l'étude du marché de l'art. Ce qui revient à envisager le rôle joué par ses acteurs (marchands-merciers, peintres-marchands, experts) dans la formation et la dispersion des collections, mais également leur rôle dans l'histoire du goût. L'histoire des collections n'est donc pas l'apanage de la seule histoire de l'art, comme le prouve le présent colloque. Elle est interdisciplinaire car la collection est précisément une œuvre polysémique : il s'agit d'une page de l'histoire sociale de l'art, de l'histoire des pratiques sociales et culturelles, de l'histoire des idées, de l'histoire du goût, mais également de l'histoire des mécanismes humains, sociaux, économiques et bien sûr juridiques.
Quelques rappels historiques sont nécessaires en préliminaire pour « planter le décor ».

I. Un siècle de collectionneurs : le XVIIIe siècle

Au temps des Lumières, collectionner devient un élément important de la culture de la société aristocratique et bourgeoise, et à ce titre partie intégrante du statut social. Dès les vingt premières années du XVIIIe siècle la réunion d'une collection est devenue un phénomène banal comme l'atteste l'apparition d'un véritable guide à l'usage des apprentis collectionneurs publié en juin 1727 dans le Mercure de France, par le polygraphe Antoine-Joseph Dezallier d'Argenville, sous le titre évocateur de « Lettre sur le choix et l'arrangement d'un cabinet curieux ». Dans cet opuscule, l'auteur prodigue des conseils à un ami imaginaire, non seulement sur les peintres dont il pourrait acquérir des œuvres, mais également sur d'autres catégories d'objets susceptibles d'être collectionnés et souvent plus abordables, tels que les estampes, les spécimens de l'histoire naturelle, la numismatique, les dessins. La variété de ceux-ci reflète la diversité des objets collectionnés. Le XVIIIe siècle constate en effet l'ouverture des collections à de nouveaux horizons, et il n'est pas rare qu'un même collectionneur ait plusieurs centres d'intérêt (histoire naturelle, numismatique, tableaux, dessins ou estampes).
Le XVIIIe siècle français constitue une remarquable pépinière de collectionneurs, dont le nombre reste cependant difficile à estimer. K. Pomian a avancé le chiffre de sept cent vingt-trois collections parisiennes au XVIIIe siècle, toutes catégories confondues, dont quatre

cent soixante-sept cabinets pour la seule période 1750-1790[3]. S'il est difficile d'expliquer un tel phénomène, « il est certain - selon Édouard Pommier - que la collection participe d'un phénomène important de la société du XVIIIe siècle, celui de l'accumulation d'objets par un groupe social qui transcende les distinctions juridiques des ordres, des moyens et des signes, qui de la résidence à la tabatière, et des tableaux aux équipages, permettent à leur possesseur de manifester une supériorité sociale désormais inséparable de la maîtrise des instruments de la connaissance et du plaisir. La collection est une parfaite démonstration de cette évolution, puisqu'en elle s'unissent les symboles de la fortune (...), du savoir (...) et du plaisir »[4]. Au XVIIIe siècle, comme au siècle précédent, la collection n'est pas seulement l'expression d'une curiosité parfois boulimique pour ce qui est rare, ancien et précieux, pour paraphraser La Bruyère. Elle est aussi et avant tout la manifestation privée d'une passion, d'une volonté de connaissance qui est aussi une aventure publique au travers de la salle de vente, de l'édition de catalogues, de l'apparition d'une littérature savante qui ne s'explique que par l'existence des collectionneurs et des érudits. L'histoire des collections est pour cette raison inséparable de la naissance d'une culture savante qui s'applique à attribuer des objets à des classes bien définies, à établir leur lieu et leur date de fabrication.

Quelles sont les sources documentaires dont dispose l'historien de l'art pour étudier cette pratique de la collection ? Quels sont les modes opératoires pour l'étude du phénomène culturel du collectionnisme ?

Les sources textuelles et visuelles de l'histoire du collectionnisme au XVIIIe siècle

Il nous faut d'abord insister sur la relative carence des sources et leur grande dispersion. Dans la plupart des cas, les sources dont dispose l'historien de l'art sont les instruments traditionnels du chercheur : inventaire après décès, catalogues de collections, récits de voyages, guides, presse périodique, correspondances d'érudits...

Qu'il s'agisse des inventaires après décès ou de ceux, plus rares qui furent réalisés du vivant du collectionneur, ils sont la source première de l'historien et sont à la base de toute étude sur l'histoire des

---

[3] K. Pomian, *op. cit.,* 1987, p. 143-144.

[4] E. Pommier, « Le problème du musée à la veille de la Révolution », *Les Cahiers du Musée Girodet,* n° 1, 1989, p. 9-10.

collectionneurs, qu'elle soit monographique ou prosopographique. Toutefois, cette source a ses limites. Comme le souligne F. Bayard, « les inventaires sont des photographies réalisées à un moment donné (généralement le décès) de la vie d'un individu. Ils ne disent donc rien sur l'histoire de la collection, la période à laquelle elle s'est formée, la manière dont elle l'a été ni comment elle a évolué »[5]. Beaucoup plus suggestifs, sont les documents de gestion des collections que sont les « catalogues domestiques ». Les catalogues imprimés sont nés, comme le rappelle Adalgisa Lugli « de la volonté de donner une image achevée du musée, de la faire circuler au-delà de la dimension physique du lieu et de la proposer comme étude et comme réflexion théorique sur la collection elle-même »[6]. Cette idée donnera naissance dans la seconde moitié du XVIe siècle aux catalogues illustrés des collections encyclopédiques. Dans le contexte français, ces catalogues se sont multipliés au XVIIIe siècle. Ils permettent de mesurer la force et les faiblesses d'une collection et révèlent au-delà, tout à la fois les choix intellectuels et les exigences de mise en ordre d'un ensemble, qu'il s'agisse de tableaux, de spécimens d'histoire naturelle ou de médailles. Certains d'entre eux ont été imprimés du vivant du collectionneur. S'agissant de cabinets de tableaux, ils ne concernent toutefois que les cabinets parisiens les plus prestigieux : celui de Louis-Antoine Crozat, baron de Thiers (1755), dont la collection de tableaux fut achetée par Catherine II et constitue le fonds de l'Ermitage ou bien le cabinet d'Ange Laurent de La Live de Jully, introducteur des Ambassadeurs et promoteur de la peinture française contemporaine. Mais lorsque l'on parle de catalogues de collection, il s'agit dans la plupart des cas de catalogues de vente. Nés à la faveur d'un développement spectaculaire du marché de l'art, en Hollande, puis en France et en Angleterre, les catalogues de vente représentent une des sources essentielles de l'histoire des collections et du marché de l'art[7]. Ils sont aujourd'hui

---

[5] F. Bayard, « Collections et collectionneurs en France à l'époque moderne », dans H. Berlan, E. Chapron, I. Luciani, G. Le Thiec éd., *Érudits, collectionneurs et amateurs. France méridionale et Italie XVIe-XIXe siècle*, Aix-Marseille, Presses de l'université de Provence, 2017, p. 88.

[6] Adalgisa Lugli, *Naturalia et Mirabilia. Il collezionismo enciclopedico nelle Wunderkammern d'Europa,* Milan, 2005, p. 65.

[7] Voir Linda Whiteley, « The language of sale catalogues, 1750-1820 », dans M. Preti-Hamard et Ph. Sénéchal éd., *Collections et marché de l'art en France 1789-1848,* Rennes, PUR, 2005, p. 35-45, et P. Michel, « Les catalogues de ventes annotés du XVIIIe siècle : une source essentielle pour l'histoire de l'art », dans C. Hurley-Griener

largement accessibles au chercheur[8]. K. Pomian a montré comment ce nouvel instrument de savoir qui se généralise dans la seconde moitié du XVIIIe siècle contribue à fixer les biographies d'artistes, la démarche, la description formelle, technique ou esthétique des œuvres, les attributions, toutes choses qui témoignent du nouveau savoir des marchands-experts[9]. Ces catalogues constituent donc une source privilégiée pour l'étude du collectionnisme et du marché de l'art de par leur double fonction commerciale et historiographique. Ils peuvent en effet être exploités sous différents angles : statistique, pour suivre les variations du goût à travers celles des prix ; stylistique pour cerner la naissance d'un savoir-faire et d'un genre nouveau, à la fois littéraire et érudit ; comparatiste, enfin, pour tenter de préciser la physionomie des experts, tant en France qu'en Angleterre ou dans les Pays-Bas. Toutefois, une approche statistique du monde des collectionneurs, réalisée à partir des catalogues de vente, pour satisfaisante qu'elle soit, reste aléatoire. Ces catalogues de vente aux enchères, aussi précieux et instructifs soient-ils, nous fournissent pourtant des données incomplètes et ne permettent tout au plus que d'approcher la réalité. On ne doit en effet jamais oublier que toutes les collections ne sont pas dispersées en vente publique, certaines étant transmises par héritage, d'autres cédées directement en bloc ou en partie, à un autre collectionneur ou à un marchand. De ce fait, les collections dispersées en vente avec ou sans catalogue ne représentent sans doute qu'une partie difficile à évaluer, du collectionnisme français. Fort heureusement, l'historien de l'art dispose d'autres sources qui peuvent être considérées comme complémentaires, telles que les relations de voyage et les guides, la presse périodique et les correspondances érudites.

Pendant longtemps les historiens ont trop négligé cette autre source imprimée que sont les relations de voyages ou les guides[10]. Plusieurs

---

et C. Barbillon éd., *Le Catalogue dans tous ses états,* Paris, Rencontres de l'École du Louvre, 2015, p. 295-310.

[8] Grâce aux bases de données du Getty Research Center (Los Angeles) accessibles sur www.getty.edu/research/institute/provenance et aux collections numériques des grandes institutions (Bibliothèque nationale de France, Bibliothèque de l'INHA).

[9] K. Pomian, *op. cit.*, Paris, 1987, plus particulièrement le chapitre intitulé : « Marchands, connaisseurs, curieux à Paris au XVIIIe siècle », p. 163-194.

[10] Nous citerons parmi d'autres relations de voyages intéressantes comme source pour l'histoire des collections : Joseph-Henry Costa de Beauregard, *Journal de voyage d'un jeune noble savoyard à Paris en 1766-1767,* éd. critique par P. Michel, Villeneuve d'Ascq, Presses universitaires du Septentrion, 2013.

publications ont montré l'utilité de cette littérature périégétique pour l'étude des collections[11]. Avec l'essor des voyages, la plupart des guides de Paris accordent une place de plus en plus grande aux « Beaux-arts » et donc aux collections. Bien que privées, celles-ci sont signalées à l'attention du voyageur au même titre que les curiosités monumentales de la Capitale française. Tour à tour Germain Brice (*Description de la ville de Paris* 9 éditions), de Jeze (*État ou Tableau de Paris*, 1761), Dezallier d'Argenville (*Voyage pittoresque de Paris*, 1re édition en 1749), Luc-Vincent Thiéry (*Guide des amateurs voyageurs à Paris*, 1786-1787), etc. évoquent dans leurs guides les principaux cabinets accessibles aux visiteurs. D'autres ouvrages bien que ne portant pas ce titre offrent les mêmes caractéristiques, tels que le Dictionnaire pittoresque et historique d'Hebert, de 1766, qui contient de riches descriptions de cabinets de collectionneurs. De telles publications furent les premières à informer les amateurs d'art sur la réputation et la nature des collections parisiennes. Par la suite, de telles sources se multiplièrent tel l'Almanach historique et raisonné des architectes, peintres, sculpteurs, graveurs et ciseleurs de l'abbé Le Brun qui eut deux éditions en 1776 et 1777. Suivant l'exemple de Dezallier d'Argenville il donne une liste de ces « sanctuaires des arts », dont les propriétaires doivent trouver une « nouvelle jouissance » dans le plaisir d'ouvrir aux amateurs et aux artistes des cabinets « qu'on ne doit pas considérer comme objets de luxe, mais d'utilité ». Il introduit une nouveauté en étendant cette liste aux principaux cabinets de province, témoignant ainsi du dynamisme des collections. Quant à la presse périodique parisienne ou provinciale, qu'elle soit savante (Journal des Savants) ou à visée plus commerciale (Affiches, Annonces et Avis divers, l'Avant-Coureur, Journal de Paris, Mercure de France, la Feuille nécessaire…) elle reste largement sous-utilisée dans la perspective de l'histoire des collections, du marché et du goût[12]. Elle fournit pourtant de nombreuses informations sur les ventes de collections, la circulation des objets, le marché de l'art, les tendances du goût.

---

[11] Voir notamment E. Jollet, « L'accessibilité de l'œuvre d'art : les Beaux-arts à Paris au XVIIIe siècle », dans *Les Guides imprimés du XVIe au XXe siècle. Villes, paysages, voyageurs,* Paris, Belin, 2000, p. 167-177 ; P. Michel, « Les Collections parisiennes et leurs visiteurs au XVIIIe siècle », dans P. Michel éd., *Collections et marché de l'art en France au XVIIIe siècle,* Bordeaux, Les cahiers du Centre François-Georges Pariset, 2002, p. 153-175.

[12] Voir sur cette question J. Châtelus, *Peindre à Paris au XVIIIe siècle*, Paris, 1991, p. 17-115.

Mais parmi ces sources, les correspondances érudites sont de loin les plus prometteuses. Dans leur rapport de synthèse élaboré en 1987 sur la question « Livre et presse : véhicules des idées », Roger Chartier et Daniel Roche, insistent sur le manuscrit et la place qu'il occupe dans le système général de la communication intellectuelle. Soulignant combien dans l'histoire de la communication épistolaire on a souvent privilégié les correspondances littéraires et à l'opposé mésestimé les correspondances érudites. Elles se trouvent en effet, le plus souvent reléguées au statut de sources sans être considérées dans leur spécificité ». L'activité épistolaire incarne le « mode de vie » de l'Homme des lumières, elle fédère les « réseaux » de l'esprit. Il s'agit de ce fait d'une source essentielle. L'une de ces correspondances érudite est bien connue, celle échangée entre le médecin avignonnais du XVIIIe siècle Esprit Calvet (1728-1810), et un autre collectionneur provençal, le marquis de Calvière[13]. Les deux hommes appartiennent à un réseau, sorte de « mini-République des Lettres provençale » mais dont le rayonnement s'étend jusqu'à Paris puisqu'ils sont en relation avec le comte de Caylus et les numismates Michelet d'Ennery et Joseph Pellerin, deux des plus grands collectionneurs de la période, en ce domaine. Une passion commune pour la collection liant ces correspondants, leurs échanges épistolaires portent donc essentiellement et naturellement sur leurs champs d'intérêt, à savoir la numismatique et l'archéologie.

Les inventaires visuels : images de la collection (gravures, dessins, peintures)

Alors que dans les pays du Nord, les Flandres notamment, on manque de catalogues écrits et publiés, en revanche on voit apparaître une sorte d'inventaire visuel, sous la forme des tableaux dits de « Cabinets d'amateurs ». Ces nombreux tableaux, surtout anversois, du XVIIe siècle, connus sous le titre de « Cabinets d'amateurs » montrent des intérieurs saturés de tableaux, de statues, de médailles, d'antiques, d'objets exotiques et naturels, et sont parfois censés restituer la

[13] Cette correspondance conservée à la Bibliothèque municipale d'Avignon a fait l'objet de nombreux travaux parmi lesquels L.W.B. Brockliss, *Calvet's Web. Enlightenment and the Republic of Letters in Eighteenth-Century France,* Oxford, University Press, 2002, et O. Cavalier, *L'Empire de Mars et des Muses. La collection du marquis de Calvière, lieutenant-général des armées du roi, 1693-1777,* Avignon-Paris, Somogy, 2002.

disposition de certains cabinets ayant réellement existé. Mais dans la plupart des cas, ceux-ci doivent être considérés comme une sorte de représentation idéale de la collection, plutôt que comme un reflet fidèle des lieux. Dans le contexte français, les représentations figurées de cabinets de collectionneurs sont rares. Celles-ci sont de deux ordres : les recueils gravés, et les représentations d'intérieurs de collectionneurs. Les recueils-gravés sont une forme de pérennisation des collections et un instrument de leur découverte à distance par leur diffusion via l'estampe. « Les recueils comme les collections déclinent l'histoire de l'art au fil d'œuvres soigneusement classées, et qui documentent artiste par artiste, école par école, le cours du temps »[14]. La première collection a en bénéficier ne fut curieusement pas une collection parisienne mais un cabinet provincial, celui de l'aixois Jean-Baptiste Boyer d'Eguilles, conseiller au Parlement d'Aix-en-Provence. Publié pour la première fois en 1709 ce recueil fut réédité par les soins de Pierre-Jean Mariette en 1744. Il inaugurait une pratique qui allait se développer dans la seconde moitié du siècle (Cabinet Choiseul, Cabinet Poullain). Ce type de recueil permettait de répertorier, de documenter et de diffuser en la pérennisant par l'image le contenu d'une collection particulière, donnant la possibilité au plus grand nombre d'y accéder virtuellement. Faire graver les tableaux de sa collection est une démarche fréquente au XVIIIe siècle, « grand siècle » de la gravure d'interprétation des maîtres principalement « flamands » alors les plus recherchés par les amateurs. Les marchands d'estampes jouèrent un rôle déterminant dans la diffusion de l'image des collections. La lettre de ces gravures qui n'omettent pas de préciser la provenance de l'œuvre reproduite (« tiré du Cabinet de M*** ») permet ainsi la reconstitution partielle d'un cabinet et dessine au-delà, les contours d'une histoire du goût à un moment donné[15].

Les différents types de questionnement autour de l'histoire des collections

Dans la conclusion des actes du colloque « Collections et marché de

---

[14] P. Griener, *La République de l'œil. L'expérience de l'art au siècle des Lumières,* Paris, Odile Jacob, 2010, p. 218.

[15] Voir sur cette question Vivian Lee Atwater, *A Catalogue and analysis of Eighteenth Century French prints after Nederlandish Baroque paintings*, Ph. D. University of Washington, 1988 (inédite).

l'art en France 1789-1848 », qui s'est tenu à l'INHA en 2005, Dominique Poulot[16] a esquissé les grandes approches et problématiques de l'histoire du collectionnisme, dégageant quelques idées forces que nous lui empruntons :

a. « La majeure partie des études du collectionnisme relevant peu ou prou de l'histoire de l'art vise à reconstruire de manière détaillée la conduite du collectionneur et son résultat, en mettant l'accent sur le contenu de ses possessions, leur étendue et leur spécificité, voire leur originalité ».

b. « Une seconde perspective, davantage répandue chez les historiens, insiste sur les fonctions des collections, leur rôle dans la construction des savoirs, dans l'élaboration d'un héritage culturel, en particulier d'un patrimoine national, ou encore sur leur place dans la consolidation ou l'affirmation de hiérarchies sociales, de statuts, comme dans la configuration de clientèles et de réseaux ».

c. « Enfin une dernière approche tend à rendre compte du collectionnisme de manière « théorique », et prend ses références, à la manière d'un « braconnage » (Michel de Certeau) dans la philosophie, la sémiologie, la théorie économique ou la psychologie ».

Quels sont les modes opératoires, les questionnements et les méthodes mises en œuvre pour l'étude du collectionnisme ? Les approches peuvent en être variées, depuis la forme la plus classique (la monographie) jusqu'aux approches les plus sociologisantes, les lectures philosophiques, voire les interprétations psychanalytiques.
Les collectionneurs du XVIIIe siècle ont été largement abordés sous l'angle d'études de cas, monographiques, suivant un plan traditionnel. Entrent notamment dans cette catégorie, pour le domaine français, les études de Cordelia Hattori sur la collection Crozat[17], celle d'Isabelle Tillerot, consacrée à Jean de Jullienne[18] et de Frédéric Bussmann sur le

---

[16] D. Poulot, « Conclusion : L'histoire des collections entre l'histoire de l'art et l'histoire », dans M. Preti-Hamard et P. Sénéchal éd., *Collections et marché de l'art en France 1789-1848,* Rennes, PUR, 2005, p. 443.

[17] C. Hattori, *Pierre Crozat (1665-1740), un financier collectionneur et mécène,* thèse, Université Paris IV-Sorbonne (sous la dir. d'A. Schnapper), 1998 (inédite).

[18] I. Tillerot, *Jean de Jullienne et les collectionneurs de son temps. Un regard singulier sur le tableau,* Paris, Maison des Sciences de l'Homme, 2010. Voir également C. M. Vogtherr et J. Tonkovitch, *Jean de Jullienne collector & Connoisseur,* cat. expo. Londres, The Wallace Collection, mars-juin 2011.

prince de Conti[19], soit deux parmi les plus grands collectionneurs du XVIIIe siècle, ou bien encore le livre de Gauthier Aubert consacré au Président de Robien[20] ainsi que plusieurs études consacrées à des collectionneurs de dessins[21].

Envisager l'étude d'un collectionneur revient donc à se poser un certain nombre de questions que Frédéric Bussmann a parfaitement résumées : « Qui était le collectionneur, quel fut son rôle au XVIIIe siècle ? Comment sa position sociale a-t-elle conditionné son goût et ses idées ? Quel est le contexte historique, social, culturel et artistique dans lequel une collection a été constituée ? Qui influença et conseilla le collectionneur ? Quels sont les critères du goût et les critères artistiques qui se développèrent et quelles en sont les motivations ? Comment le cabinet fut-il présenté et accueilli ? Et enfin, comment la collection fut-elle finalement dispersée ou vendue ? »[22]. Cela revient à comprendre un collectionneur dans son époque, à cerner la démarche inédite ou non qui l'a animé, à discerner enfin en quoi il est singulier, voire unique ou si à l'opposé sa stratégie de collectionneur l'inscrit dans un temps, une norme ou un milieu. Dans ce type d'approche, une attention toute particulière doit être accordée à la culture du collectionneur, envisageable à travers l'analyse de la composition de sa bibliothèque. Mais de telles études ont leurs limites. En dépit de leur intérêt, ces approches monographiques « ne permettent pas de rendre compte de ce que fut la collection dans la pensée des hommes du XVIIIe siècle, qui, surtout, demeurent trop souvent construites autour du seul intérêt porté

---

[19] F. Bussmann, *Un Prince collectionneur. Louis-François de Bourbon Conti et ses collections au palais du Temple à Paris*, Paris, Maison des Sciences de l'Homme, 2012. Voir également *Les Trésors des princes de Bourbon Conti,* cat. expo. L'Isle Adam, Musée d'Art et d'histoire Louis-Senlecq, mai-oct. 2000, Paris, Somogy, 2000.

[20] G. Aubert, *Le Président de Robien gentilhomme et savant dans la Bretagne des Lumières*, Rennes, PUR, 2001.

[21] R. Bacou, *Le Cabinet d'un grand Amateur. P.-J. Mariette 1694-1774,* cat. expo. Paris, Musée du Louvre, 1967 ; P. Rosenberg et L. Barthélémy-Labeeuw, *Les dessins de la collection Mariette. École française,* Milan, Electa, 2011 ; V. Kobi, *Dans l'œil du connaisseur. Pierre-Jean Mariette (1694-1774) et la construction des savoirs en histoire de l'art,* Rennes, PUR, 2017 ; J. Labbé et L. Bicart-Sée, *La Collection de dessins d'Antoine-Joseph Dezallier d'Argenville reconstituée d'après son Abrégé de la vie des plus fameux peintres*, Paris, 1996 ; F. Arquié-Bruley, J. Labbé et L. Bicart-Sée, *La Collection Saint Morys au Cabinet des Dessins du Musée du Louvre*, Paris, 1987 et J.-F. Méjanès, *Les collections du comte d'Orsay : dessins du musée du Louvre,* cat. expo, Paris, Musée du Louvre, 1983.

[22] F. Bussmann, *op. cit.*, 2012, p. 3.

à la personnalité du collectionneur et aux caractères intrinsèques de la collection »[23]. De fait, les monographies de collectionneurs ont généralement pour inconvénient de l'isoler dans sa pratique. Aujourd'hui on a plutôt tendance à l'appréhender comme élément d'un réseau, qu'il soit géographique, social[24] ou par champ de spécialité (les antiquaires, dans le sens donné à ce mot au XVIIIe siècle, les naturalistes, les numismates etc.).

La collection a fait également l'objet d'approches thématiques élaborées autour de l'étude des collectionneurs de tel ou tel artiste (le goût pour les gravures de Rembrandt, le goût pour la peinture ou pour la peinture française contemporaine)[25], ou tel ou tel domaine : les dessins[26], les petits bronzes[27], les antiquités classiques, la sculpture moderne, l'histoire naturelle[28], les médailles[29].

Une autre démarche consisterait à envisager l'étude d'une pratique dans un territoire géographique déterminé (local, régional, national). Or, si les travaux portant sur les collections parisiennes sont nombreux, le

---

[23] I. Tillerot, *op. cit.*, 2010, p. 7.

[24] I. Tillerot (*op. cit.*, 2010) dans son étude de la collection de Jean de Jullienne a élargi son champ d'investigation à un cercle de collectionneurs proches de l'entrepreneur des Gobelins envisageant leurs stratégies de collection.

[25] Nous renvoyons notamment à P. Michel, *Peinture et plaisir. Les goûts picturaux des collectionneurs parisiens au XVIIIe siècle,* Rennes, PUR, 2010.

[26] P. Michel, « Collections de dessins et marché de l'art en France au XVIIIe siècle », dans H. Pauwels, A. Van den Kerkhove et L. Wuyts éd., *Liber Memorialis Erik Duverger. Bijdragen tot de kunstgeschiedenis van de nederlanden,* Wetteren, 2006, p. 169-220. Signalons également la thèse en cours de Delphine Chambon, *Collectionner le dessin en France au XVIIIe siècle*, Université de Lille 3 (sous ma direction). Voir également Ch. Michel, « Le goût pour le dessin en France aux XVIIe et XVIIIe siècles : de l'utilisation à l'étude désintéressée », *Revue de l'Art,* n° 143, 2004, p. 27-34.

[27] Sur les collections de sculpture voir G. Scherf, « Collections et collectionneurs de sculptures modernes », dans Th. W. Gaehtgens, Ch. Michel, D. Rabreau et M. Schieder éd., *L'Art et les normes sociales au XVIIIe siècle,* Paris, 2001, p. 147-164 et P. Michel, « Le goût pour les petits bronzes de collection en France au XVIIIe siècle », dans M. Favreau et P. Michel, éd. *L'objet d'art en France du XVIe au XVIIIe siècle : de la création à l'imaginaire*, Bordeaux, Cahiers du Centre François-Georges Pariset, 2007, p. 141-169.

[28] Voir notamment l'excellent livre de B. Daugeron, *Collections naturalistes entre science et empires 1763-1804,* Paris, publications scientifiques du Museum d'Histoire naturelle, 2009.

[29] Th. Sarmant, *La République des médailles. Numismates et collections numismatiques à Paris du Grand Siècle au Siècle des Lumières*, Paris, H. Champion, 2003.

champ du collectionnisme provincial reste lui très largement à défricher[30]. Si l'enquête a été menée en ce qui concerne les bibliothèques, il reste beaucoup à faire en ce qui concerne les collections d'objets.

Dans son Almanach historique et raisonné des architectes, peintres, sculpteurs, graveurs et ciseleurs qui eut deux éditions en 1776 et 1777, l'abbé Le Brun donne une liste des principales collections de son temps, visibles à Paris et dans les provinces. Les noms livrés montrent que, au cours de la seconde moitié du XVIIIe siècle, la passion de collectionner était partagée par tous les milieux ou presque : la noblesse d'épée, de l'administration, des finances, tout comme par les membres du premier et du tiers état, les abbés, les riches bourgeois, les magistrats, les marchands mais aussi les artistes. L'historien peut donc saisir les pratiques des collectionneurs à partir de l'étude d'un groupe de collectionneurs considéré comme un observatoire de la pratique[31]. La démarche sociologique étant ici appliquée aux collectionneurs et à un groupe social en particulier : la haute aristocratie, les financiers.... Une telle approche se donne pour objectif de mettre en évidence (ou d'isoler), de préciser, voire de nuancer selon le cas, « les différences qui marquaient le goût, les moyens de se distinguer et les attitudes culturelles des divers groupes au sein de l'élite française »[32]. Une question l'emporte dans ce type d'approche : l'échantillon retenu constitue- t-il un milieu cohérent dont les collections représenteraient les valeurs ? Cela revient à vérifier si l'on peut isoler un groupe restreint d'individus homogènes, mû par un commun intérêt par exemple pour un certain type de peinture, comme l'a fait Colin B. Bailey pour un groupe de collectionneurs de la fin du XVIIIe siècle[33]. Pour ce faire, il

---

[30] On signalera cependant parmi les publications récentes V. Krings et C. Valenti dir., *Les Antiquaires du Midi. Savoirs et mémoires XVIe-XIXe siècle,* Paris, 2010 et E. Chapron, I. Luciani et G. Le Thiec dir., *Érudits, collectionneurs et amateurs. France méridionale et Italie XVIe-XIXe siècle*, Aix-Marseille, Presses universitaires de Provence, 2017.

[31] Ce qu'a fait O. Bonfait, « Les collections picturales des financiers à la fin du règne de Louis XIV », *XVIIe siècle,* n° 151, avr.-juin 1986, p. 125-151 et le même, « Les collections des parlementaires parisiens au XVIIIe siècle », *Revue de l'Art,* 1986, n° 73, p. 28-42. Nous citerons encore la thèse (inédite) de Élodie Kong, *Les financiers et l'art en France dans la seconde moitié du XVIIIe siècle,* Université Lille 3 (dir. P. Michel), 2016.

[32] F. Bussmann, *op. cit.*, 2012, p. 4.

[33] Colin B. Bailey, *Patriotic Taste. Collecting Modern Art in the Pre-Revolutionary Paris,* New Haven-London, Yale University Press, 2002.

faut interroger en premier lieu les corpus de ces collections, les liens de convergence et de divergence entre eux. En un mot, rechercher si au sein de ce groupe, l'on peut repérer des stratégies collectives ou individuelles de collection.

Quelques questionnements ou axes forts de la recherche sur le collectionnisme

Interroger le sens des collections, artistiques ou naturalistes revient à questionner les moyens de constitution des collections, les modalités de leur formation. Or, les enjeux économiques apparaissent indissociables de ceux des collections. Le niveau de fortune est en effet un élément constitutif de la pratique de la collection. Il s'agit d'un aspect qui ne peut être éludé et qui pourtant est souvent évacué des études des historiens de l'art sur les collectionneurs. Ce qui revient dans l'idéal à étudier la nature et la structure de leur fortune, leur provenance, mais également leur degré de mobilisation. Quelle est la part de leur fortune consacrée à leur activité de collectionneur ?

La formation d'une collection : les moyens de l'appropriation

Comment un collectionneur a-t-il constitué sa collection ? De quels moyens disposons-nous pour appréhender l'histoire de sa formation ? Quelles sont les modalités et les voies d'enrichissement de la collection ? L'entrée des objets dans une collection peut se faire selon des modalités différentes : l'héritage, l'achat, la commande, le don, l'échange, la spoliation...
Au XVIIIe siècle la collection est rarement l'œuvre commune de plusieurs représentants d'une même famille ; les collections « dynastiques » constituent l'exception dans le contexte français. Le cas de la collection d'Orléans fruit de plusieurs générations est à ce titre exceptionnel. Le plus souvent, la formation d'une collection est une aventure individuelle. Une des caractéristiques des grandes collections de la seconde moitié du XVIIIe siècle est la rapidité avec laquelle elles furent constituées. La collection du prince de Conti est à ce titre exemplaire ; elle témoigne d'une véritable *furor collecionnis* selon les termes de Fréderic Bussman. Il paraît en effet incroyable que le prince ait pu réunir dans une période relativement brève, environ dix ans, une collection de plus de 1500 tableaux. Il était connu qu'il achetait des

collections entières et que les brocanteurs de tous poils faisaient le siège de son hôtel.

Pour former une collection, l'achat en ventes publiques apparaît comme la forme d'acquisition la plus commune. Du moins est-elle la plus repérable. L'existence de nombreux exemplaires de catalogues de ventes annotés, avec le prix et le nom de l'acquéreur, permet de retracer quelques-unes de ces acquisitions.
En l'absence de marchands spécialisés dans certains domaines (archéologie, numismatique…), l'enrichissement des collections se faisait à l'occasion de trouvailles, de fouilles ou au cours de voyages, et, le plus souvent, par achat ou échange entre antiquaires ou numismates. L'essentiel du marché numismatique était alimenté par des voies détournées et par des découvertes lointaines, dans le Midi, en Italie ou au Levant. Thierry Sarmant[34] a montré que la communauté savante des numismates fonctionne en vase clos, selon des règles bien établies. Les médaillistes entretenaient des commerces littéraires en France et à l'étranger, aussi bien pour s'enrichir d'informations nouvelles que de pièces manquant à leur petit trésor monétaire. Ces échanges avaient leurs usages et leurs rites. Certaines correspondances érudites permettent d'envisager ces pratiques, telle celle déjà mentionnée d'Esprit Calvet, docteur et professeur de médecine à Avignon qui constitue une source de première main ou bien encore celles du numismate Pellerin à Paris ou de Jean-François Séguier à Nîmes[35].

Le cabinet du collectionneur : espace social et espace de savoir : sociabilité mondaine et pratiques savantes

Depuis longtemps, les bibliothèques et les cabinets sont des lieux d'échange sociaux et intellectuels. Les collectionneurs ouvrent volontiers les portes de leur cabinet afin d'en montrer les richesses. Le

---

[34] T. Sarmant, *La République des médailles ; Numismates et collections numismatiques à Paris du Grand Siècle au Siècle des Lumières,* Paris, Champion, 2003.

[35] D. Roche est le premier à avoir attiré l'attention sur celle-ci. Voir D. Roche, *Les Républicains des lettres. Gens de culture et Lumières au XVIIIe siècle,* Paris, Fayard, 1988, p. 263-280. Cette correspondance fait l'objet d'une publication électronique par les soins de l'UMR 7303 Telemme (CNRS. Université Aix-Marseille) et l'Institut Européen Séguier (seguier.org).

cabinet du naturaliste, au même titre que la galerie de tableaux, est au XVIIIe siècle tout à la fois un espace de sociabilité et un lieu du partage du savoir. Aborder cette question revient à s'intéresser aux conditions d'accès à l'art dans une ville comme Paris au XVIIIe siècle, à la place et au rôle joué par les collections privées dans la formation d'un espace du savoir. Accessible au public - ou du moins à un certain public - la collection devient un espace d'échange, d'élaboration et de circulation des savoirs. À une époque où l'idée d'un musée public accessible à tous commençait juste à être posée, il faut bien considérer que les possibilités s'offrant à ceux qui s'intéressaient à l'art étaient limitées (églises, expositions académiques ou libres, commerce d'art et ventes publiques). Dans ce contexte, les collections privées se présentent comme une alternative à la quasi inaccessibilité des collections royales (elles ne furent qu'en partie visibles à partir de 1750 au Luxembourg). Seules en effet, elles permettaient d'avoir une vue d'ensemble de l'art européen, qu'il soit ancien ou moderne. Déjà, la collection du duc d'Orléans au Palais-Royal avait ouvert la voie, « ce prince ayant donné des ordres pour les faire voir dans la matinée aux Artistes, aux Amateurs & aux étrangers » et un catalogue en avait été imprimé[36]. Mais bien que celle-ci « fonctionne comme un véritable musée public bien avant le Louvre », Pascal Griener estime à juste titre que « l'histoire des collections n'a pas saisi l'importance programmatique de la galerie du duc d'Orléans, au Palais-Royal »[37].

Au XVIIIe siècle, le cabinet du collectionneur est un lieu de savoir et de transmission de celui-ci et les objets qui le composent sont des objets de connaissance, des objets matériels qui concrétisent un savoir. Il convient donc de dessiner les contours d'une pratique mondaine ou savante et de montrer le rôle joué par les collections et leurs initiateurs dans la constitution des disciplines historiques ou scientifiques.

Pratiques mondaines et savantes au sein de la collection

Une telle approche revient à considérer les pratiques savantes autour des collections : le travail in camera, c'est-à-dire une véritable pratique des objets qui nous amène à nous intéresser à l'usage social et intellectuel de toute collection. Les collections de médailles et

---

[36] L. F. Dubois de Saint-Gelais, *Description des tableaux du Palais Royal,* Paris, 1727, p. v-vi.

[37] P. Griener, *op. cit.,* 2010.

d'antiques constituent par exemple des observatoires privilégiés pour comprendre l'évolution des pratiques antiquaires en France et en Europe. Il en est de même des cabinets naturalistes qui deviennent des lieux de recherche, des laboratoires des sciences. L'importance de ces collections, constituées tant par des particuliers que par des scientifiques, est donc réelle. Elles permettent de dresser l'inventaire des productions naturelles de nos régions et de susciter leur étude, contribuant ainsi au progrès des sciences naturelles. De même, la galerie de tableaux devient au XVIIIe siècle le lieu d'une expérience à vocation cognitive comme le rappelle notre collègue Pascal Griener dans son ouvrage *La République de l'œil.* Si de nombreux cabinets de collectionneurs étaient accessibles et favorisaient cette éducation de l'œil, le cabinet du banquier Pierre Crozat se distinguait parmi les collections du XVIIIe siècle par la place qu'il tenait dans la vie culturelle parisienne. De fait, au XVIIIe siècle la collection n'est pas une pratique solitaire mais un plaisir partagé. Parmi les collectionneurs enthousiastes qui montrent volontiers leur collection, le graveur d'origine allemande Johann-Georg Wille occupe une place de choix. Lieu de sociabilité artistique, le cabinet de tableaux et de dessins de Wille est également un espace de la sociabilité mondaine[38].

Les fins de la collection : enjeux des collections et motivations des collectionneurs

En 1788 Watelet et Levesque pouvaient écrire : « On est connaisseur par étude, amateur par goût, et curieux par vanité »[39]. Une telle définition, bien que lapidaire, a le mérite de poser clairement la question centrale des motivations d'un collectionneur. Il faut examiner en ce lieu les valeurs dont la collection est investie, c'est-à-dire l'interprétation de la collection, la question fondamentale de la (ou des) motivation(s) du collectionneur. Peut-on parler de la collection comme objet de plaisir, de collections objets de connaissance ou de collections ostensibles ou bien encore de collections spéculatives ?
Vous me permettrez de faire ici une autocitation. Dans mon livre

[38] Voir E. Décultot et M. Espagne, F.-R. Martin éd., *Johann Georg Wille (1715-1808) et son milieu. Un réseau européen de l'art au XVIIIe siècle,* Rencontres de l'École du Louvre, Paris, 2009.
[39] Watelet et Lévesque, « Curieux », dans *Encyclopédie méthodique*, Paris, 1788, t. I/1, p. 171.

Peinture et Plaisir. Les goûts picturaux des collectionneurs parisiens au XVIIIe siècle, je constatais que : « Si les rédacteurs des catalogues de vente sont pratiquement unanimes à vanter avec parfois quelque emphase et exagération, la qualité des collections dont ils se voient confier la dispersion, il est infiniment plus rare qu'ils nous transmettent des témoignages sur les intentions et la démarche du collectionneur »[40]. De fait, les éclairages sur ce sujet sont rares. Toutes les collections présentent un certain nombre de caractéristiques exemplaires : goût du savoir, volonté encyclopédique, besoin d'émotions, caractère privé voire secret, rareté et coût des objets, désir d'accumulation, etc. Pour autant, il n'est pas aisé de rechercher les motivations personnelles d'un collectionneur : « Amusement numismatique, plaisir des yeux sont des expressions qui reviennent fréquemment sous la plume des collectionneurs pour montrer l'imbrication du sensible et de la science, de la distinction sociale et de la recherche d'une délectation ». Par ces quelques mots D. Roche a fort bien résumé l'éventail des motivations du collectionneur.

La collection comme tradition

Un cas exemplaire nous est fourni dans le cas français par le prince de Conti. Louis-François de Bourbon Conti, prince du sang, grand prieur de l'ordre de Malte se mit relativement tard à collectionner les œuvres d'art. Il réussit malgré tout à réunir en un peu plus de dix ans entre 1766 et 1776 une des plus grandes collections d'art de l'époque. Mais cette collection fut en définitive le fruit d'une longue tradition où le fait de collectionner faisait partie de la représentation princière, reflétant autant cette idée traditionnelle de la fonction d'une collection que les prédilections personnelles du prince. Il s'agissait donc avant tout d'une collection représentative qui correspondait au rang et aux ambitions politiques de son initiateur. Conti s'inscrivait ainsi dans la tradition des collectionneurs princiers. Les dépenses de luxe faisaient partie de l'habitus du prince, de sa manière d'être, mais aussi de la « culture des apparences » comme le souligne F. Bussmann. Elles correspondaient à l'idéal du gentilhomme ; un prince du sang doit d'autant plus tenir son rang. Mais dans ce cas précis, il faut également tenir compte de l'émulation, des modèles. La collection beaucoup plus riche du duc

---

40 P. Michel, *Peinture et plaisir. Les goûts picturaux des collectionneurs parisiens au XVIIIe siècle*, Rennes, PUR, 2010, p. 371.

d'Orléans au Palais-Royal a pu fournir un modèle au prince de Conti. Quoi qu'il en soit, dans bien des cas moins relevés socialement, la collection fut incontestablement un *status symbol*, un élément d'une stratégie de la distinction.

La collection comme *status symbol*

L'émulation joua vraisemblablement un rôle non négligeable dans la formation de certaines collections. Les antécédents célèbres fournissent des modèles de bon goût à suivre. Sous l'impulsion des livres de Jürgen Habermas[41] et de Reinhart Kosselek[42], la recherche a mis en valeur la nouvelle volonté des élites de se distinguer socialement par leur savoir, par leur goût littéraire ou artistique. Au-delà du plaisir personnel, la collection a incontestablement une fonction bien affirmée, un rôle éminemment social à jouer. Dans cette perspective, la collection vaudrait donc surtout pour un « signe de culture ». Le prestige social et culturel lié à une collection est souvent associé à une notion de goût. Cette motivation vaut également pour les cabinets scientifiques. Certains d'entre eux traduisent le statut social et culturel de leur propriétaire. La richesse de certaines collections en témoigne ; elle est généralement fonction du niveau de fortune et du rang social du collectionneur. Les savants, tel Lamarck, ont d'ailleurs souvent condamné cette ostentation. Les scientifiques faisant exception, ils forment des cabinets importants sans avoir nécessairement des moyens financiers démesurés.

La collection comme passion

C'est fort heureusement et à toutes les époques la motivation la plus répandue et dont nous rencontrons de nombreux témoignages dans la littérature d'art ou dans les correspondances privées. Ces dernières fournissent et de loin, les témoignages les plus sincères, les moins sujets à la critique historique. Un collectionneur normand, le baron de Saint-Victor, écrit au numismate parisien Pellerin, le 4 janvier 1771, à propos de sa collection numismatique : « Enfin, Monsieur, quelque expérience que j'aye déjà faite autrefois de la faiblesse de mes lumières, il faut que

---

[41] J. Habermas, *Strukturwandel der Öffentlichkeit,* Francfort, 1969.
[42] R. Kosselek, *Kritik und Krise. Eine Studie zur Pathogenese der Bürgerlichen Welt*, Francfort, 1973.

je renonce pour jamais à porter aucun jugement sur une Médaille, si je m'abuse sur celle-ci, pardonnés moi ce détail, mais un amant passionné ne tarit point sur le détail des charmes de sa maîtresse, la jouissance n'a point encore détrompé mes yeux, parce que j'ai oublié que j'étais amant, lorsque que j'ai pris la fonction de juge »[43].
Mais la collection peut également être un palliatif à l'ennui, au désœuvrement. Il faut bien l'admettre, les motivations des collectionneurs sont parfois d'un autre ordre, elles varient en fonction de l'âge des « grippés » comme le confesse le marquis de Calvière au médecin Esprit Calvet dans une lettre du 6 janvier 1772 : « Je me rappelle fort bien qu'autre fois quand j'aimais les filles, je me souciais fort peu des Médailles, mais à présent que les médailles sont presque mon unique passion, je sens que les filles sont prodigieusement déchues auprès de moy, et même auprès de mon imagination qui étoit la plus difficile à guérir »[44]. La collection vient donc parfois combler les vides de l'existence, de l'absence.

Espace et dispositif de la collection : lieux et matérialité de la collection

Passant en revue les points faibles des études sur le collectionnisme D. Poulot constatait en 2005 que « À la différence des histoires de musées, constamment soucieuses de sites urbains occupés, des architectures érigées, de la disposition des pièces, l'histoire des collections s'abstrait trop souvent des lieux de conservation et de jouissance organisée par le collectionneur »[45]. De fait, cet intérêt pour les espaces de la collection n'est devenu véritablement significatif qu'assez récemment. On s'intéresse en effet depuis quelques années à l'histoire des espaces de la collection, ce que les anglo-saxons appellent *The Display of art*, à la rencontre de la dimension intellectuelle et matérielle de l'activité savante[46]. Les collections se déploient dans un

---

[43] Paris, Bibliothèque nationale de France, Ms NAF 1074, f° 156. Rouen, le 4 janv. 1771.
[44] Avignon, Bibliothèque Ceccano, Ms 2356, f° 93v°. Lettre du 6 janv. 1772.
[45] D. Poulot, « Conclusion : L'histoire des collections entre l'histoire de l'art et l'histoire », dans M. Preti-Hamard et Ph. Sénéchal éd., *Collections et marché de l'art en France 1789-1848,* Rennes, PUR, 2005, p. 438.
[46] Voir notamment T. W. Gaehtgens & L Marchesano, *Display Art History. The Düsseldorf Gallery and its Catalogue*, Los Angeles, The Getty Research Institute, 2011.

espace physique au sein de la maison du collectionneur, soit par une répartition dans l'ensemble de la demeure, soit au sein d'un espace spécialisé, le plus souvent le cabinet ou la galerie qui connaît un regain d'actualité à la fin du XVIIIe siècle.

Les perspectives ouvertes invitent à envisager l'espace, non plus seulement comme cadre matériel plus ou moins contingent d'un projet intellectuel, mais comme étant une de ses dimensions constitutives. Comme le souligne Rafael Mandressi : « les espaces de savoir font sens par leurs usages, par les intentions qui ont informé leur aménagement, par les objets qui y sont disposés, par les typologies architecturales en jeu (cabinet, galerie...), par leurs évolutions et métamorphoses »[47]. Dans le cas français, faute d'études spéciales[48], la disposition des collections particulières est beaucoup moins bien connue que celle des collections royales et comme nous l'avons dit, les représentations figurées en sont rares pour le XVIIIe siècle[49].

En 1999 dans sa leçon inaugurale de la chaire européenne au Collège de France, Thomas Gaehtgens a précisément abordé la question de L'Image des collections en Europe au XVIIIe siècle, appelant de ses vœux une véritable réflexion sur le sujet. Il y posait un certain nombre de questions : les collectionneurs vivent-ils avec leurs œuvres d'art ? Qu'en font-ils ? Existe-t-il des manières différentes de les conserver et de les présenter ? Peut-on constater des différences nationales ou sociales ? Que nous apprennent les sources picturales sur la manière dont les œuvres étaient appréciées ? Comment l'ordre matériel des collections, le dispositif dans le cas d'une galerie de tableaux, le rangement physique dans des armoires dans le cas des cabinets naturalistes, nous est-il connu ? Quelles ont été les différentes manières de présenter les œuvres qui ont existé ? En matière picturale, les

---

[47] R. Mandressi, « Espaces, institutions, artefacts : figures des savoirs entre architectures et pratiques », dans Ch. Jacob éd., *Les lieux de savoir, espaces et communautés,* Paris, Albin Michel, 2007, p. 706.

[48] Nous renvoyons à notre étude P. Michel, « Lieux et dispositifs de la collection en France dans la seconde moitié du XVIIIe siècle », dans J. Rasmussen éd., *La Valeur de l'art. Exposition, marché, critique et public au XVIIIe siècle*, Paris, Honoré Champion, 2009, p. 131-159.

[49] À l'exception des relevés dessinés du cabinet Bonnier de la Mosson de l'architecte Jean Courtonne (Paris, Bibliothèque de l'INHA) ou du « Catalogue des tableaux de Jean de Jullienne », Paris, 1756, Ms, New York, The Pierpont Morgan Library, publié intégralement pour la première fois et étudié par I. Tillerot, *Jean de Jullienne et les collectionneurs de son temps. Un regard singulier sur le tableau,* Paris, Maison des Sciences de l'Homme, 2010.

accrochages ont-ils varié au fil du temps, des lieux et des milieux sociaux ? Quelles règles ont présidé à ces aménagements et à leurs modifications ?
Souvent, dans la demeure du XVIIIe siècle, en France du moins, la collection est dispersée dans l'ensemble de l'espace domestique. Mais déjà un mouvement se dessine dans la seconde moitié du siècle. On constate notamment une tendance à l'autonomisation de la collection de tableaux par sa concentration dans un espace spécifique, la galerie par exemple. Dans l'hôtel aristocratique du XVIIIe siècle, la galerie est parfois un espace mixte destiné à présenter en sus de l'accrochage des tableaux de sa collection, des objets variés. C'est le cas chez le financier Paul Randon de Boisset avant 1777, comme le montre un dessin de Gabriel de Saint-Aubin (Lyon, Musée des arts décoratifs). Dans la plupart des cas, il ne semble pas avoir existé de principes d'accrochage des œuvres. Les tableaux ne sont répartis ni selon les écoles, ni selon la chronologie, ni même selon les sujets, comme le montre par exemple l'accrochage des tableaux dans la maison de Jean de Jullienne tel que nous le dévoile un exceptionnel document, le Recueil Jullienne de la Pierpont Morgan Library de New York. Pendant une bonne partie du XVIIIe siècle, l'accrochage des tableaux, qu'il s'agisse d'une collection privée ou de la présentation d'une centaine de tableaux des collections royales au Luxembourg, peut être qualifiée d'éclectique ; elle se faisait par la plus stricte indifférence à l'historicisme de l'art et de la spécificité des Écoles. Ce dispositif qui favorisait les confrontations, permettait de faire mieux ressortir par comparaisons et oppositions, les caractéristiques formelles des uns et des autres. Le cabinet du collectionneur constituait donc pour l'artiste comme pour l'amateur un espace de formation aux « manières » des peintres. Ainsi, « la comparaison entre les différents genres servait de chemin pour étayer le jugement… »[50]. On était donc loin des préconisations du marchand Le Brun qui défendait l'idée pour le Muséum national d'une présentation par écoles[51]. La symétrie resta le principe d'accrochage favori dans les intérieurs des collectionneurs, y compris lorsque, comme chez le duc de Choiseul, les tableaux n'étaient pas exposés dans une galerie prestigieuse mais dans les pièces de réception de l'ancien

---

[50] Andrew Mc Clellan, « Rapports entre la théorie de l'art et la disposition des tableaux au XVIIIe siècle », dans É. Pommier éd., *Les Musées en Europe à la veille de l'ouverture du Louvre,* Paris, Musée du Louvre et Klincksieck, 1995, p. 567-582.
[51] D. Poulot, *Musée, nation, patrimoine 1789-1815,* Paris, Gallimard, 1997, p. 203.

hôtel Crozat. Les miniatures de la célèbre « tabatière Choiseul » peinte en 1771 par le miniaturiste Louis Nicolas van Blarenberghe (coll. privée) avec des vues de la demeure du duc de Choiseul, ministre de Louis XV est « l'une des sources les plus explicites de la manière dont un grand collectionneur vivait avec ses œuvres »[52]. Ces vues très précises nous introduisent dans la familiarité du collectionneur et nous décrivent le rapport de Choiseul aux tableaux de sa collection. Intégrée au cadre de vie, « la peinture n'était plus subordonnée à un système décoratif. C'est elle qui déterminait à présent l'ambiance d'un intérieur en offrant des points de vue nombreux et variés vers lesquels les visiteurs pouvaient aussi se tourner de temps en temps pendant la conversation »[53].

Même lorsqu'il s'agissait de simples amateurs, le geste de collectionner était, dans nombre de cas, étroitement associé à la volonté d'aménager son lieu d'habitation.

La fin de la collection : transmission ou éclatement

Dans l'immense majorité des cas, la mort du collectionneur est suivie de la mise en vente et donc du démantèlement de sa collection qui est souvent l'œuvre d'une vie. Les exemples ne manquent pas au XVIIIe siècle. La collection d'objets d'art et surtout de dessins et d'estampes que Pierre-Jean Mariette était parvenu à réunir et à compléter eut le sort de toutes les collections : elle fut mise en vente moins d'une année après sa mort, en 1775.

Pour qu'une collection survive à son inventeur, des dispositions testamentaires particulières sont nécessaires. Le collectionneur exerce ainsi au-delà de sa mort un pouvoir de décision par ses dispositions testamentaires. Celles-ci subordonnent expressément le legs à l'engagement de ne pas la disperser. Dans son testament de 1750, Dezallier d'Argenville lègue à son fils sa collection de dessins réunie sous la forme de 30 volumes à la condition expresse que celui-ci « le conserve a toujours et le conserve en son entier »[54]. Vœu qui ne fut pas respecté. Les exemples de transmission à la collectivité sont infiniment

---

[52] T. Gaehtgens, *L'image des collections en Europe au XVIIIe siècle,* Collège de France. Chaire européenne. Leçon inaugurale, jeudi 29 janv. 1999, p. 15.

[53] T. Gaehtgens, *op. cit.,* 1999, p. 16.

[54] Paris, Archives nationales, Minutier Central des notaires, Étude LII, 353. Testament du 16 oct. 1750 et codicille du 15 mai 1760.

rares au XVIIIe siècle. Nous en citerons trois qui concernent tous la province : vers 1770 Clément de Lafaille, contrôleur ordinaire des guerres, secrétaire perpétuel de l'Académie de La Rochelle, lègue à sa mort à l'Académie, son médaillier, ses livres et surtout son cabinet d'histoire naturelle, décrit par Dezallier d'Argenville comme l'un des plus renommés. Il y joint une somme de douze mille livres pour l'entretien des collections, qui doivent être rendues publiques. Celles-ci sont installées dans une maison contiguë à l'hôtel de ville, acquise en 1782 avec une partie des fonds. Ce cabinet est ouvert au public en 1789 et l'est toujours. De même, en 1778, l'érudit nîmois Jean-François Séguier fait don de ses collections qui seront réunies en un musée public à sa mort en 1785. Enfin un peu plus tard, en 1810, le médecin avignonnais Esprit Calvet léguait sa bibliothèque et son cabinet de médailles et d'antiques et sa collection d'histoire naturelle à la Ville d'Avignon. Ces trois donations ont au moins deux points communs : elles concernent toutes la province et sont toutes issues d'une démarche patrimoniale. Or, comme l'a souligné fort justement E. Pommier ce geste patrimonial : « se décèle surtout dans les villes où une longue tradition municipale et la présence de vestiges de civilisations antiques ont favorisé le développement d'une forte conscience historique »[55]. On peut donc dire que de ce point de vue la province a précédé Paris.

Rare au XVIIIe siècle, une telle volonté de pérennisation sera beaucoup plus fréquente au XIXe siècle, siècle des musées : ainsi ont agi un certain nombre de collectionneurs - Du Sommerard (en 1843) dont le nom est attaché aujourd'hui au musée de Cluny à Paris, Sauvageot (au Louvre 1856), Boucher Crèvecoeur de Perthes (1867), Guimet (1889), Gonse (1893), Caillebotte (1894) etc. - soit des ensembles riches et divers qui ont alimenté, voire constitué des musées.

Les legs ont parfois posé aux institutions qui les ont accueillies des problèmes juridiques parfois insolubles. Mais dans certains cas, il faut le dire, le legs à l'institution sonne aussi le glas d'une collection car elle court le risque d'être absorbée, digérée par la masse du musée ou de la bibliothèque à laquelle elle est agrégée. Feuillet de Conches, auteur des Causeries d'un curieux (1862) le dit avec raison à propos des cabinets d'estampes : « À peine leurs collections, amassées avec tant d'amour, classées à force de savoir, de travaux et de veilles, leur ont-elles un moment donné les joies de la possession, en traversant leur cabinet,

---

[55] E. Pommier, *Le problème du musée à la veille de la Révolution*, Les Cahiers du musée Girodet, n° 1, 1989, p. 16.

qu'elles sont allées s'engloutir dans la Bibliothèque nationale, ce « vaste gouffre », comme l'appelait Terrasson, destinée commune de toute collection de monuments écrits »[56]. Mais il s'agit d'une autre histoire !

Conclusion

Dans l'avant-propos du catalogue du cabinet Quentin de Lorangère, en 1744, le célèbre marchand Gersaint brosse ce magnifique portrait du curieux et donne surtout une justification à cette pratique :
« Il faut nécessairement que tout homme ait quelque amusement ; son esprit fatigué d'une étude, & d'un travail continuel, ou accablé d'affaires & d'occupations journalières demande du relâche, & de la dissipation ; ce sont ordinairement nos passions qui nous dictent nos plaisirs & nos amusemens, & nous ne nous en formons guères que d'une espèce à les pouvoir satisfaire ; mais un Curieux a souvent l'avantage & le mérite de n'être point livré à ces passions fortes & si familières à la nature humaine : l'objet de la curiosité remplit les vuides de son loisir : amusé par ce qu'il possède, ou occupé par les recherches de ce qu'il désire de posséder, il ne lui reste que les momens suffisans pour pouvoir travailler au progrès de sa curiosité, & son Cabinet devient le centre de tous ses plaisirs, & le siège de toutes les passions »[57].
Mais le collectionneur joue aussi le rôle de filtre et dans bien des cas la collection peut être considérée comme « l'antichambre du musée » pour reprendre une expression de Dominique Pety, du moins lorsque l'œuvre personnelle est comme nous l'avons vu précédemment, pérennisée par le legs à l'institution muséale. Eugène Piot résumait en 1842 dans l'Introduction à son Cabinet de l'Amateur et de l'Antiquaire tout ce que nous devons à ces généreux donateurs de nos musées et rendait un vibrant hommage à tous ceux et à toutes celles qui, atteints du virus, ont voulu partager leur passion de la collection.
« Grâce à l'amateur, rien ne s'est perdu dans la défroque que les siècles laissent après eux en tombant sans retour dans le gouffre de l'éternité. Il a conservé tous ces mille détails dont se compose la physionomie d'un siècle. L'un a choisi les armures, l'autre les meubles, celui-ci les vases,

---

[56] F. Feuillet de Conches, *Causeries d'un curieux. Variétés d'histoire et d'art tirées d'un cabinet d'autographes et de dessins*, Paris, 1862, II, p. 479-480.
[57] Gersaint, *Catalogue de la vente du cabinet Quentin de Lorangère,* Paris, 1744, p. 1-3.

cet autre les manuscrits ou les médailles ; et, soyez tranquille, du jour où cette honnête passion est entrée dans un esprit, la collection sera complète, fallut-il aller chercher au fond de l'Espagne le fourreau qui manque à cette rapière, au fond de la Grèce ou de l'Asie-Mineure la médaille absente ou introuvable ; fallut-il remuer jusqu'aux fondations cyclopéennes les terrains où se trouvaient les vases étrusques ; la lame de Tolède trouvera sa gaine ; la page déchirée sera recousue à sa place, le médaillier verra bientôt briller dans tout l'éclat de son oxyde la médaille dont il n'existe aucun double à Londres, le vase étrusque contemporain d'Évandre prendra position en tête de la série. N'est-ce donc pas une belle mission que d'aller ainsi ramasser

Il faut dire que la littérature, notamment celle du XIXe siècle, d'une richesse exceptionnelle en la matière, s'est largement emparée de ce singulier personnage qu'est le collectionneur, de ses manies et de ses travers, nous livrant une incomparable galerie de portraits, que ce soient ceux du Cousin Pons de Balzac, ou de M. de Menussard d'Horace de Vieil-Castel, personnage de cette formidable galerie des Français peints par eux-mêmes (1853) « qui se complaît dans l'insensibilité de sa maîtresse (la porcelaine), dans la matérialité de son idéalisation »[58] ou bien encore le Gardilanne de Champfleury personnage de la nouvelle intitulée Le violon de faïence, qui « aimait les beaux meubles, les tableaux des maîtres, les dentelles anciennes, les curiosités de l'Inde et du Japon, les émaux de Limoges, les eaux-fortes les plus rares, les ivoires, les verreries de Venise, les somptueuses étoffes du Levant, les faïences de Henri II, les miniatures, les armes, les tabatières, les Raphaël et les Vélasquez, les bahuts et les crédences ; enfin, il aimait tout ce qui est beau, précieux ou hors de prix »[59]. Le collectionneur fait alors son entrée fracassante dans le champ littéraire, il trouve sa place dans les physiologies, aux côtés du bourgeois et de l'artiste, même si le discours romantique « cantonne le collectionneur dans le stéréotype du vieux maniaque » (D. Péty). Le récit excentrique, comme le montre Dominique Pety, lui accorde de fait une place éminente, notamment dans les écrits de Champfleury (*Le Fuenzès*, 1847 ou *Le violon de faïence*, 1862), ou *Les Aventures de M. Bric-à-brac*, roman zoologique, archéologique et paléontologique d'E. de La Bédolière et P. Bernard

---

[58] Horace de Vieil-Castel, « Les collectionneurs », dans *Les français peints par eux-mêmes*, Paris, Curmer, 1840-1842, t. I, p. 121-128.
[59] Champfleury, *Le violon de faïence*, Paris, Hetzel et Cie, (s.d.), p. 3-4.

(de 1842). En avançant dans le siècle, il conquiert également le roman réaliste, ce qui nous renvoie à l'exemple bien connu des frères Goncourt avec leur *Renée Mauperin*, de 1864, le *À Rebours* de Huysmans (1884) ou le non moins célèbre *Bouvard et Pécuchet* de Flaubert (1881). Depuis, la sociologie, la philosophie, l'anthropologie, l'ethnologie et la psychanalyse se sont à leur tour intéressées au personnage et à l'acte de collectionner, donnant naissance notamment, aux thèses de Jean Baudrillard, de Krisztof Pomian, de Werner Muensterberger[60] et plus récemment de Pierre Wajcman.

[60] W. Muensterberger, *Le collectionneur : anatomie d'une passion,* Paris, Payot, 1996.

Collectionnisme public et privé en comparaison

Antoinette MAGET DOMINICE
Professeur junior en valeur des biens culturels et recherche de provenance
Institut d'histoire de l'art
Ludwig-Maximilians-Universität Munich (Allemagne)

Aborder les problématiques liées aux collections privées ne va pas sans aborder l'histoire et l'existence des collections publiques, tant les deux sont intimement liées. En effet, on constate qu'à travers le temps, les collectionneurs privés et les conservateurs de musées publics se jaugent, se concurrencent et enrichissent mutuellement leurs activités, dans des modalités et des cadres variés.

Qu'est-ce que le collectionnisme et que comprend-on sous ce terme ?

Le terme de collectionnisme se profile dès le début du XXIe siècle dans la recherche en sciences humaines, plus particulièrement en histoire de l'art. Il est auparavant plus connu de la recherche en médecine, domaine dans lequel il décrit une activité à tendance pathologique, la tendance forte à accumuler des objets de toute nature[1]. C'est la définition que l'on trouve encore dans le Larousse, selon lequel le collectionnisme est « le besoin pathologique de rassembler des objets hétéroclites inutiles et sans valeur marchande. »

En histoire de l'art, le collectionnisme est l'activité de constitution d'une collection, la création d'un ensemble de biens culturels dont l'un des buts est la conservation[2]. À celui-ci s'ajoutent d'autres objectifs, qui varient selon la personne qui collectionne : entité muséale publique, elle est animée d'autres motivations que la personne privée. Et c'est là que se situe le cœur de la comparaison entre collectionnisme public et privé.

[1] H. Codet, *Essai sur le collectionnisme*, Paris, Jouve & Cie, 1921.
[2] V. not. B. Vouilloux, « Le discours sur la collection », *Romantisme*, 2001, n° 112, La collection, p. 95-108.

De la frontière entre collectionnisme public et collectionnisme privé

Tant au XIXe siècle qu'aujourd'hui, la frontière ne se laisse toutefois pas si aisément identifier entre les deux types de collectionnisme. Les lignes bougent, les synergies existent et les personnes se connaissent. C'est ainsi qu'il s'agit de tout d'abord considérer les composantes qui caractérisent le collectionnisme public, du XIXe siècle à aujourd'hui, et comment celui-ci s'est inscrit dans une politique que l'on peut qualifier de « globale ». Puis d'aborder le statut acquis par les objets dans les collections publiques, pour enfin analyser les grandes caractéristiques du collectionnisme privé et les liens qu'il entretient avec le collectionnisme public.
L'on verra, durant toute la période considérée, que les mécanismes acquisitifs sont souvent approchants ou même semblables, que les objectifs parfois s'accordent ou que les buts peuvent varier, mais aussi que comparer collectionnisme privé et collectionnisme public est aussi une histoire de rapprochements et d'éloignements.

1. Collectionnisme public – Caractéristiques principales

Le XIXe siècle est celui de la fondation et de la consolidation des projets muséaux d'envergure en Europe. Tout particulièrement à Berlin et à Paris, mais aussi à Londres et dans d'autres grands centres urbains[3], les dirigeants politiques chapeautent la constitution de collections qui portent leurs ambitions en matière d'hégémonie politique sur le plan national et international. Le collectionnisme public est en effet un instrument politique, qui s'illustre dans de nombreux domaines de compétences de l'État.

1.1. Le musée et ses collections comme outil de politique nationale

La première caractéristique du collectionnisme public, et sans doute la plus centrale, est qu'il sert la politique nationale, au même titre que

[3] V. not. P. Fisher, "Local Meanings and Portable Object: National Collections, Literatures, Music and Architecture", *in* G. Wright, *The Formation of National Collections of Art and Archaeology*, Hannover/London, UP of New England, 1996, p. 15-37; A. Meyer, B. Savoy, "Towards a Transnational History of Museums. An Introduction", *in Id*, *The Museum is Open – Towards a Transnational History of Museums 1750-1940*, Berlin/Boston, De Gruyter, 2014, p. 1-16.

d'autres domaines régaliens. Au XIXe siècle, d'une manière assez générale, le musée – et partant l'activité d'enrichissement de ses collections, le collectionnisme – contribue à la réalisation d'une politique nationale dont les objectifs sont l'expression de la munificence du souverain ou du gouvernement, la légitimation du système et l'éducation du peuple.
À ce titre, les gouvernements trouvent dans l'institution muséale un lieu de conciliation entre temps et absolu, entre déroulement chronologique logique et temps cyclique[4]. Il convient de souligner que ces objectifs sont portés par des moyens financiers relativement restreints et qu'au XIXe siècle, en dehors des capitales, les initiatives privées sont déterminantes.

1.1.1. Collectionnisme public et munificence

Aux origines des grandes collections publiques qui se « font » au XIXe siècle transparaît le souhait de démontrer la munificence d'un souverain ou d'un gouvernement. Aussi, l'enrichissement des collections et le développement des musées peuvent être attribués à la figure de la personne régnante ou dirigeante.

Nombreuses sont les représentations du prestige et du pouvoir dans le domaine des collections publiques, mais certaines sont particulièrement parlantes, à l'image du tableau réalisé par François-Auguste Biard en 1855, *Une soirée au Louvre chez le Comte de Nieuwerkerke*[5]. Cette image illustre de manière exemplaire le prestige qui découle de l'union entre lieu de pouvoir et palais des arts. La scène immortalisée sur la toile peinte par Biard se déroule en fin de semaine à Paris, lors de l'un des célèbres « vendredis du Louvre » organisés par le comte de Nieuwerkerke. L'homme occupe, à la date de la réalisation de cette toile, la fonction de directeur général des Musées nationaux, avant de devenir quelques années plus tard surintendant des Beaux-arts. Il dispose à ce titre d'un appartement de fonction au Louvre, dans le cadre duquel il convie l'élite artistique et sociale de la capitale[6]. De deux à

[4] J. Baudrillard, *Le système des objets*, Paris, Denoël / Gonthier, 1968, p. 115.
[5] F.-A. Biard, *Une soirée au Louvre chez le Comte de Nieuwerkerke*, 1855, Huile sur toile, Musées et domaine nationaux du Palais de Compiègne, No. Inv. FPN 3802. V. *Le Comte de Nieuwerkerke. Art et pouvoir sous Napoléon III*, Exposition au Musée national du Château de Compiègne, 6 oct. 2000-8 janv. 2001, Paris, RMN, 2000.
[6] V. également la toile de Charles Giraud, *Intérieur du cabinet du Comte Émilien de*

quatre cents invités, artistes, hommes de lettres, hauts fonctionnaires, diplomates et aristocrates se retrouvaient à l'occasion de ces soirées, organisées durant le carême. Elles contribuaient aussi à relayer dans les cercles influents de la société l'image d'un empereur protecteur des arts et de la culture.

La confusion – volontaire ou non – entre personnalité du souverain et collections publiques est accentuée en France par le fait que sous Napoléon III, les objets d'art sont inscrits sur la liste civile, qu'ils soient conservés dans les musées ou dans les résidences impériales[7]. Ils sont inaliénables et imprescriptibles, mais la confusion règne dans les esprits (surtout ceux de ses détracteurs). Or selon le sénatus-consulte du 12 décembre 1852, l'Empereur a la jouissance des œuvres mais n'en a pas la propriété, les objets appartenant à la dotation de la Couronne[8].

Cette image contredit néanmoins la réalité des faits, car si le gouvernement français, à l'image de ses voisins, cherche à dominer le jeu politique en se positionnant également dans le domaine muséal et à communiquer sur une certaine opulence, le budget consacré aux acquisitions reste limité. Quelques crédits supplémentaires extraordinaires sont parfois accordés[9] mais le gouvernement impérial communique essentiellement sur des achats spectaculaires et politiques. On pense bien évidemment à l'achat de la collection Campana en 1861 mais aussi à l'arrivée du produit des fouilles réalisées en Macédoine, en Asie mineure et en Syrie et qui constituèrent les collections du musée Napoléon III, brièvement ouvert pour quelques mois en 1862. Néanmoins, l'objectif de Napoléon III de développer les musées et d'en tirer parti dans l'idéologie conduit Thomas Greenwood à écrire en 1888, dans une présentation des institutions culturelles en Europe que : « [...] In 1852, Napoleon III decreed that a million pounds sterling be spent in clearing away these [= the old buildings erected between the old Louvre and the Tuileries], and uniting the two palaces. The expenditure of so

Nieuwerkerke, directeur général des musées impériaux, au Louvre, 1859, Huile sur toile, Musée du Louvre, No. Inv. RF1990-4, ou la collection.

[7] V. Catherine Granger. *L'Empereur et les arts. La liste civile de Napoléon III. Mémoires et documents de l'École des chartes*, t. 79, 2005, p. 39-50.

[8] AMN H20 Commission d'examen des archives en 1870, 22 nov. 1870, rapport de la commission.

[9] A. Bertinet, *Les musées de Napoléon III. Une institution pour les arts (1849-1872)*, Mare & Martin, 2015, p. 81.

large a sum has given France the finest Museum buildings probably in the world. [...] »[10].
Dans la future capitale de l'Allemagne, la publication annuelle des rapports administratifs prussiens permet de considérer le budget attribué chaque année aux musées, et partant la somme consacrée à l'augmentation et à l'enrichissement des collections. Aussi en 1884, plus d'un tiers du budget annuel accordé par l'administration de l'éducation est consacré aux acquisitions, le reste pour la mise en valeur et la conservation des collections ainsi que pour le fonctionnement[11]. À cette somme est ajouté un crédit de 2 millions de Reich Mark à répartir entre tous les musées prussiens, à titre exceptionnel en raison de la création d'une antenne à Smyrne[12], mais aussi pour des acquisitions supplémentaires.

1.1.2. Collectionnisme public et légitimation

Une dimension supplémentaire du collectionnisme public est son rôle dans la consolidation des gouvernements, car le collectionnisme public est aussi un outil de légitimation politique. Les collections sont développées et enrichies afin de contribuer à écrire l'histoire, telle que se la souhaite le gouvernement et telle que le peuple doit la comprendre. Cette recherche de légitimation explique ainsi les nombreuses fouilles menées sous le Second empire en Macédoine et en Cappadoce. Napoléon III y cherche les traces d'une lignée « directe » avec les grands peuples des siècles passés. C'est lui aussi qui donne l'ordre de mener des fouilles en France afin de retrouver l'emplacement d'Alésia[13]. En France, la filiation et la légitimation se recommandent alors de l'Empire romain[14].

---

[10] T. Greenwood, *Museums and Art Galleries*, London, Simpkin, Larshall and Co., 1888, p. 327-328.

[11] *Zentralblatt für die gesamte Unterrichtsverwaltung in Preussen*, Januar-Februar Heft, Berlin: Wilhelm Herz, 1884, p. 292-293.

[12] Kapitel 122 Titel 1 bis 6: « Mehr Aufwendung für die Königlichen Museen zu Berlin sind erfolgt durch die Errichtung der Stelle eines in Smyrna zu domizilierenden Abtheilungs-Direktors, einer Registratorstelle, zweier Direktorial Assistentenstellen, einer Konservatorstelle und mehrere Unterbeamtenstellen im Betrage vom 83'755 M. », *idem*, p. 312.

[13] V. not. M. Reddé, « Introduction : Alésia et la mémoire nationale française », *Anabases*, 9 | 2009, 13-24.

[14] Cette tendance se remarque également par le transfert de biens culturels en provenance des territoires en cours de colonisation, comme cela fut le cas quelques

En Prusse, la seconde partie du XIXe siècle correspond à la construction de l'Allemagne moderne et l'empereur cherche à démontrer sa légitimité[15]. À cette fin, il en appelle à l'histoire de l'humanité et au développement des civilisations sur le pourtour du bassin méditerranéen. Arrivés à Berlin, les objets sont répartis entre l'Altes et le Neues Museum, afin de contribuer à écrire une histoire de l'Empire prussien qui remonte aux origines de la civilisation européenne[16]. Ainsi à Berlin, le bâtiment construit par Stüler pour le Neues Museum s'articule autour d'un corps central abritant la cage d'escalier et propose ainsi un contraste dynamique à la rotonde érigée par Schinkel pour l'Altes Museum. Contraste architectural[17], mais constante intellectuelle : les deux bâtiments renferment l'idée d'une marche à travers tout l'effort de l'histoire humaine pour tendre à l'Esprit absolu[18]. Cet objectif se reflète jusque dans l'architecture du Neues Museum. De part et d'autre de l'imposante cage d'escalier, le visiteur découvre des fresques qui illustrent cette évolution de l'humanité et culmine, dans les étages supérieurs, par les peuples germains. La montée d'escalier symbolise l'ascension héroïque de l'humanité en direction d'un but idéal. Il ne s'agit pas ici uniquement de la contemplation de l'art mais

---

années plus tôt pour les biens en provenance d'Algérie. V. not. sur les premières collections du Musée algérien au Louvre N. Oulebsir, *Les usages du patrimoine, Monuments, Musées et politique coloniale en Algérie*, Paris, Éditions de la Maison des sciences de l'homme, 2004, p. 76-77.

[15] B. Anderson, *L'imaginaire national. Réflexions sur l'origine et l'essor du nationalisme*, Paris, La Découverte, 2002 (1996, orig. 1983), p. 95 ; E. Hooper-Greenhill, *Museums and the Shaping of Knowledge*, London / New York, Routledge, 1992, p. 193.

[16] D. Crimp, « The End of Art and the Origin of the Museum », *Art Journal*, vol. 46, n° 4, Winter 1987, p. 264.

[17] Contraste qui porte à interrogation, puisque comme le fait remarquer Michael F. Zimmermann, les éléments présentés à l'extérieur par l'un sont repris à l'intérieur par l'autre. Il s'agirait ainsi plus d'une inversion « privée/publique » que d'une réelle rupture : « Stüler gelang keine derart wirksame Synthese unterschiedlicher historischer Anregungen wie seinem Lehrer Schinkel. Doch er bot in dem nach aussen bescheidenen Bau ein einzigartiges Repertoire stilistischer und technischer Möglichkeiten seiner Zeit. […] spitzte die Idee des Museums zu, das in seiner Architektursprache und seiner Dekoration insgesamt dieses bildungsbürgerliche Konzept zur Schau stellte. », Michael F. Zimmermann, « Einleitung », *in* Peter Bloch (Hrsg.), *Berlins Museen, Geschichte und Zukunft*, Zentralinstitut für Kunstgeschichte München, München: Deutscher Kunstverlag, 1994, p. 15.

[18] Douglas Crimp, « The End of Art and the Origin of the Museum », *Art Journal*, vol. 46, n° 4, Winter 1987, p. 264.

également de l'éducation pragmatique[19]. Les fresques réalisées par Wilhelm von Kaulbach et basées sur des récits aussi bien mythologiques que bibliques[20], illustrent, sur les murs de la cage d'escalier, l'histoire de l'évolution du monde en quatre cycles qui se répondent. La décoration monumentale du Neues Museum ne dépare pas au sein de l'ensemble des musées situés sur le territoire allemand au XIXe siècle. Presque tous présentent dans leurs espaces de circulation des fresques où sont peintes de manière grandiose la transmission de l'art et sa compréhension par un rappel au passé[21].
À ce sujet, dans sa *Lettre de Humboldt*, Roland Recht souligne que « Les stratégies du choix de la mise en valeur du patrimoine, de la politique de création artistique, sont des manifestations de la même volonté du pouvoir de construire l'histoire. La vision du pouvoir est une vision de l'histoire. Et le musée en tant qu'il est un système de représentation, appartient à cette idéologie du pouvoir au premier chef, il constitue l'espace historique où le public le plus large peut accéder aux images dans lesquelles ce pouvoir se reconnaît et sur lesquelles il fonde sa légitimité culturelle »[22]. À Berlin, ces stratégies sont d'autant plus construites que se trouvent sur une même île le palais de l'Empereur, la cathédrale et les musées.
Au XXe les gouvernements bâtissent moins – mais jalonnent toutefois

---

[19] C. Ballé, E. François, *Publics et projets culturels. Un enjeu des musées en Europe*, Paris, L'Harmattan, 2000, p. 38.

[20] Il devient possible, par l'étude de chacun des décors réalisés dans les musées germaniques, de définir quelques tendances dans l'ornementation. On dénombre ainsi les fresques à inspiration mythologique et biblique, celles qui permettent l'appréhension du contexte historique et politique du bâtiment, celles où domine l'illustration de l'évolution des arts. Ce dernier groupe ne présente qu'une unité limitée, puisque la thématique se retrouve en arrière-plan des deux autres. Ainsi à Leipzig, la source d'inspiration de Theodor Grosse est la mythologie grecque et la bible hébraïque. V. pour une description exhaustive des fresques du Neues Museum, M. Schasler, *Die königlichen Museen von Berlin. Ein praktisches Handbuch zum Besuch der Galerien, Sammlungen und Kunstschätze derselben*, Berlin, C. Parthey, 1860, p. 136-145.

[21] Certains des bâtiments muséaux sont ornés de fresques, non pas dans leurs espaces intérieurs, mais en façade : l'Altes Museum à Berlin et la Neue Pinakothek à Munich, mais aussi le Musée Thorvaldsen à Copenhague. V. not. J. J. Sheehan, *Geschichte der deutschen Kunstmuseen. Von der fürstlichen Kunstkammer zur modernen Sammlung*, München, C.H. Beck, 2002, p. 200.

[22] R. Recht, *La lettre de Humboldt. Du jardin paysager au daguerréotype*, Paris, Chr. Bourgeois, 1989, cité par J.-L. Déotte, *Oubliez ! Les ruines, l'Europe, le Musée*, Paris, L'Harmattan, 1994, p. 93.

leurs capitales de gestes muséaux. C'est la prolongation de l'élan instauré au XIXe siècle qui se retrouve par exemple dans l'ouverture de la New Tate Gallery à Londres, dans le musée du quai Branly à Paris ou encore à Berlin dans le rassemblement de toutes les collections sur l'emplacement de l'île aux musées, dans l'ancien château en cours de reconstruction[23].

Les enjeux de recherche, d'éducation et de prestige dominent la politique muséale. Les musées sont comme des vitrines liées aux espaces qu'ils représentent. Et dans la compétition que se livrent les États au niveau mondial, les musées en sont l'un des instruments – hier comme aujourd'hui[24].

1.1.3. Ambition d'éducation

De plus, les musées sont les symboles d'une volonté politique et publique d'édification du plus grand nombre[25]. On observe là une extension des buts purement politiques vers des objectifs sociaux, portés par l'organisation des institutions et la présentation des collections.

L'ambition d'éducation que portent les musées s'illustre dans des bouleversements au niveau organisationnel tout d'abord. Les horaires de visite sont étendus, les collections sont également accessibles les week-ends. Les règlements de visite sont assouplis, on permet l'entrée aux hommes, aux femmes et aux enfants et même, aux ouvriers. État de fait dont se désole Mérimée, qui se plaint qu'à Paris, « une foule de bonnes, d'ouvriers et de soldats viennent se promener dans la galerie par désœuvrement »[26]. Néanmoins, l'iconographie d'époque présente d'une manière générale des visiteurs à la tenue et aux atours bourgeois. En effet le musée reste, malgré sa volonté d'ouverture, une sorte de galerie d'apparat et continue d'ignorer une partie de la population.

---

[23] V. not la thèse de F. von Bose, *Das Humboldt-Forum. Eine Ethnografie seiner Planung*, Berlin, Kadmos, 2016.

[24] V. sur ce sujet les travaux récents sur la diplomatie culturelle, not. B. Wallis, « Selling Nations. International Exhibitions and Cultural Diplomacy », *in* I. Rogoff, D. J. Shermann (eds.), *Museum culture. Histories, Discourses, Spectacles*, London, Routledge, 1994, p. 265-283.

[25] V. not. D. Poulot, *Une histoire des musées de France, XVIIIe-XXe siècle*, Paris : La Découverte, 2008, p. 143-150.

[26] P. Mérimée, « Les grands maîtres au musée de Madrid », *L'Artiste*, Paris, juill. 1870-nov. 1871, p. 342.

Aujourd'hui la mission d'éducation se trouve au cœur des préoccupations des collections publiques et celle-ci se diversifie, dans ses supports et dans ses dynamiques.

1.2. Enrichissement des collections

Pour servir les objectifs politiques que leur imposent les gouvernements et leurs ambitions encyclopédiques, les institutions publiques organisent l'enrichissement et la présentation des collections. Les acquisitions se font sur le marché, par l'acceptation de dons ou de legs mais aussi par l'envoi de missions scientifiques.

Ces ambitions sont ainsi alimentées primairement par des achats plus ou moins importants mais dont les arrivées sont assez largement communiquées et dont on trouve notamment la trace dans la presse. Le deuxième outil d'enrichissement est constitué par l'envoi de missions scientifiques, qui réalisent des fouilles et dont le produit rejoint les collections nationales, enfin par une étroite relation avec les collectionneurs privés

On remarque également que la deuxième partie du XIXe siècle est teintée de rivalités entre les trois grandes puissances européennes à l'époque, la France, l'Allemagne et la Grande-Bretagne. Cette concurrence transparaît également dans l'activité des conservateurs sur le continent européen, dans un climat de rivalités et d'émulation[27]. Les grandes puissances envoient certains de leurs conservateurs à l'étranger afin d'obtenir des informations plus fiables sur l'état des collections. Des rapports sur la qualité, la documentation et la présentation des objets se trouvent dans les archives. Ces missions contribuent au développement encyclopédique des collections, car l'on cherche sans cesse à égaler son voisin. Et ce climat d'émulation se retrouve bien évidemment dans le collectionnisme, enrichissant le débat scientifique, stimulant le marché, augmentant l'audience dans les musées et dynamisant les publications[28].

---

[27] D'une part avec l'envoi de scientifiques chargés de comparer les collections et, d'autre part, avec la fondation de musées servant les mêmes buts (création en 1852 du musée de Mayence puis en 1867 celui de Saint-Germain-en-Laye, tous deux dédiés aux antiquités nationales). V. not. A. Schnapp, « Archéologie et tradition académique en Europe aux XVIIIe et XIXe siècles », *Annales. Économies, Sociétés, Civilisations*, 37e année, vol. 5, 1982, p. 760-777, 773-774.

[28] E. Emery, L. Morowitz, "From the living room to the museum and back again", *Journal of the History of Collections* (2004) 16 (2), p. 285-309, p. 286.

Le dépècement de la collection Campana au début des années 1860 permet d'identifier cette rivalité, puisqu'une véritable course-poursuite s'engage alors entre les grandes capitales européennes pour acheter tout ou partie de la collection[29]. Les gouvernements envoient des experts à Rome, ceux-ci complotent et exercent des pressions sur les uns et les autres.

D'autant plus que l'administration pontificale ayant levé les mesures de restriction à l'exportation (et même les taxes), les appétits s'affûtent. Finalement en mai 1861 la France, après l'Angleterre et la Russie et avant la Belgique, acquiert près de 12000 objets[30]. Cette concurrence s'exprime également sur le terrain, dans les territoires du pourtour méditerranéen. Les missions scientifiques se voient parfois refuser des permis de fouilles ou mettre des entraves supplémentaires à l'envoi d'objets vers les métropoles[31].

On constate enfin que durant le Second Empire, les donateurs réguliers du Louvre englobent les élites impériales et les artistes, mais aussi les conservateurs des musées impériaux. Et qu'avec la multiplication des propositions, le Louvre finit par refuser certaines collections[32].

Un phénomène identique se développe en Grande-Bretagne et en Prusse. Les dons sont soigneusement étudiés, d'une part en raison de la qualité des objets proposés mais aussi en raison des coûts qu'engendre leur arrivée et des moyens limités dont disposent les institutions.

Aujourd'hui, on note que la combinaison d'une baisse des financements publics, d'une raréfaction de biens culturels sur le marché et du renforcement des dispositions légales en matière de provenance etc. conduisent à une modification des politiques d'acquisition. Les institutions privilégient les acquisitions portant véritablement sur la durée, d'objets significatifs et dont l'intégration dans les collections existantes est pertinente. Les missions de fouilles sont devenues des

---

[29] V. not sur la Collection Campana, F. Gauthier, L. Haumesser, A. Trofimova (dir.), *Un rêve d'Italie. La collection du marquis Campana*, Exposition au Musée du Louvre, 7 nov. 2018 au 11 févr. 2019, Paris, Musée du Louvre/Liénart, 2018.

[30] V. not. G. Nadalini, « La collection Campana au musée Napoléon III et sa première dispersion dans les musées français (1862-1863) », *in Journal des savants,* année 1998, vol. 2, n° 1, p. 183-225 ; F. Gaultier, L. Haumesser et A. Trofima (dir.), *Un rêve d'Italie. La collection du marquis Campana*, Paris, LienArt, 2018.

[31] Sur la révision de la pratique longtemps en vigueur en Égypte et relative au partage de fouilles, v. not. A Maget, *Collectionnisme public et conscience patrimoniale, Les collections d'égyptologie en Europe*, Paris, L'Harmattan, 2009, p. 243 et s.

[32] A. Bertinet, n. 7, p. 86-87.

missions de collecte d'informations scientifiques, à de fort rares exceptions. Les collections publiques développent une politique d'acquisition audacieuse ainsi qu'elles soignent leur renommée, puisque ces deux qualités attirent donateurs et testateurs. Les donations dépendent en effet fortement de l'image dont dispose l'institution parmi les élites, locales et internationales. Car, aujourd'hui plus encore qu'hier, les institutions publiques se doivent de recourir à des rapprochements avec les collectionneurs privés afin de pouvoir continuer à remplir leurs objectifs, sans pour autant piétiner leurs fondements éthiques.

1.3. Collectionnisme public et temporalité

Chateaubriand, dans ses *Mémoires d'outre-tombe*, parlant de sa visite à Potsdam du château de Frédéric le Grand, estime que « Ce n'est pas l'homme qui arrête le temps, mais le temps qui arrête l'homme »[33]. Or le temps représente un enjeu minime pour le collectionnisme public. Portées par un appareil d'État organisé indépendamment des personnes, les missions d'enrichissement des collections, de leur présentation et partant de concordance avec les objectifs politiques exprimés, ne dépendent pas d'une chronologie limitée par la vie et la mort d'une personne. Ce détachement de la temporalité humaine constitue l'une des caractéristiques et l'une des forces du collectionnisme public.

2. Collectionnisme public et objets

Le collectionnisme public sert les objectifs de realpolitik et dans ce contexte, touche à la dimension immatérielle des objets qui rejoignent les collections. En premier lieu, l'entrée d'un objet dans une collection publique a une conséquence sur la symbolique de l'objet lui-même. Son statut évolue, sa signification et le message qu'on lui fait porter sont modifiés[34]. L'objet est sorti de son contexte et en quelque sorte « libéré » de sa fonction première, pour devenir un objet « d'art » et de patrimoine, qui plus est national. Les objets religieux par exemple, sont sortis de leur contexte dévot et de leur fonction cultuelle, pour rejoindre des lieux d'exposition souvent esthétiques et grevés d'un message politique.

---

[33] F.-R. de Chateaubriand, *Mémoires d'outre-tombe*, vol. I, p. 145.

[34] Emery, Morowitz, n. 23, p. 288.

En second lieu, les acquisitions se font sur le très long terme et selon des critères fixés par un plenum. Les entrées reflètent les goûts de leur temps et la figure des conservateurs influents à une période, mais les différences s'aplanissent sur la durée[35]. De plus, les champs patrimoniaux au sein desquels se font les choix n'apportent rien à la personnalité du conservateur, ce qui ne le freine pas à explorer des domaines moins attractifs[36]. On peut ici citer Delacroix, qui en 1862 souligne que « une collection offerte à l'étude doit se composer, non seulement de beaux objets, mais encore de tous ceux qui, dans un ordre de mérite moins élevé, permettent toutefois de suivre et de juger les tâtonnements à travers lesquels l'art est arrivé à sa perfection »[37].
Enfin, non seulement le choix des objets sert des objectifs politiques, mais également leur accrochage, leur présentation. Les institutions publiques cherchent, dans leur grande majorité, à atteindre une certaine objectivité scientifique et à rendre les développements compréhensibles. L'accrochage suit généralement des critères chronologiques, géographiques… qui alimentent « l'idéologie » derrière le musée. De plus, cette muséographie s'inscrit soit au sein d'un complexe muséal structuré et compact géographiquement, comme l'Île aux musées à Berlin, soit encore dans une constellation d'institutions en devenir, avec par exemple à Paris le Musée du Louvre, le Musée des Antiquités nationales à Saint-Germain ou à Londres avec le British Museum, et le Musée de South Kensington.
C'est ainsi que l'objet, dépouillé de sa signification première, se voit sorti du temps et revêtu d'une symbolique dont les enjeux échappent à son créateur[38].

---

[35] Ce sont deux éléments qui différencient diamétralement le collectionnisme public du collectionnisme privé. En effet, le collectionneur n'a qu'une vie pour constituer sa collection et ses choix sont guidés par sa compréhension personnelle et un certain goût pour l'art. V. not. G. Adriani, „Ein Museum für Neue Kunst", *in* G. Adriani (Hrsg.), *KunstSammeln*, Ostfildern, 1999, p. 10; H. P. Thurn, „Menschen als Sammler. Vom Naturzwang zum Kulturvergnügen", i B. Past (Hrsg.): *SammelARTen Aspekte der Aneignung in Kunst und Kultur.* Oberhausen, 2009, p. 10.

[36] G. Ridler, *Privat gesammelt – öffentlich präsentiert. Über den Erfolg eines neuen musealen Trends bei Kunstsammlungen*, transcript Verlag, 2012, p. 70-71.

[37] *Journal des Débats*, 9 nov. 1862.

[38] V. à ce sujet not. K. Pomian, « Musée et patrimoine », *in* H. P. Jeudy (éd.), *Patrimoines en folie*, Paris, Éditions de la Maison des sciences de l'homme, 1990, p. 177-198.

3. Collectionnisme privé

Ayant considéré les caractéristiques principales du collectionnisme public, il convient de s'arrêter brièvement sur les éléments qui irriguent le collectionnisme privé. De même que pour le collectionnisme public, le collectionnisme privé a pour objectif la thésaurisation d'objets. En revanche, ceux-ci sont rassemblés primairement pour le prestige social qu'ils confèrent, pour le « pouvoir magique » qu'ils contiennent et pour l'aura qu'ils dégagent, comme expression de l'appartenance à un groupe social et de la loyauté à celui-ci, comme stimulation de la curiosité et enfin pour la satisfaction esthétique qu'ils procurent.
Les collections privées d'art contemporain sont à ce titre, particulièrement éloquentes en ce qui concerne l'expression d'un statut social[39]. Et les ambitions philanthropiques surgissent plutôt après quelque temps, ou au moment d'anticiper ou de régler une succession.

4. Rapprochements entre collectionnisme public et privé

Les points de contact entre les deux modes de collectionnisme remontent à l'origine des musées et à l'ouverture des « cabinets de curiosité » ainsi que de galeries privées, souvent nobiliaires, comme l'a bien montré Patrick Michel[40]. On constate en effet que durant la période qui va du milieu du XIXe siècle à aujourd'hui, le collectionnisme public est secondé dans l'achèvement de ses objectifs par les collectionneurs privés.

Ceux-ci peuvent, on l'a abordé, consentir des dons ou des legs, ou participer à des acquisitions. Le musée public est alors considéré comme réceptacle de la passion d'une vie, du travail de sélection selon des critères personnels et comme prolongation de sa présence humaine. On observe aussi que les collections privées ne se satisfont plus de contribuer à la richesse des collections publiques, mais qu'elles en adoptent les codes, les objectifs et les contraintes. C'est une nouvelle

---

[39] V. not. les monographies qui s'y consacrent, comme K. L. Holzmann, *Sammler und Museen, Kooperationsformen der Einbindung von privaten zeitgenössischen Kunstsammlungen in die deutsche Museumslandschaft*, Wiesbaden, Springer, 2016; Ridler (n. 36).

[40] V. P. Michel, *Les collections privées en France au XVIIIe siècle : une approche méthodologique,* p. 39.

logique qui se profile, une expression nouvelle de la philanthropie des collectionneurs.
Et l'on voit que les collections privées s'ouvrent au public, sous une forme muséale ou plus intimiste, que des musées privés s'ouvrent mais aussi que des objets sont mis à la disposition d'une institution publique par le biais de prêts à long terme. Le rapprochement entre public et privé revêt de nouvelles formes en ce début du XXIe siècle, s'ouvre et se ferme, à l'image de la situation qui prévaut à Baden-Baden, entre la fondation Frieder Burda et la Kunsthalle. La Kunsthalle, institution publique qui dépend du ministère de la recherche, de la science et des arts du Bade-Wurtenberg, a été fondée en 1909 et est abritée dans un bâtiment de style classique. En voisinage direct depuis 2004, la collection de la fondation Frieder Burda est une collection d'art moderne et contemporain, comprenant environ un millier d'œuvres et rassemblée par le collectionneur depuis 1986[41].

Cette proximité géographique – les deux collections sont présentées dans des bâtiments reliés par une passerelle vitrée – paraît symptomatique de la nécessité qu'ont les deux formes de collectionnisme à échanger et à cohabiter, mais aussi des attentes ou des compréhensions parfois contraires des uns et des autres.
Cet état de fait se retrouve dans la communication de l'une et de l'autre des institutions. Aussi, pour la fondation privée, « Le Musée Frieder Burda se veut un musée autonome tout en entretenant une relation fraternelle avec la Kunsthalle qu'il vient compléter. C'est pourquoi ce passage de verre est comme un cordon ombilical tendu entre les deux bâtiments et qui peut s'ouvrir et se fermer. »[42]. En vis-à-vis, la Kunsthalle annonce sur son site que l'institution remplit une « obligation d'éducation publique »[43] et que « Le Musée Frieder Burda, en voisinage direct, abrite la collection du mécène d'art Frieder Burda. La Kunsthalle elle, ne reflète pas le goût personnel de la direction et de ses collaborateurs, mais se trouve confortée de manière plus marquée encore, dans sa volonté d'agir au sein de la société. L'emplacement à

---

[41] G. Ridler, *op. cit* (n. 29), p. 205-208 ; J. Benhamou-Huet, *Global collectors – Collectionneurs du monde* Paris/Bordeaux, Phébus, 2008, p. 84-87.
[42] https://www.museum-frieder-burda.de/fr/musee/architecture/ (consulté le 2 juill. 2017).
[43] Traduction de l'auteur – „einen „öffentlichen Bildungsauftrag"". V. http://www.kunsthalle-baden-baden.de/kunsthalle/kunsthalle-heute (consulté le 2 juill. 2017).

côté d'un musée privé constitue une constellation idéale pour renouveler la réflexion sur les obligations d'une institution culturelle publique au début du XXIe siècle »[44].
Dans une interview accordée en 2004 et publiée dans l'un des catalogues de la collection Burda, le collectionneur définissait cette cohabitation comme « une coopération prometteuse entre la mission culturelle de l'État et l'engagement de particuliers pour l'art »[45].

Remarques conclusives

D'un point de vue juridique, il est intéressant de souligner que le collectionnisme recourt depuis plus de deux siècles aux mêmes outils : achats, dons, legs et, pour les institutions publiques, envoi de missions scientifiques. En revanche, le cadre juridique dans lequel ces enrichissements ont lieu a évolué. Développement de dispositions de protection du patrimoine culturel, prise de conscience éthique et consécration de celle-ci dans des codes de déontologie, restriction au mouvement des biens culturels… Cela conditionne les acquisitions et exige de penser autrement la complétude des collections.
Par ailleurs, les ressources financières des collections publiques étant oscillantes et tendant ces dernières années à baisser, celles-ci dépendent toujours plus étroitement du dynamisme du secteur privé pour pouvoir continuer à assumer leurs missions.

Enfin, et ce n'est pas une conclusion mais plus une invitation à la discussion sur le caractère ténu de la distinction entre collectionnisme public et privé, sur la frontière qui existe entre eux deux, Daniel Buren déclarait récemment, durant une interview au sujet de l'œuvre qu'il venait de terminer à la Fondation Louis Vuitton en 2016, *l'Observatoire de la lumière* et par laquelle il a recouvert les surfaces vitrées d'une sorte de damier multicolore et transparent, que « L'espace public est

---

[44] Traduction de l'auteur. "[…] zeigen, sondern sich dem Willen, in die Gesellschaft hineinzuwirken, noch stärker als bisher verpflichten. Die Platzierung neben einem privaten Museum bietet dabei eine optimale Ausgangslage, um den öffentlichen Auftrag einer staatlichen Kunsthalle am Anfang des 21. Jahrhunderts neu zu thematisieren" http://www.kunsthalle-baden-baden.de/kunsthalle/kunsthalle-heute/ (consulté le 2 juill. 2017).

[45] Traduction de l'auteur. – „Ein zukunftsweisenes Miteinander von staatlichem Kulturauftrag und private Kunstengagement". F. Burda, « Nicht auf Zeit », *in Stiftung Frieder Burda*, 2004, p. 7-9, 8.

forcément politique »[46]. Ainsi, les convergences du secteur privé et public en matière de collection pourraient être une continuation de la politique portée par les États en matière de musées.

46 Daniel Buren, Interview par V. Duponchelle, *Le Figaro* [en ligne], 3 juin 2016 < http://www.lefigaro.fr/arts-expositions/2016/06/03/03015-20160603ARTFIG00251-daniel-buren-l-espace-public-est-forcement-politique.php> (consulté le 2 juill. 2017).

La collection source de savoir : les figures du collectionneur « scientifique » en histoire naturelle

Michel VAN PRAËT
Professeur émérite au Muséum national d'Histoire naturelle de Paris
Conservateur général du patrimoine

« L'introduction du contexte de constitution des collections naturalistes en Europe, est l'occasion de souligner que ces collections sont, dès la fin du XVIe siècle, liées à la structuration des sciences. Alors que les sciences se professionnalisent progressivement pendant les siècles suivants, le profil du collectionneur scientifique sera de ce fait pluriel. Des scientifiques, travaillant au sein d'institutions cherchant à constituer des collections exhaustives des productions de la nature s'identifieront progressivement d'amateurs ne collectionnant qu'une partie des objets naturels. Ces collectionneurs privés privilégient la rareté ainsi que des valeurs esthétiques ou symboliques mais excluent de nombreux éléments fréquents dans la nature, dont la conservation est délicate. Quelles que soient les ruptures liées aux évolutions des sciences, amateurs et professionnels continuent d'entretenir des liens contribuant à l'enrichissement des collections dans certains domaines des sciences naturelles. Plus globalement, ils sont tous soumis à un ensemble de règles communes en rapide évolution qui, dans un but de protection de la biodiversité, encadrent la collecte, le marché et le mouvement des collections naturalistes…, règlementations qui, paradoxalement ne considèrent pas l'apport de ces collections au débat public en faveur de la protection des espèces et en limitent parfois l'usage social.

Le collectionneur scientifique : une figure plurielle

Les sciences dites « exactes » sont aujourd'hui généralement associées à l'image de professionnels rétribués pour travailler dans des équipes au sein de laboratoires de recherche. Néanmoins leur professionnalisation ne fut que progressive. L'image contemporaine du scientifique demeure, jusqu'au XIXe siècle, pour partie insuffisante à décrire les liens entre amateurs et professionnels, entre acteurs privés et publics, en particulier dans le domaine des sciences de la nature où les collections jouent un rôle structurant. Des naturalistes majeurs, comme C. Darwin ou G. Mendel, devraient ainsi être considérés comme des amateurs, si l'on distingue le professionnel de l'amateur par le fait que le premier dispose de compétences validées par un diplôme et est salarié à temps plein pour effectuer des recherches dans ce domaine (Cohen et Drouin, 1989).

La définition du collectionneur « scientifique » sera ainsi plurielle pendant plusieurs siècles et ce n'est que progressivement que l'on pourra, à des époques distinctes selon les pays européens, distinguer des amateurs, constituant dans certains domaines naturalistes des collections à thématique scientifique, des professionnels construisant leur démarche scientifique autour de collections se constituant au sein d'institutions universitaires et de musées.

Les collectionneurs figures fondatrices des sciences de la nature

Une histoire des collections scientifiques qui serait fondée sur une distinction entre amateurs et professionnels devrait être menée en distinguant finement époques et régions européennes depuis le XVIe siècle (Pomian, 1987). Plus globalement, l'importance majeure des collections scientifiques dans le développement de la science européenne peut par contre être soulignée pour l'ensemble des sciences de la nature (Pearce, 1989 ; Van Praët, 2008, 2012).

La démarche scientifique se constitua du XVIe au début du XIXe siècle en Europe sur la base d'une collecte et d'une étude des « productions de la nature » par des individus dont l'activité personnelle majeure était souvent liée au domaine de la santé[1]. L'iconographie la plus souvent reproduite dans les ouvrages traitant de l'histoire des musées, la vue du cabinet d'histoire naturelle du pharmacien napolitain F. Imperato qui précède le texte de sa *Dell'Historia Naturale* (1599), témoigne de ce lien fondateur en Europe entre d'une part la constitution de collections, leur conservation et leur présentation au sein de cabinets scientifiques et, d'autre part le développement des sciences naturalistes et médicales. À Paris, le jardin royal des plantes médicinales et son cabinet, l'actuel

[1] Qu'ils exercent localement ou qu'ils accompagnent les campagnes d'exploration et plus tard la colonisation de contrées ultramarines, ces personnels de santé, en particulier les chirurgiens de marine et les médecins militaires, constituent pendant plusieurs siècles des acteurs essentiels des collectes scientifiques et vont contribuer à la constitution des cabinets et musées d'histoire naturelle.

Muséum national d'histoire naturelle, dont la création remonte à un édit royal de 1626, fait figure de précurseur quand l'édit de 1635, qui en fixe le fonctionnement, attribue à des docteurs en médecine des rétributions pour exercer non plus la médecine, mais des fonctions de "garde du cabinet » et de « démonstrateur ». Cette professionnalisation précoce à Paris, coexiste avec des situations où des acteurs laïcs ou religieux du secteur de la santé et dans certains cas de l'horticulture, constituent la majorité des « scientifiques-collecteurs-collectionneurs » en Europe.
Cette figure du scientifique en voie de professionnalisation coexiste également avec celle de collecteurs privés dont les revenus leur permettent de constituer des collections. Certains ont pu être à l'origine d'institutions scientifiques majeures et la constitution des collections de l'Ashmolean Museum de l'université d'Oxford, ouvert en 1683, illustre ainsi les liens entre amateurs et institutions, recherche et horticulture. E. Ashmole avait offert en 1677 sa collection à l'université d'Oxford dans le but de constituer un musée, après avoir été fait docteur en médecine en 1669 par cette université, sa collection était elle-même, pour partie, constituée des collections des Tradescant, une famille d'horticulteurs et voyageurs naturalistes.
Plus récemment, l'histoire du British Museum reflète, comme dans le cas du Jardin royal des plantes médicinales, les liens qui unissent la genèse des musées scientifiques et la médecine. Il est créé au milieu du XVIIIe siècle, à partir du legs par Hans Sloane (1660-1753), médecin qui présida le Royal College of Physicians et la Royal Society, de sa collection d'ouvrages et collections, principalement d'histoire naturelle et médailles. Le British Museum ouvre au public en 1759 comme un musée polythématique autour d'une riche bibliothèque. Dans le courant du XIXe siècle des tensions internes quant aux finalités du musée se font jour et le département d'histoire naturelle s'autonomise pour être finalement transféré en 1880 dans le quartier de South Kensington et y devenir le Natural History Museum (Stearn, 1998). Cette scission du British Museum au XIXe siècle est l'un des multiples exemples de la séparation progressive des arts et des sciences dans la culture occidentale, qui s'accompagne d'une spécialisation thématique de nombreux musées et collections au XIXe siècle.

Classer et ordonner la Nature conduit à organiser les collections

Décrire et nommer les « productions de la nature » est, dès le XVIe siècle, un enjeu majeur de naturalistes, mais l'adoption de normes de nomenclature partagées nécessitera deux siècles de débats. En 1736, dans sa revue de la littérature botanique, le médecin et botaniste C. Linné[2] mentionne les auteurs et leurs ouvrages en fonction de leurs apports à la botanique. Il y donne une valeur supérieure aux « Methodici » proposant des principes généraux de classification (par rapport aux « Collectores ») et se place lui-même dans cette catégorie des « Methodici », à laquelle il rattache plusieurs dizaines d'autres botanistes, ce qui témoigne de l'importance attachée par les naturalistes à la définition de classifications normalisées. Pour l'ensemble du vivant, le système de classification de Linné ne commencera néanmoins à s'imposer, en termes de normes de nomenclature des espèces, que plus de vingt ans plus tard, à la suite de la dixième édition de son ouvrage *Systema Naturae*, où il généralise, en 1758, sa nomenclature binomiale[3].

Cette problématique des nomenclatures taxinomiques croise les approches philosophiques de la perception du vivant. Ainsi, plusieurs philosophes, comme G.W. Leibniz, J.-J. Rousseau ou J.W. Goethe, avant et lors de la diffusion des principes linnéens, vont débattre des principes de classification, en particulier en botanique, et des implications philosophiques de tel ou tel type de classification. Ils consultent dans ce cadre des collections, voire sont eux-mêmes, comme pour les trois philosophes mentionnés ci-dessus, des collectionneurs naturalistes que le terme « amateur » ou « scientifique » est impropre à caractériser (Drouin, 2008). L'une des collections botaniques acquises par Rousseau constitue par ailleurs, encore aujourd'hui, un outil de référence scientifique comportant des types taxinomiques conservés au Muséum national d'histoire naturelle à Paris.

Ce développement de la nomenclature est structurant des sciences de la nature et doit conduire à analyser de manière critique l'expression « cabinet de curiosités ». Les naturalistes européens définissent, dès leurs ouvrages de la fin du XVIe siècle, leurs collections comme des éléments de compréhension de l'histoire naturelle[4] et attribuent

---

[2] Linné, 1736, *Bibliotheca botanica*.

[3] Si les normes de nomenclatures taxinomiques dérivent des principes proposés par Linné, les concepts fixistes de classification de celui-ci étaient, déjà à l'époque, très débattus et sont aujourd'hui remplacés par d'autres approches structurées par la théorie évolutionniste du vivant.

[4] F. Imperato, précédemment cité, introduit dès 1599 son ouvrage *Dell' Historia Naturale* par une illustration légendée non pas « cabinet de curiosités » mais « Rittrato del museo di Ferrante Imperato ».

rapidement une dimension péjorative à l'expression cabinet de curiosités qui recouvrait pour eux des collections non scientifiques. Au début de la Révolution française les savants du « Jardin national des Plantes et de son Cabinet d'Histoire naturelle » dans une note à la Convention, établie à l'initiative de Lamarck, écrivent « Toute collection d'histoire naturelle n'est pas comme telle essentiellement utile : l'ordre, la détermination et un certain état des objets, sont des conditions indispensables pour qu'une collection de ce genre ait le degré d'utilité qui peut la rendre précieuse et lui mériter un grand intérêt (...). On voit, en effet, souvent des collections d'histoire naturelle dont l'objet en quelque sorte est de former spectacle et peut-être d'offrir une image de la richesse et du luxe du propriétaire (...) des collections telles que je viens de les décrire ne sont utiles à rien ; elles constituent de simples cabinets de curiosités, et non de vrais cabinets d'histoire naturelle ». Ils motivent ainsi leur demande de développement et réorganisation de l'institution, aux motifs que faute des moyens nécessaires le cabinet d'histoire naturelle de l'établissement ne serait rien de plus qu'un cabinet de curiosités. Ils seront entendus et le décret du 10 juin 1793 adopte de surcroît l'appellation de « Muséum d'Histoire naturelle » qui marque l'abandon de toute référence au terme de cabinet pour les collections scientifiques en France.
Le développement des classifications et la stabilisation de normes de nomenclature, à la charnière des XVIIIe et XIXe siècles, conduit les scientifiques à réorganiser alors le rangement des collections par ensembles botaniques, zoologiques et minéralogiques selon les principes de taxonomie et à séparer collections d'arts et de sciences. L'évolution des sciences de la Nature se traduit alors par une profonde réorganisation des salles des musées et conduit parfois à une scission des collections scientifiques et artistiques des institutions, comme cela a été mentionné dans l'exemple du *British Museum*. Cette réorganisation des collections permet d'assimiler les salles des musées d'histoire naturelle du XIXe à des réserves visitables organisées comme des bibliothèques de spécimens où ceux-ci sont classés selon les principes linnéens (Van Praët, 2012).

Avec l'adoption de normes de nomenclature, les naturalistes du XIXe siècle disposent d'outils méthodologiques de classification pour ordonner le vivant et par la même leurs collections. Dans le même temps, les progrès en matière de conservation du matériel biologique, qu'il s'agisse de spécimens en liquide ou naturalisés, assurent aux collectes une pérennité dont ne bénéficiaient pas celles des grandes explorations et colonisations antérieures. La conjonction de techniques efficaces de conservation et les grandes explorations et campagnes coloniales du XIXe siècle vont contribuer à un enrichissement durable des collections naturalistes européennes et à la constitution des collections américaines. Si quelques collections de trophées de chasse exotiques sont constituées alors par certains aristocrates et capitaines d'industrie, le XIXe va surtout être marqué par la constitution des grandes collections scientifiques des institutions universitaires et des musées à vocation publique.

Collectionneurs institutionnels et collectionneurs privés, liens et ruptures

La professionnalisation des sciences et des évolutions internes de celles-ci, avec l'émergence de nouvelles disciplines, contribue depuis la fin du XIXe siècle à diversifier la nature des collections scientifiques. Ces deux processus contribuent également à permettre de distinguer de plus en plus les professionnels, travaillant au sein d'institutions universitaires et muséales, des collectionneurs privés dont les collections vont de moins en moins représenter la totalité de la diversité du monde naturel.

Néanmoins, les uns et les autres partageant les mêmes normes internationales de description et de dénomination des espèces, les liens entre eux demeurent importants jusqu'à aujourd'hui dans les domaines particuliers où les amateurs constituent des collections naturalistes. Le but ultime des collectionneurs privés étant, en termes d'obtention de spécimens rares, la découverte d'espèces nouvelles, les normes internationales de dénomination et de description de celles-ci nécessitent une collaboration avec les scientifiques des collections publiques. Toute nouvelle espèce n'étant reconnue qu'après publication de sa description selon des règles précises et le spécimen « type » devant être consultable[5], les établissements scientifiques et les musées

[5] L'actuel Code international de nomenclature zoologique fait suite aux règles internationales de nomenclatures zoologiques rédigées après le premier congrès international de zoologie en 1889, tandis que l'actuel International Code of Botanical Nomenclature est issu des travaux initiés par le congrès international de botanique de 1905. L'un et l'autre sont régulièrement mis à jour et constituent les références des conventions internationales et des droits nationaux.

spécialisés ont, de fait, été les institutions les plus fréquentes de conservation des types collectés et décrits, y compris par les collectionneurs scientifiques privés. Ceux-ci entretiennent dans ce contexte des relations suivies avec les collections publiques et il est courant qu'ils leur lèguent leurs collections ou du moins leurs spécimens les plus rares. Au-delà des grands musées précédemment cités, comme le *British Museum* ou *l'Ashmolean Museum*, certains musées français d'histoire naturelle trouvent également leur origine dans un don ou legs originel et continuent parfois de s'enrichir, en particulier en entomologie, conchyologie et paléontologie, par le même processus de dons de collections privées souvent issues de collectes personnelles[6].

Si certaines disciplines des sciences de la Nature, en développant des démarches expérimentales et en s'intéressant aux processus biologiques, se sont construites en tension avec les collections et les musées, d'autres ont au contraire étendu les collections à de nouveaux domaines, au-delà des trois disciplines traditionnelles de la zoologie, de la botanique et de la minéralogie. C'est le cas lors de la constitution de la paléontologie comme discipline dans le courant du XIXe siècle. Dans cette discipline, les liens entre collectionneurs privés et professionnels ont d'emblée eu un rôle important dans la constitution des collections, jusqu'à aujourd'hui, en posant d'ailleurs des questions éthiques et juridiques, le marché des fossiles étant soumis à des règles particulièrement diverses d'un pays à un autre[7].

D'autres disciplines, comme l'anthropologie, se constituent et se structurent de manière plus complexe. À la fin du XIXe siècle, l'anthropologie physique mobilise essentiellement des scientifiques dont les premières générations seront des médecins mais, rapidement, l'anthropologie culturelle s'enrichit de démarches professionnelles mais aussi d'apports de collectionneurs privés voire d'artistes qui

---

[6] Les musées français d'histoire naturelle, relevant de collectivités locales, interrogés en 2017, ont répondu recevoir, pour près de la moitié d'entre eux, d'une dizaine à plusieurs centaines de spécimens par an sous forme de dons, principalement en entomologie, conchyologie et paléontologie.
Les dations sont par contre extrêmement rares. On peut mentionner celle des minéraux de l'écrivain et académicien Roger Caillois, ainsi que celle des volcanologues Maurice et Katia Krafft. Ces deux dations furent faites au profit du Muséum national d'Histoire naturelle.

[7] La Lettre de l'OCIM a consacré en 2013 son numéro 147 à la problématique « collections paléontologiques : statuts et circulation ».

contribueront, comme Picasso, à une reconnaissance de la créativité artistique des cultures africaines et océaniennes et à l'enrichissement des collections privées et publiques.

Plus globalement, la professionnalisation des sciences conduit, depuis la toute fin du XIXe siècle, à ce que les collectionneurs scientifiques soient, si l'on considère l'importance scientifique des collections, des acteurs institutionnels constitués d'établissements scientifiques (universitaires ou muséaux) où œuvrent des professionnels, quelle que soit la diversité de leurs statuts (universitaires, conservateurs, ingénieurs, chercheurs).

Plusieurs grandes collections naturalistes constituées à la même époque par des initiatives privées sont de fait des institutions scientifiques, quel que soit le statut aristocratique des collectionneurs. C'est par exemple le cas du Musée océanographique de Monaco, conçu de 1889 à 1910 par le Prince Albert 1er (1848-1922), ou du Musée royal d'Afrique centrale, créé de 1905 à 1908 à Tervuren par Léopold II (1835-1909), suite à l'exposition universelle de Bruxelles de 1897. Albert 1er de Monaco doit être considéré comme un naturaliste scientifique majeur[8] ; il en est de même au Japon si l'on considère les collections de l'empereur Shôwa (1901-1989), qui signe de son prénom « Hirohito » de nombreuses recherches de biologie marine. Les motivations initiales de Léopold II furent, pour une part, liées à des intérêts plus personnels. Elles rejoignent ceux de l'aristocratie européenne pour les explorations, les chasses et les trophées exotiques. C'est également pour partie le cas des collections de Philippe d'Orléans (1869-1926)[9] ; il demeure que ces diverses collections ont contribué à l'enrichissement de collections nationales et furent intégrées dans des musées d'histoire naturelle.

---

[8] Le prince Albert 1er organisa et participa à de nombreuses campagnes océanographiques sur ses navires l'Hirondelle et la Princesse Alice, qui permirent la collecte et la description de plusieurs espèces nouvelles. Il créa l'Institut océanographique et l'Institut de paléontologie humaine à Paris, ainsi que le musée océanographique à Monaco. À l'inauguration de celui-ci en 1910 il déclarait : « j'ai voulu réunir dans un même éclat les deux forces directrices de la civilisation, l'Art et la Science ».

[9] Sa collection fut léguée au Muséum national d'histoire naturelle et exposée dans un bâtiment particulier, des années 1930 à 1960, avant d'intégrer les présentations de la galerie de l'évolution. Voir sa biographie publiée par M.-F. Lafon.

Les difficultés de conservation, élément discriminant pour les collections privées

Conserver sur le long terme les collections naturalistes, nécessite des méthodes parfois complexes selon la nature minérale ou organique de celles-ci. Si les roches et minéraux posent quelques contraintes, la conservation des éléments biologiques pose dans de nombreux cas des difficultés du fait de leur complexité et de leur coût.
Le manque de maîtrise des principes de conservation des matières organiques réduit la durée de vie des collections du XVIe siècle au milieu du XVIIIe siècle et seuls les éléments susceptibles d'être conservés à sec font l'objet de collections. Si les plantes se conservent bien par dessiccation dans les herbiers, la conservation durable des animaux se limite pendant plusieurs siècles à celle de certains de leurs éléments tels que les squelettes ou les coquilles[10]. La mise au point depuis la fin du XVIIIe de processus de conservation en liquide et de méthodes de taxidermie a permis d'élargir la diversité des collections, néanmoins la technicité des préparations en liquide fait que de nombreux domaines ont toujours été peu représentés dans les collections privées. L'immense groupe des mollusques n'est par exemple collectionné que sous forme de coquilles des espèces qui en comportent. Si les progrès de la taxidermie ont permis la constitution de collections privées d'oiseaux et mammifères naturalisés, la taille des spécimens a conduit à limiter le nombre des collectionneurs aux catégories sociales disposant d'espaces appropriés et de moyens financiers permettant d'assurer la préservation des montages taxidermiques sur le long terme.

Alors que les collections naturalistes des institutions scientifiques continuent jusqu'à aujourd'hui de tendre à échantillonner l'ensemble du monde minéral et du vivant[11], les collections privées portent principalement, entre autres du fait des contraintes de conservation et

---

[10] Les insectes et les animaux de petites tailles étaient également préservés par dessiccation, mais la méconnaissance des processus d'acidification des graisses et les attaques par les parasites font que peu de ses préparations ont été conservées jusqu'à aujourd'hui.

[11] Ces collections scientifiques mobilisent régulièrement de nouvelles techniques de conservation pour répondre aux avancées des questionnements scientifiques, par exemple en considérant préserver les composés moléculaires des organismes mis en collection afin de faciliter les études génétiques.

d'entretien évoquées précédemment, sur les insectes, les coquilles de mollusques, les fossiles macroscopiques et certains éléments minéralogiques selon des principes prenant souvent en compte l'esthétique et la rareté. Ainsi, dans les collections de mammifères et d'oiseaux, cela peut conduire certains amateurs à acquérir davantage d'individus mâles, avec leurs parures de parade sexuelle, aux dépens des formes juvéniles et des femelles souvent moins colorées[12].

Collecteurs et collectionneurs, amateurs et scientifiques face à l'évolution des textes de protection de la nature

Naturalistes amateurs et collectionneurs privés sont, comme les scientifiques et les institutions publiques collectant, conservant et exposant des collections, soumis aux codes internationaux de nomenclature mais aussi à un ensemble de conventions internationales, à des directives et un règlement européens, ainsi qu'à des lois nationales visant à protéger les espèces[13].
La « convention sur le commerce international des espèces de faune et de flore sauvages menacées d'extinction » (CITES) adoptée en 1973 à Washington dans le but de contrôler les mouvements des spécimens, vivants ou morts, des espèces concernées est le texte le plus souvent cité[14]. Elle ne s'applique pourtant qu'indirectement en Europe où la Communauté européenne a adopté en 1996 un Règlement qui en durcit les principes de mise en œuvre et élargit la liste des espèces concernées[15]. Ce règlement impose entre autres lors du transport de ces spécimens, y compris à l'intérieur d'un même État, que ce soit à des fins de vente, de prêt à une exposition ou d'étude scientifique… des

---

[12] Les dons aux musées peuvent ainsi induire, dans ces deux groupes, un déséquilibre du *sex ratio* des spécimens. Cela a récemment été souligné dans une étude polémique (Cooper N. *et al*. 2019. Sex biases in bird and mammal natural history collections. *Proceedings of the Royal Society B: Biological Sciences*, 286 (1913): 20192025-20192025. doi: 10.1098/rspb.2019.2025) alors que la problématique est plus globalement de veiller à une collecte exhaustive de spécimens aux divers stades de développement et de pondérer les dons et collectes de formes chatoyantes.

[13] Sur la genèse du droit de l'environnement, consulter l'ouvrage coordonné par J. Fromageau et M. Cornu, eds, *Genèse du droit de l'environnement, Fondements et enjeux internationaux*, l'Harmattan, 2001.

[14] La CITES est régulièrement mise à jour pour tenir compte de l'évolution de la situation des espèces ; https://cites.org/fra/disc/text.php

[15] Le Règlement CE 338/97 est régulièrement mis à jour ; http://eur-lex.europa.eu/legal-content/FR/ALL/?uri=celex:31997R0338.

autorisations administratives comme les certificats intra-communautaires (CIC) délivrés en France par les directions régionales de l'environnement, de l'aménagement et du logement (DREAL)[16].
Les lois et réglementations françaises ne posent pas pour autant nécessairement des principes identiques à ceux existants dans d'autres États européens. Ainsi, ramasser un animal mort, appartenant à une espèce protégée, est un délit que le collecteur soit un musée ou un collectionneur privé en France, mais pas nécessairement dans tel ou tel autre État européen.
Dans le cas des CIC précédemment évoqués, la mise en œuvre peut être compliquée en raison de la diversité des interprétations au sein d'une même administration. Une consultation des musées d'histoire naturelle français en 2017 a révélé une diversité d'interprétations selon les DREAL qui amena certains musées d'histoire naturelle, lors de la fusion des régions françaises, à refaire leurs demandes de CIC, leur nouvelle DREAL ne reconnaissant pas les autorisations précédemment délivrées.
À l'opposé de l'objectif fondamental de protection de la biodiversité, grâce à la protection d'espèces définies par ces divers textes, l'interprétation de certains d'entre eux conduit à ne plus pouvoir mener certaines actions de culture scientifique. Des expositions n'ont pas pu se réaliser et l'itinérance des spécimens naturalisés d'espèces en danger est soumise à tant d'aléas administratifs que les prêts entre musées sont évités. Contrairement à l'itinérance des œuvres promue par les musées d'art et d'histoire, les espèces emblématiques de l'altération de la biodiversité ne sont plus mobilisées lors des itinérances d'expositions scientifiques que sous des formes virtuelles alors même qu'elles existent dans les réserves. Elles peuvent même faire l'objet d'autodafés comme récemment en France dans le cas de la destruction des stocks de défenses d'éléphants, sans chercher à mobiliser ce que pourrait apporter en termes de sensibilisation à la protection des espèces, la monstration de la masse des défenses entrées par des voies illégales en France.
Très récemment, la Convention sur la diversité biologique (CDB) a été complétée en 2010 par le « protocole sur l'accès aux ressources

[16] Les procédures dites « simplifiées » d'autorisations pouvant être accordées à des personnes préalablement agréées doivent concerner le préteur et l'emprunteur ; elles sont de fait peu opérationnelles, seuls quelques grands musées scientifiques ayant l'agrément.

génétiques et le partage juste et équitable des avantages découlant de leur utilisation », dit protocole de Nagoya qui fait également l'objet d'applications nationales différentes selon les États. En France, la récente publication en 2016 et 2017 de décrets et arrêtés d'application de ce protocole[17] conduit, dans un contexte d'affichage, parfois dogmatique, de la protection des espèces, certains acteurs à considérer que tout spécimen susceptible de conserver des traces de matériel génétique est concerné, même s'il n'avait pas été mis en collection dans le but d'une étude génétique[18].

Durant la même période, dans un but de protection des rhinocéros et éléphants, un décret d'interdiction du commerce de l'ivoire d'éléphants et de la corne de rhinocéros mettait en cause jusqu'aux possibilités de restauration des instruments de musique et objets d'art comportant de l'ivoire[19]. Il n'a été modifié pour permettre l'utilisation d'ivoire prélevé avant 1947[20] qu'après d'âpres échanges entre des interlocuteurs des milieux de l'environnement, de la culture et des sciences.

Dans la période récente, la protection de l'environnement a privilégié, en France, un affichage volontariste qui se retrouve dans le titre de la loi de 2016 intitulée « pour la reconquête de la biodiversité, de la nature et des paysages ». Pour autant, cette loi ne se place pas dans une perspective de coévolution de l'humanité et de la nature (Van Praët *et al.*, 2017), et a conservé, en dépit de critiques, le terme de « reconquête » caractéristique d'une vue de dominatrice de la nature. En application de cette loi, le décret de novembre 2017 « relatif à

---

[17] Décret n° 2016-1615 du 21 nov. 2016 portant publication du protocole de Nagoya du 29 oct. 2010 sur l'accès aux ressources génétiques et le partage juste et équitable des avantages découlant de leur utilisation, relatif à la convention sur la diversité biologique, signé par la France le 20 sept. 2011 à New York. NOR : MAEJ1632439D.
- Décret n° 2017-848 du 9 mai 2017 relatif à l'accès aux ressources génétiques et aux connaissances traditionnelles associées et au partage des avantages découlant de leur utilisation. NOR : DEVL1702693D.
- Arrêté du 8 nov. 2017 relatif aux formulaires de déclaration et de demande d'autorisation d'accès aux ressources génétiques et aux connaissances traditionnelles associées. NOR : TREL1726666A.

[18] Les débats n'ont permis de limiter que des aspects rétroactifs vis-à-vis des collections déjà constituées.

[19] Arrêté du 16 août 2016 relatif à l'interdiction du commerce de l'ivoire d'éléphants et de la corne de rhinocéros sur le territoire national. NOR : DEVL1615873A.

[20] Arrêté du 4 mai 2017 portant modification de l'arrêté du 16 août 2016 relatif à l'interdiction du commerce de l'ivoire d'éléphants et de la corne de rhinocéros sur le territoire national. NOR : DEVL1638253A.

l'encadrement des usages portant sur des spécimens d'animaux d'espèces non domestiques ou des végétaux d'espèces non cultivées », modifie le code de l'environnement et va régir pour les années à venir une partie des règles que doivent suivre collectionneurs privés et publics[21].
La récente multiplication des textes encadrant la constitution et la gestion des collections naturalistes publiques comme privées, brièvement évoquée ci-dessus, a été menée du point de vue de l'environnement. Quelle qu'ait été la réalité des débats entre acteurs de sa protection et de son exploitation, ces débats ont globalement omis la place des collections en termes de sources de savoirs pour les communautés scientifiques et la société.
L'ambiguïté initiale du terme de « commerce » apparu dans la convention CITES, n'a été développée que de manière négative dans les textes ultérieurs. Ceux-ci tendent à considérer tout spécimen mort comme ayant été à priori tué pour être collecté en vue d'un commerce lucratif. Ils mettent ainsi le collecteur et le collectionneur, y compris scientifique, dans l'obligation de devoir justifier l'origine du spécimen, ce qui est compréhensible, mais le place en position de suspect, y compris quand il développe une action sans but lucratif, de recherche ou de culture scientifique, dans une perspective de protection desdites espèces et plus globalement de la biodiversité. Acteurs de la protection et de l'exploitation de l'environnement ont enfermé le politique et le législateur dans une démarche où le contrôle s'opère en dépit du but recherché, ici l'usage lucratif ou non des collections naturalistes, ou plus précisément en assimilant tout échange autour de celles-ci comme ayant un but lucratif. Quelles que soient les difficultés qu'il peut y avoir à contrôler le but non lucratif d'un transport de spécimen scientifique, le développement nécessaire des connaissances devrait justifier une attention accrue de ce point de vue dans les conventions, lois et réglementations à venir.

Dans un contexte où le virtuel et ses acteurs mobilisent les images d'espèces symboliques, souvent seulement représentatives d'une faible

[21] Loi n° 2016-1087 du 8 août 2016 pour la reconquête de la biodiversité, de la nature et des paysages. NOR : DEVL1400720L.
Décret n° 2017-1583 du 17 nov. 2017 relatif à l'encadrement des usages portant sur des spécimens d'animaux d'espèces non domestiques ou des végétaux d'espèces non cultivées et modifiant le code de l'environnement. NOR : TREL1636829D.

part de la biodiversité, collectionneurs, scientifiques et médiateurs des sciences de la nature se trouvent mis au défi de réaffirmer le potentiel des collections et l'importance d'en favoriser l'accès pour le développement des connaissances, le partage de celles-ci et les débats sociétaux que justifient les objectifs de coévolution de l'humanité au sein de l'ensemble du vivant.

Bibliographie

Cohen Y. et Drouin J.-M., 1989, *Les amateurs de sciences et de techniques,* Cahiers d'histoire et de philosophie des sciences, 27, p. 7-10.
Drouin J.-M., 2008, *L'herbier des philosophes*, Seuil éd.
Fromageau J. et Cornu M. eds., 2001, *Genèse du droit de l'environnement. Fondements et enjeux internationaux*, L'Harmattan éd.
Imperato F., 1599, *Dell'Historia Naturale.*
Lafon M.-F., 1999. *Philippe, duc d'Orléans 1869-1926, explorateur, navigateur, naturaliste*, Boubée éd.
Lamarck J.-B., 1790, *Mémoire sur les cabinets d'histoire naturelle*, Bibliothèque centrale du Muséum, Archive Y2 1068 & 103 981.
Linné C., 1736, *Bibliotheca botanica.*
Pearce S., 1989, *Museums studies in material culture* (Pearce dir.), Leicester University Press éd.
Pomian K., 1987, *Collectionneurs, amateurs et curieux : Paris, Venise, XVIe-XVIIIe siècle*, Bibliothèque des histoires, Gallimard éd.
Stearn W. T., 1998, *The Natural History Museum at South Kensington*, The Natural History Museum ed.
Van Praët M., 2008, *Muséums et collections d'histoire naturelle : quelle place dans l'histoire des musées,* Histoire de l'art, 62, p. 11-18.
Van Praët M., 2012, *Cultures scientifiques et musées d'histoire naturelle en France*, p. 71-87, Art et Science, Les Essentiels d'Hermès, CNRS Éditions.
Van Praët M., Duée P.-H et Mignard J.-P, 2017, *Une éthique pour habiter la Terre autrement*, pp. 319-334. *L'expérience de nature comme bien commun. Le souci de la nature. Apprendre, inventer, gouverner* (Fleury C. et Prévot A.-C. éds.), CNRS Éditions.

National laws on private collections: problems and solutions

Elina N. MOUSTAIRA
Professor of Comparative Law
School of Law
National and Kapodistrian University of Athens

Introduction

"Why collect, especially when it involves choosing to participate in a criminal market?", it is asked. Various reasons are put forth. Cultural edification of the public or scholars is one of them. Hoping to gain a cultural capital is another one. Self-realization and public service are often offered as explanations[1].
Private collectors often use terms such as "falling in love" with the artworks they [want to] acquire. In recent years, private collectors in several countries make public interventions, appearing thus as giving more weight to the rational element, that is, the focus of attention is not anymore the concept of passion, but an intellectual project[2].

The opacity of the art collecting activity

A usual complaint in many countries is the opacity of the whole "system of art" and especially of the creation and enrichment of private collections. A recent Spanish study confirms that. It is noted that "Taken into account of the private character of the individual collections, it is not possible to offer a global statistic on the amount of the artworks acquired by Spanish buyers, or to offer some general characteristics"[3]. This opacity – not only in Spain – was the reason for which Jean Baudrillard published an article in *Libération*, with the title « Le

---

[1] S. Mackenzie/D. Yates, Collectors on illicit collecting: Higher loyalties and other techniques of neutralization in the unlawful collecting of rare and precious orchids and antiquities, *Theoretical Criminology* 2015, 1-18.
[2] E. N. Moustaira, *Art Collections, Private and Public: A Comparative Legal Study*, Springer, 2015, 7.
[3] C. Mc Andrew, *El mercado español de arte en 2012*, Barcelona, Fundación Arte y Mecenazgo, 2012, 63.

complot de l'art ». He expressed his dislike to the actual conception of culture, speaking about the art system as a perfectly organized net, almost invincible, in which whoever enters with the aim to attack it, in the end is converted to a part of it. According to him, in this system, the art has no vital function, has lost the transcendence, the culmination of a phase of a total visualization that has reached the Occident. In this conspiracy, everybody is victim and complice at the same time.

In Spain, the number of the private collectors is rather small. Even smaller is the number of the collectors who speak about their collections. According to a recent study, private collecting in Spain has to walk a long road before being considered as a socially and culturally established practice, politically protected and stimulated by an adequate legislation[4].

Art Galleries – Contemporary Art

Art Galleries are among the most powerful players/factors in the field of contemporary art collecting. All artists, especially those who have a high international market value exhibit their new works in art galleries, before any exhibition in artforums or museums (if they have that chance), in order to occupy for a certain time a central place of the artworld. New artists know that exhibitions in an art gallery may help them live from their own art. Still, the relationship between artists and galleries is not an easy one.

Internet has helped collectors have a direct access, in real time, to works of art that are offered for sale. This has also augmented the competition of new, very rich, collectors.

Issues of unfair competition, or misleading advertising, privacy, bank datas, e-commerce often arise in cases of promotion of artworks in web. Galleries with an international activity create "Back-Offices". Contacting rich collectors all over the world is a priority for them, every workday. Related to that is the fact that many galleries open subsidiaries in other countries or big spaces near international airports. This is a real centrifugal power in the landscape of galleries[5].

---

[4] M. D. Jiménez-Blanco, *El coleccionismo de arte en España. Una aproximación desde su historia y su contexto*, Barcelona, Fundación Arte y Mecenazgo 132-133.

[5] R. Fleck, *Das Kunstsystem im 21. Jahrhundert. Museen, Künstler, Sammler, Galerien*, Passagen Verlag, 2013, 63-65.

Art Market

It is estimated (according to the datas of TEFAF of Maastricht) that there are more than 400.000 professionals all over the world, working in art market. That means about 2.000.000 work posts and more posts/activities connected directly or indirectly with the art market.
In the EU, during the first decade of the 21st century exports of art have been more that imports. In 2008, Italy became the third biggest market in EU, replacing Germany. Galleries and antiquaries, in this country, in 2008 were 5.775, giving work to about 25.000 persons. There were also about 200 auction houses[6].

Art dealers - Collectors

One of the latest – or perhaps the latest – lawsuits over valuable artworks that reached London courts is the following: Count Giovanni Volpi di Misurata had entered into a partnership with Old and Modern Masters Ltd, a London-based dealer, in 2014, giving the dealer a 50 percent share in the paintings by 16th Century Dutch artist Anthonis Mor and permission to sell them in exchange for 1.5 million euros. Volpi sued the dealer for breach of the partnership agreement over the paintings. The dealer denied any wrongdoing, arguing that concerns over how the family came into possession of the works caused problems for potential buyers.
As the reportage states, "The opaque art world, where the most prized works exchange hands for eye watering amounts of money, throws up multiple court battles across the globe between collectors, dealers and auction houses over fraud, authenticity, and money laundering."[7]
The most crucial issues here and in other cases are provenance of the artworks and authenticity. Clear chain of ownership is most important.

---

[6] S. Segnalini, Il (cosidetto) diritto dell'arte nella formazione del giurista: ricognizione dell'esistente e proposte possibili, *in*: G. Ajani/A. Donati (eds.) *I diritti dell'arte contemporanea*, Umberto Allemandi & Co., Torino 2011, 191.
[7] J. Hodges, "Mussolini's Aide, His Son and a Spat Over Dutch Master's Art" https://www.bloomberg.com/news/articles/2017-03-06/mussolini-s-aide-a-prince-and-the-fight-over-dutch-master-s-art

Authenticity of Artworks

Artworks are often sold "for stratospheric sums"[8]. The buyers – usually collectors – want to be sure about the authenticity of the artworks they buy, since it could not be excluded that these items are fakes or that they have been forged, or misattributed or reattributed.
"Can the principle of caveat emptor (buyer beware) apply to issues of appraisal and authentication in the largely unregulated art market?", it is asked[9]. This is a question put by a U.S. scholar, regarding U.S. law, but obviously a question about the liability of art experts may concern all national laws.
As it is pointed out, in USA an appraisal is not by itself a warranty of authenticity, under the Uniform Commercial Code. Nevertheless, when one donates [art] property and submits an appraisal to the Internal Revenue Service (IRS) for purposes of tax deduction, one must include a statement of authenticity. Therefore, "for tax purposes, such an appraisal is de facto a representation of authenticity"[10].
Although in that country a professional expert, when performing services for a client, "has the duty to have that degree of learning and skill ordinarily possessed by reputable [members of the profession], practicing in the same or a similar locality and under similar circumstances"[11], appraising personal property – works of art included – in USA is unregulated. That is, the profession is mostly self-regulated. In the 1980's, the Appraisal Foundation, a non-profit organization was established and it oversees ever since the publication of the Uniform Standards of Professional Appraisal Practice (USPAP). These Standards are only useful guidelines, they are not legally binding.
There are fundamental differences in burden of proof concepts among EU and non-EU jurisdictions.
Under Swiss civil law, the factual question whether a work of art is an authentic work or not must be proven to a "predominant degree of

---

[8] V. Wiener, Appraising Art in the Stratosphere: The Dynamics of Steve Wynn's Elbow and Other Valuation Situations, *Journal of Advanced Appraisal Studies* 65, 75 (2008).
[9] J. B. Prowda, *Visual Arts and the Law. A Handbook for Professionals*, Lund Humphries in association with Sotheby's Institute of Art, 2013, p. 203.
[10] J. B. Prowda, *Visual Arts and the Law. A Handbook for Professionals*, Lund Humphries in association with Sotheby's Institute of Art, 2013, p. 204.
[11] S. M. Levy, Liability of the Art Expert for Professional Malpractice, 1991 *Wisconsin Law Review* 595, 600.

probability" (überwiegende Wahrscheinlichkeit). This degree of probability must be established according to the experiences of life; and the accuracy of this material fact must be proven through objective factors[12].

Auction houses

Secrecy and anonymity in the art world can be reckless and may be blamed for many scandals in this world and for contributing to Money-Laundering. Art Market is criticized for lacking security and transparency[13].
A notorious example is that of the Knoedler gallery in New York, 165 years in business. Collectors paid about $80 million to purchase unknown "masterpieces", brought to market by a Long Island art dealer. The "masterworks", allegedly come from a mystery collector, had in fact been created by a forger in his Queens garage.
Concerns about anonymity were intensified last years, when the Panama Papers were released, which gave many details about the use of corporate veils to conceal ownership, avoid taxes and enable crime. Christie's said, last February, that its policy has been strengthened during the last months, and that it now requires agents who want to sell works through the auction house to tell the name of the owner they represent.
The situation is far from simple. Veils have been and are being used to obscure ownership of arts. Even when big cases become notorious, like that of Rybolovlev v. Bouvier, over matters that include the money from the Sotheby's sale, secrecy is still being defended. Other cases are also famous/notorious, like that of the seizure of "Hannibal", an $8 million painting by Jean-Michel Basquiat brought into the U.S. by Edemar Cid Ferreira, a jailed ex-Brazilian banker who converted some of his laundered money into a massive art collection". At the time he moved the painting into USA, he claimed that it was worth $100[14].
So far, efforts to reduce anonymity in art sales have had no result. In 2012, a New York appeals court ruled that auction houses had the

[12] E. N. Moustaira, *Art Collections, Private and Public: A Comparative Legal Study*, Springer, 2015, 100.
[13] A. L. Bandle, *The Sale of Misattributed Artworks and Antiques at Auction*, Edward Elgar Publishing, 2016, 336.
[14] S. Rubenfeld, Art World's Response to Money-Laundering Concerns Draws Critics, *The Wall Street Journal*, Feb. 27, 2017.

obligation to let buyers know the identity of sellers. But the decision was overturned on appeal[15].

As far as art authentication is concerned, the situation in USA is the following: At the beginning and during the first half of the 20th century, auction houses acted as intermediaries between sellers and purchasers and disclaimed all representations and warranties to the works they auctioned. In only a few cases, courts awarded purchasers rescission of contract based on fraud claims.

In 1966, New York enacted legislation on the creation and negation of express warranties in the sale of fine art. In 1968, the legislation limited the application of the warranties to sales by art merchants to non-merchants and further restricted the power to negate such warranties.

In 1973, Sotheby's offered for the first time warranty to clients. In 1977, Christie's did the same. Nowadays, both auction houses extend their limited warranties for 5 years from the date of the relevant auction, while the UCC warranty extends 4 years. These warranties refer only to the work's authorship and not to physical condition or provenance[16].

People working in the big, international, auction houses argue that they have to deal with multiple problems. In Sotheby's, there is a department exclusively dedicated to legal problems and trying to set procedures and rules that would respond to the rules of each country as well as to the rules of the international treaties. These procedures and rules refer to the contracts of intermediation, to the certification of artworks, to the percentage due to the artists, on the transactions of their artworks, to the possibility of certain States to acquire or "notify" artworks considered as significant national cultural heritage, etc.

Sotheby's has 40 offices all over the world and 8 selling locations: London, New York, Paris, Amsterdam, Hong Kong, Milan, Geneva, Zurich. People working in Sotheby's believe that clear and uniform rules for each of these instances, would be necessary in order to assure the absolute respect of the laws and to guarantee the maxima transparency of the whole operation[17].

---

[15] G. Bowley & W. K. Rashbaum, "Has the Art Market Become an Unwitting Partner in Crime?", *The New York Times*, Feb. 19, 2017.

[16] J. B. Prowda, *Visual Arts and the Law. A Handbook for Professionals*, 2013, 208.

[17] C. Dwek, Norme necessarie e norme inefficienti nella pratica di una casa d'aste internazionale, *in*: G. Ajani/A. Donati (eds.) *I diritti dell'arte contemporanea*, Umberto Allemandi & Co., Torino 2011, 109.

Donations - Tax evasion

Private museums in USA, "a part of American culture", have proliferated in the last decade. Many are those who claim that the US tax system, as far as art is concerned, "is rigged toward the wealthy".
U.S. network of museums relies on a tax code that encourages rich collectors to share their art. The Association of Art Museum Directors estimates that more than 90% of art collections held in public trust by American museums were donated by private individuals. Collectors (usually wealthy ones) save millions of dollars in federal taxes by donating art and money to museums and art foundations. The difference between them and the private museums is that the founders of the latter "can deduct the full market value of any art, cash and stocks they donate"; that is, private museums are tax-exempt and many are those that say there should be a clear public benefit, and it should not be entirely at the discretion of the person running the museum or foundation"[18].

Let it be mentioned here, that in order for a donation to a museum in USA to qualify for a tax deduction, it must satisfy 3 general requirements: it must be to a qualifying institution (e.g. a non-profit museum), it must be of qualifying property and it must display proper intent and not be made in exchange for goods and services. Donor may deduct the fair market value of the donations; unfortunately, in case of offered antiquities, their value assessment is inherently subjective and often the donors "manipulate the assessed value in the worst"[19].

In Italy too, there is a difference in donations' tax deduction, between private persons and business entities. Private persons who want to make a donation in favor of public entities, foundations, non-profit associations which are active in the artistic or cultural sector, may have a tax deduction of 19%. On the contrary, business entities may deduct from their income the full amount of their contributions to the artistic-cultural sector.

To this disparity of tax treatment is owed the fact that in Italy business entities make many more such donations than private persons (the law 142/21.11.2000 has a difficult formulation and for this reason not all

---

[18] P. Cohen, "Writing Off the Warhol Next Door", *The New York Times*, Jan. 10, 2015, citing the comment of Robert Storr, (then) Dean of the Yale School of Art.

[19] D. Yates, (2016) "Museums, collectors, and value manipulation: tax fraud through donation of antiquities", *Journal of Financial Crime* 2016, 173, 180.

commercialists know about that possibility).
In December 2009 were presented the results of a research on a sample of 1000 persons of ages between 25 and 64, that Civita Association in collaboration with the Ministero per i Beni e le Attività Culturali had made. It seems that the motivations to donate in favor of art and culture move beyond the simple fiscal benefit. The persons that participated in that research had declared that a major motive for them would be the transparency of administration of the funds that are/would be collected from the donations. They wanted to be certain that their donations would be really destined to the cultural entity that they would have chosen.
A proposal by the Ministero per i Beni e le Attività Culturali, for a registry for the "istituzioni ammesse a ricevere contributi e liberalità", for the entry in which, the cultural institutions should guarantee particularly high standards of transparency and correctness in the administration of the funds collected, would perhaps be a positive step[20].

Immunity of collections from suit or seizure[21]

Loan of cultural objects to institutions in other states sometimes causes fear to the prospective lenders (either states or private persons) that they could be seized by third-party claimants who would take advantage of the change in jurisdiction[22].
Claims by third parties may arise in 3 cases: 1) a government, a company or an individual may claim to be the owner of a cultural object, file a suit asking to have that ownership recognized, and seek to take possession of the object; 2) a claimant may ask for the seizure of a cultural object – treated as an asset – in order to enforce a judgment

---

[20] P. Sandretto Re Rebaudengo, Il diritto dell'arte a esistere nel diritto, *in*: G. Ajani/A. Donati (eds.) *I diritti dell'arte contemporanea*, Umberto Allemandi & Co., Torino 2011, 89, 95-96.
[21] E. N. Moustaira, *Art Collections, Private and Public: A Comparative Legal Study*, Springer, 2015, 117-119.
[22] See N. Palmer, Adrift on a Sea of Troubles: Cross-Border Art Loans and the Specter of Ulterior Title, 38 *Vanderbilt Journal of Transnational Law* 947, 950 (2005): "Public exhibition exposes cultural objects to widespread scrutiny, alerting potential claimants".

issued against the owner; 3) the cultural object may be seized as part of a criminal investigation[23].
Immunity from seizure or suit statutes' aim is to prevent either the seizure of borrowed cultural objects that might have been ordered by a court or other legally imposed restraint on their physical movement or a suit against them.
Concerns about seizure of borrowed cultural objects first arose in the early 1960s when U.S. museums thought about borrowing artworks from the Soviet Union. Soviet Union, worried that claims might be made against these artworks (that had been nationalized after the 1917 revolution) while being in USA, asked for some guarantee that they would be given back to Russia after the agreed time.
In 1965, the [Federal] Immunity from Seizure Act (22 U.S.C. sec. 2459) was adopted. It was followed by legislation in four states: New York (Arts and Cultural Affairs Law, sec. 12.03), Rhode Island (General Laws, sec. 5-62), Texas (Civil Practice and Remedies Code, sec. 3-61), and Tennessee (Tennessee Code, sec. 28-3-115).
In the following years, more countries adopted such laws[24]. In Canada, five provinces have enacted immunity from seizure laws: Manitoba (Foreign Cultural Objects Immunity from Seizure Act, C.C.S.M. 1987, c. F-140), Québec (Code of Civil Procedure R.S.Q. 1976, c. C-25), Ontario (Foreign Cultural Objects Immunity from Seizure Act, R.S.O. 1990, c. F.-23), British Columbia (Law and Equity Act, R.S.B.C. 1996, c. 253), and Alberta (Foreign Cultural Property Immunity Act, R.S.A. 2000, c. F-17).
France enacted such a law in 1994, Germany in 1998 (Gesetz zum Schutz deutschen Kulturgutes gegen Abwanderung, BGBl. I 1955, 501, as amended by Gesetz zur Umsetzung von Richtlinien der Europäischen Gemeinschaften, 26.5.1998), Belgium in 2002, Austria in 2003, Switzerland and Lichtenstein in 2005, Israel and United Kingdom in 2007, Finland, Czech Republic, and Japan in 2011, Hungary in 2012,

---

[23] C. Forrest, Immunity from Seizure and Suit in Australia: The Protection of Cultural Objects on Loan Act 2013, *International Journal of Cultural Property* 21 (2014) 143, 144; D. Getz, The History of Canadian Immunity from Seizure Legislation, *International Journal of Cultural Property* 18 (2011) 201, 205-209.

[24] All these details about legislations are taken from the articles of *C. Forrest*, Immunity from Seizure and Suit in Australia: The Protection of Cultural Objects on Loan Act 2013, *International Journal of Cultural Property* 21 (2014) 144 and *D. Getz*, The History of Canadian Immunity from Seizure Legislation, *International Journal of Cultural Property* 18 (2011) 201, 203.

and Australia in 2013 (Protection of Cultural Objects on Loan Act).
In some of these countries, the relevant legislation provides broad protection to cultural objects lent by foreign countries. This is the case for example of USA and of United Kingdom. It is pointed out though, that it will be the courts that will determine how far this protection reaches[25].
The Australian Act, borrowing the scheme followed by U.K. respective legislation[26], establishes institutional immunity, that is, immunity arises only when cultural objects are imported in the country under an agreement between a lender and a borrowing institution that has been approved by the minister. In many other countries, as it is mentioned, such as Canada, France, Germany and Israel, in order that immunity is granted, a specific request has to be filed which will specify the objects for which immunity is being asked.
Comments on this recent Australian law, point out that "it remains to be seen whether this statute with such a wide immunity will function as intended"[27].
Cultural Heritage Law Committee of the International Law Association completed in 2014 a Draft Convention on Immunity from Suit and Seizure for Cultural Objects Temporarily Abroad for Cultural, Educational or Scientific Purposes. This Draft Convention is intended for eventual adoption by an international or regional organization and ratification of it by states[28].

Artists' rights

It is argued that if we want to restitute to Art a public role, it is necessary to put the artist in the center of the so called System of Art and recognize his/her professional dignity[29].
Artists' rights are the so called moral rights.
Scholars in USA often refer to a divide between author-oriented civil

---

[25] L. M. Kaye, Art Loans and Immunity from Seizure in the United States and the United Kingdom, *International Journal of Cultural Property* 17 (2010) 335, 354.
[26] A. O'Connell, The United Kingdom's Immunity from Seizure Legislation, *Modern Law Review* 72 (2009) 783.
[27] C. Forrest, Immunity from Seizure and Suit in Australia: The Protection of Cultural Objects on Loan Act 2013, *International Journal of Cultural Property* 21 (2014) 163.
[28] See Summary of ILA's 76th Conference – Washington 2014, April 12, 2014, p. 13.
[29] A. Detheridge, Quali diritti per l'arte contemporanea?, *in*: G. Ajani/A. Donati (eds.) *I diritti dell'arte contemporanea*, Umberto Allemandi & Co., Torino 2011, 25, 29.

law countries and user-oriented common law countries[30]. This divide has been historically marked by the presence or absence of moral rights in copyright law[31].
In 1990, the U.S. Copyright Act was amended and only visual artists were named possessors of "moral rights". According to the Visual Artists Rights Act of 1990, visual artists enjoy the same protection as authors. Numerous articles were written on this law[32]. Several scholars considered this novelty as at least strange, since copyright was always concerning texts[33].
The term "moral right" was adopted as the direct translation of the French term "droit moral", which was established in the 19th century. Still, there are voices pointing out that the so called moral rights[34] could follow the German term "Urheberpersönlichkeitsrecht" and be called or rather described as authorial rights of personality[35].
In numerous countries moral rights have been guaranteed since many years, following mainly the French conceptual paradigm, not being identical the legal regulations of all the civil law countries though[36].
Under French law there are 4 moral rights[37], the following:
1) The Right of Disclosure (Droit de divulgation), Code de la propriété intellectuelle, article L. 212-2.
2) The Right to Withdraw from Publication or to Make Modifications (Droit de retrait ou de repentir), Code de la propriété intellectuelle, article L. 121-4.

---

[30] E. N. Moustaira, *Art Collections, Private and Public: A Comparative Legal Study*, Springer, 2015, 22-24.
[31] S. G. Bonneau, Honor and Destruction: The Conflicted Object in Moral Rights Law, 87 *St. John's Law Review* 47, 48 (2013).
[32] S.P. Liemer, How We Lost Our Moral Rights and the Door Closed on Non-Economic Values in Copyright, 5 *John Marshall Review of Intellectual Property Law* 1 (2005).
[33] R. Tushnet, Worth a Thousand Words: The Images of Copyright, 125 *Harvard Law Review* 683, 685 (2012).
[34] The artists' creative minds and souls as embodied in their works, see *J.R. Applebaum*, The Visual Artists Rights Act of 1990: An Analysis Based on the French *Droit Moral*, 8 *American Journal of International Law & Policy* 183 (1992).
[35] S.R. Munzer/K. Raustiala, The Uneasy Case for Intellectual Property Rights in Traditional Knowledge, 27 *Cardozo Arts & Entertainment Law Journal* 37, 68 (2009).
[36] G. Dworkin, The Moral Right of the Author: Moral Rights and the Common Law Countries, 19 *Columbia-VLA Journal of Law & Arts* 229, 230 (1995).
[37] J. B. Prowda, *Visual Arts and the Law. A Handbook for Professionals*, Lund Humphries in association with Sotheby's Institute of Art, 2013, p. 102 – 105.

3) The Right of Attribution (Droit à la paternité), Code de la propriété intellectuelle, article L. 121-1.
4) The Right of Integrity (Droit ou respect de l'œuvre), Code de la propriété intellectuelle, article L. 121-1.
According to most U.S. scholars, moral rights are divided into 3 categories: the right of integrity, the right of attribution, and the right of disclosure[38]. Other scholars divide them further, either into 5 categories (attribution, integrity, disclosure, withdrawal, and resale royalties)[39] or into four categories (rights of publication, paternity, integrity, and withdrawal)[40].

Let me mention here the "Artworks' Transfer Agreement", first of its kind, published in 1971 by New York art dealer (especially conceptual art) and curator Seth Siegelaub and lawyer Robert Projansky. Aim of this agreement was to formally define and protect artists' rights at the sale of their works. It was translated into French, German, Italian and Dutch and became an internationally standard artist agreement – still is.

Collecting archaeological material

It has often and repeatedly been stated that there is a causal relationship between the demand for archaeological material and the excavation, both legal and illegal, of the archaeological sites. An exhaustive registry of all heritage objects in a country could be an efficient enough preventive measure, effective enactment of it though is not an easy thing to do. As it is pointed out, it is the regulation of the demand side of the market that should be focused on. The fact that cultural objects at some parts of the world, which have been on public display for hundreds of years, have become target of major theft during the last decades (example, the cultural objects within Bolivian churches) is an evidence of a clear connection between global demand and local theft. "Theoretically…, a disruption of the demand for objects will eventually

---

[38] R. R. Kwall, Preserving Personality and Reputational Interests of Constructed Personas Through Moral Rights: A Blueprint for the Twenty-First Century, 2001 *University of Illinois Law Review* 151, 152.
[39] S.P. Liemer, Understanding Artists' Moral Rights: A Primer, 7 *Boston University Public Interest Law Journal* 41, 45-46 (1998).
[40] J. M. Dine, Authors' Moral Rights in Non-European Nations: International Agreements, Economics, *Mannu Bhandari*, and the Dead Sea Scrolls, 16 *Michigan Journal of International Law* 545, 550 (1995).

trickle down to the supply and the motivation to rob" these objects will be lost[41].

Collectors should refuse to buy antiquities for the provenance of which they would not have enough or any information. If they did that, the illicit trade in antiquities would be diminished[42]. Internet market in antiquities of unknown provenance is unfortunately flourishing, either because customers/buyers are ignorant or because they are indifferent. As it is pointed out, "the experience of eBay U.S.A. shows that in the absence of effective oversight self-regulation is likely to fail, and concerned public or professional bodies need to step forward and respond to the challenge". eBay should be monitored regularly, non-domestic antiquities should be accompanied by an image of valid export documentation, otherwise be removed from the market, and criminals should be convicted[43].

---

[41] D. Yates, Church Theft, Insecurity, and Community Justice: The Reality of Source-End Regulation of the Market for Illicit Bolivian Cultural Objects, *European Journal of Criminal Policy* 2014, 445, 456.

[42] M. Kersel, The lure of the artefact? The effects of acquiring eastern Mediterranean material culture, *in*: A.B. Knapp & P. Van Dommelen (eds) *The Cambridge Prehistory of the Bronze and Iron Age Mediterranean*, Cambridge University Press, 2015, 367, 375.

[43] N. Brodie, The Internet Market in Antiquities, *in*: *F. Desmarais* (ed.), *Countering Illicit Traffic in Cultural Goods: The Global Challenge of Protecting the World's Heritage*, Paris: ICOM, 2015, 11, 18.

II

La protection publique des collections privées

Sous la présidence de Marina Schneider

II

L'exposition publique des collections privées

La notion de collection en droit français

Mathilde ROELLINGER
Juriste
Ancien avocat au Barreau de Paris

Depuis plusieurs années, la collection d'art privée est à l'honneur dans les expositions muséales. Certaines d'entre elles resteront dans les esprits, notamment la collection de Gertrude Stein exposée au Grand Palais en 2011, et plus récemment la collection de Sergueï Chtchoukine présentée au sein de la fondation Louis Vuitton. Ces expositions reconstituent des ensembles qui n'existent plus après la dispersion de la collection par leurs anciens propriétaires ou leurs descendants. Comment expliquer cet engouement ? La présentation de telles collections prestigieuses sont porteuses d'un intérêt tant d'un point de vue historique qu'artistique. Cette reconstitution retranscrit aussi l'histoire des goûts d'une époque. Une collection privée en France n'est pas soumise à un statut juridique général. Elle est avant tout considérée comme un ensemble de biens mobiliers corporels. Malgré l'absence de statut juridique, la collection privée est « saisie » par le droit français, au sens où le droit va tenir compte de ses particularités afin, dans certains cas, de la protéger. La protection d'une collection implique d'éviter la dispersion de ses éléments, de maintenir son intégrité et de la valoriser. Il sera ici question d'appréhender la notion de collection privée en essayant d'en dégager ses critères constitutifs. Lors de l'étude de ces critères, nous nous poserons la question de savoir si la collection est appréhendée par le droit en raison des liens qu'elle entretient avec le collectionneur ou bien alors, si la collection est envisagée par le droit de manière autonome pour sa valeur intrinsèque.

Dans la première partie, il sera fait état de plusieurs cas de jurisprudence qui démontrent l'existence de liens étroits entre le collectionneur et la collection. Ce sont ces liens qui ont justifié une protection de cette dernière (**I**).

Dans la seconde partie, la collection sera appréhendée par le droit pour sa valeur et sa cohérence. Seront alors évoquées la notion de collection en matière de circulation des biens culturels, ainsi que les nouvelles dispositions de classement des ensembles historiques mobiliers qui permettent d'éviter leur dispersion (**II**).

I. Caractérisation de la collection privée par ses liens avec le collectionneur

1. Une protection au titre de l'œuvre de l'homme

C'est à travers une qualification juridique à la fois prétorienne et *sui generis* d'"œuvre de l'homme" que la Cour d'appel de Paris, dans un arrêt du 25 mai 1988, a accordé une protection à une collection de voitures anciennes réunie par les frères Schlumpf[1]. Les industries des Schlumpf ont été mises en liquidation judiciaire. La collection de voitures est devenue ensuite la propriété du syndic de faillite. La collection est alors vendue à l'Association du Musée national de l'automobile de Mulhouse à travers un traité à forfait en 1981. Les deux frères ont assigné l'Association du Musée de l'automobile de Mulhouse et l'Association pour la gestion du Musée dans le but que le musée soit exclusivement désigné par leur nom, c'est-à-dire « Musée Schlumpf, sous quelque forme et à quelque titre que ce soit ». La Cour d'appel a fait droit aux demandes des collectionneurs en considérant que : « l'œuvre du collectionneur, née de son initiative et sa volonté affirmée, mérite en elle-même, la protection judiciaire nécessairement inhérente à une œuvre de l'homme qui porte témoignage d'une époque déterminée ou d'un génie créateur ». La Cour a décrit l'acte de collection comme étant : « l'action de réunion et de collection et la passion qui ont inspiré leurs auteurs ont constitué et continuent de constituer un message et un témoignage dont l'initiative créatrice mérite protection comme étant l'expression d'un droit de la personnalité voisin du droit moral et la manifestation d'une action hors du commun ». La Cour a reconnu ainsi l'existence de liens entre les collectionneurs et la collection de voitures, cette dernière devenant l'expression d'un droit de la personnalité voisin du droit moral. Or le droit moral se caractérise précisément par le lien intime entre l'auteur et sa création. Ce sont ces liens étroits et l'empreinte portée par le collectionneur sur sa collection qui ont justifié une protection judiciaire.

---

[1] Cour d'appel de Paris, 1re chambre section A, 25 mai 1988, Assoc. du Musée national de l'automobile de Mulhouse et autres Consorts Schlumpf, Dalloz Sirey 1988, jurisprudence, p. 542.

En effet, la Cour d'appel a imposé dans l'arrêt que l'appellation « Collection Schlumpf » soit utilisée sur tous les supports de communication relatifs au Musée national de l'automobile. La juridiction a également ordonné le maintien en l'état d'une pièce dédiée à la mémoire de la mère des collectionneurs Schlumpf. Ce qu'il faut retenir de l'arrêt est qu'une collection d'objets pourrait être qualifiée d'une œuvre de l'homme à condition de remplir les conditions suivantes : des objets corporels (meubles) réunis ou agencés selon le dessein d'une personne individuelle, et que cette collection ainsi réunie soit porteuse d'un message ou d'une signification qui demeure pertinente, et d'une action qui sorte de l'ordinaire. Cependant, il faut tempérer l'existence d'une actuelle protection de la collection privée à travers cette qualification prétorienne d'œuvre de l'homme. En effet, l'arrêt Schlumpf reste une jurisprudence isolée.

2. Une protection de la collection privée par le droit d'auteur

Dans un autre arrêt rendu par la Cour d'appel de Paris, la collection privée d'Henri Langlois présentée dans une exposition a été qualifiée d'œuvre de l'esprit. Henri Langlois, cinéphile et collectionneur de films et de tous les objets relatifs au cinéma, a conçu pas moins d'une cinquantaine d'expositions sur l'histoire du cinéma. La dernière d'entre elles, celle inaugurée en 1975, appelée le « Musée du Cinéma Henri Langlois » a été l'objet d'un litige opposant d'un côté, le Comité de défense du Musée du Cinéma Henri Langlois, l'Association Henri Langlois et les héritiers d'Henri Langlois, et de l'autre, la Cinémathèque française. Cette exposition « Musée du Cinéma Henri Langlois » était une mise en scène de la collection d'Henri Langlois, racontant l'histoire du cinéma. Le conflit a surgi lorsqu'il a été question de déménager la Cinémathèque française et donc le Musée du Cinéma Henri Langlois en les déplaçant du Palais de Chaillot au Palais de Tokyo. Les héritiers ont cherché à encadrer ce déménagement afin d'éviter une altération de la collection et de sa présentation. Les héritiers du collectionneur ont eu gain de cause. Dans son arrêt du 2 octobre 1997, la Cour d'appel a considéré que : « l'exposition dénommée 'Musée du Cinéma Henri Langlois' [...] constitue une œuvre de l'esprit, bénéficiant de la protection légale ». La juridiction a donné : « acte aux consorts Langlois de ce qu'ils autorisent la translation de l'exposition au Palais de Tokyo sous réserve que l'esprit ne soit pas altéré[2] ». La qualification d'œuvre de l'esprit a obligé le dépositaire du Musée du Cinéma Henri Langlois, c'est-à-dire la Cinémathèque française, à respecter l'esprit de l'exposition Musée Henri Langlois lors de son déménagement au Palais de Tokyo. C'est sous l'angle de l'exposition que la Cour d'appel a considéré la collection d'Henri Langlois comme étant une œuvre de l'esprit. Ainsi, la Cour a retenu que la présentation de l'exposition est faite dans « un ordre et selon une scénographie originale ». Il s'agirait « d'une création résolument personnelle », dès lors qu'elle « exprime à la fois l'imaginaire d'Henri Langlois et ses conceptions propres de l'histoire du cinéma et reflétant ainsi sa personnalité ». Le critère principal qui a justifié une protection par le droit d'auteur est le fait d'avoir glissé la collection dans une exposition, ce qui implique un agencement de la collection par le collectionneur. Cela rejoint les propos d'Umberto Eco pour qui la collection est comme un « trésor ou théâtre du monde[3] », impliquant à la fois une part de mise en scène et la présence d'un public. L'intérêt de la qualification d'œuvre de l'esprit est qu'elle rend compte des liens étroits tissés entre l'auteur et sa collection, ici mise en scène dans un contexte d'exposition. Si l'arrêt concernant la collection des voitures Schlumpf était une première étape dans ce cheminement, le présent arrêt en franchit une autre. L'arrêt du Musée du Cinéma Henri Langlois amplifie encore ce lien en qualifiant l'exposition comme étant une œuvre de l'esprit. L'œuvre de l'esprit porte par définition l'empreinte de son auteur, tandis que le droit moral de l'auteur sur l'œuvre traduit un lien intime entre les deux. Si l'on tente de synthétiser les critères de la collection pour aboutir à une protection par les droits d'auteur, il s'agirait d'un rassemblement dans un même lieu physique d'objets matériels sélectionnés par une personne, qui sont mis en scène dans le cadre d'une exposition destinée au public, étant précisé que l'exposition doit refléter la personnalité de son auteur.

Une autre figure juridique s'intéresse aux liens entre une personne et un objet : les souvenirs de famille. Sont qualifiés de souvenirs de famille, « les objets se caractérisant par un rattachement des souvenirs et des manuscrits au passé familial et à la famille[4] ». Des objets d'art

---

[2] Cour d'appel de Paris, 1re chambre section A, 25 mai 1988, Assoc. du Musée national de l'automobile de Mulhouse et autres Consorts Schlumpf. Dalloz Sirey 1988, jurisprudence, p. 542.
[3] Umberto Eco et Isabella Pezzini, *Le musée, demain*, Casimiro, 2015, p. 20.
[4] CA Paris 1re chambre Section A, 7 déc. 1987, n° Numéro JurisData : 1987-604174 sur les manuscrits d'Émile Zola.

appartenant à la famille d'Orléans ont ainsi reçu la qualification de souvenirs de famille en raison de leur « rapport direct avec divers membres de la famille d'Orléans[5] » et pour être pourvus « d'une grande valeur affective ». Pour une collection privée satisfaisant aux critères de souvenirs de famille, ce régime permettrait d'éviter la dispersion définitive et irrémédiable de ses composants entre les héritiers et de maintenir l'indivision. Toutefois, la qualification de souvenir de famille est rarement accordée par les juridictions.

II. Figure autonome de la collection, indépendante de son créateur

La collection est aussi appréhendée par le droit pour sa valeur intrinsèque indépendamment de ses liens avec son créateur. Les collections en mains privées peuvent recevoir une protection émanant du droit du patrimoine[6]. Le premier exemple est donné par une disposition sur la circulation des biens culturels (**1**). Le second est fourni par les nouveaux articles L.622-1-1 et L.622-1-2 du Code du patrimoine qui permettent un classement au titre de monument historique des ensembles historiques mobiliers (**2**).

1. La collection protégée par la législation sur la circulation des biens culturels

L'introduction d'une définition légale de la collection est récente en droit français. La législation sur la circulation des biens culturels s'est saisie de la définition de la collection à travers un décret n°2001-894 du 26 septembre 2001 codifié sous l'article R.111-3 du Code du patrimoine, lequel précise : « constitue une collection, un ensemble d'objets, d'œuvres et de documents dont les différents éléments ne peuvent être dissociés sans porter atteinte à sa cohérence et dont la valeur est supérieure à la somme des valeurs individuelles des éléments qui le composent. La valeur et la cohérence de la collection s'apprécient en fonction de son intérêt pour l'histoire ou pour l'histoire de l'art, des civilisations, des sciences et des techniques ». Le collectionneur ou l'entité créatrice sont totalement absents de la définition. Seules compte la cohérence et la valeur de la collection. La cohérence est mesurée au

---

[5] Civ. 2e, 29 mars 1995, n° 93-18.769.

[6] Il faut noter que la pérennité des collections privées est aussi assurée par des mécanismes de droit privé (donations, legs avec charges, fondations).

regard des conséquences qui résulteraient d'une dissociation des éléments de l'ensemble. Ensuite, la collection doit, par la réunion des objets, engendrer une valeur « qui est supérieure à la somme des valeurs individuelles des éléments qui la composent ». Il s'agit d'une valeur patrimoniale. En effet, la cohérence et la valeur s'apprécient « en fonction de l'intérêt de la collection pour l'histoire ou pour l'histoire de l'art, des civilisations, des sciences et des techniques ». Cette définition large a toutefois un usage limité. Elle s'applique uniquement à certaines catégories de collections dont l'exportation est subordonnée à l'obtention d'un certificat d'un bien culturel[7]. En raison de sa formulation en des termes généraux, il serait possible de s'appuyer sur cette définition de la collection telle que précisée par l'article R.111-3 du Code du patrimoine pour bâtir un régime juridique de la collection. La nouvelle loi CAP, dans sa définition des ensembles historiques mobiliers s'en est inspirée en reprenant notamment la notion de cohérence.

2. Le classement à titre de monument historique des ensembles et des collections

Les ensembles mixtes[8] et les collections constituent des entités spécifiques avec un intérêt patrimonial, dont la protection effective imposait un ajustement en matière de classement d'objets mobiliers au titre des monuments historiques. Une des innovations importantes de la loi du 7 juillet 2016[9] en matière de protection des objets mobiliers a été

[7] L'annexe 1 à laquelle renvoie l'article R.111-1 du Code du patrimoine qui envisage la collection pour certaines catégories d'objets culturels, appréhendée de manière isolée et en collection : « les collections archéologiques », « gravures, estampes, sérigraphie et lithographies isolées... ou en collection », « incunables et manuscrits, y compris les lettres et documents autographes littéraires et artistiques, cartes géographiques, atlas, globes, partitions musicales », « affiches et cartes postales », « les livres et partitions musicales isolés ou en collection», « collection et spécimens provenant de collection de zoologie, de botanique, de minéralogie, d'anatomie », ainsi que les « collections présentant un intérêt historique, paléontologique, ethnographique, numismatique ou philatélique ».

[8] Ensembles mixtes, au sens de combinaison d'un immeuble et de plusieurs meubles qui présentent des liens historiques ou artistiques entre eux.

[9] Loi n° 2016-925 du 7 juill. 2016 relative à la liberté de la création, à l'architecture et au patrimoine, *JORF* n° 0158 du 8 juill. 2016, l'article 75 de la loi insère deux nouveaux articles après l'article L.622-1 du Code du patrimoine : art. L.622-1-1 et 622-1-2.

de rendre possible le classement d'un ensemble ou d'une collection d'objets mobiliers et d'instaurer dans des conditions exceptionnelles une servitude de maintien *in situ* d'objets dans un immeuble classé. Tout d'abord, l'article L.622-1-1 du Code du patrimoine offre une protection spécifique pour les ensembles historiques mobiliers lesquels sont : « un ensemble ou une collection d'objets mobiliers dont la conservation dans son intégrité et sa cohérence présente un intérêt public au point de vue de l'histoire, de l'art, de l'architecture, de l'archéologie, de l'ethnologie, de la science ou de la technique peut être classé au titre des monuments historiques comme ensemble historique mobilier par décision de l'autorité administrative, après avis de la Commission nationale du patrimoine et de l'architecture ». La loi instaure la notion d'ensemble historique mobilier, qui est définie dans l'étude d'impact du projet de loi comme : « un ensemble mobilier est composé de biens dont la réunion en tant qu'ensemble s'inscrit dans l'histoire de ces biens, et dont l'intérêt patrimonial comme ensemble est supérieur à celui de chaque objet constituant cet ensemble[10] ». Cette définition est une référence explicite à la collection telle qu'elle est envisagée par l'article R.111-3 du Code du patrimoine : une valeur patrimoniale supérieure se dégage de l'ensemble par rapport aux objets considérés individuellement. La collection est envisagée pour sa valeur intrinsèque lorsqu'elle forme un tout cohérent et que le démembrement des composantes nuirait à l'essence de la collection. Là encore, il faut observer l'absence de lien avec la personne ou l'entité qui a rassemblé ladite collection. Il est uniquement question des liens des objets entre eux. Les conséquences du classement de la collection ou de l'ensemble d'objets comme un ensemble historique mobilier sont principalement le maintien des objets ensemble et l'interdiction de diviser ou disperser l'ensemble en lots ou en pièces, notamment par voie d'aliénation[11]. La loi prend soin de préciser que les effets du classement « s'appliquent à chaque élément de l'ensemble historique mobilier classé et subsistent pour un élément s'il est dissocié de l'ensemble ». Si le classement des collections et des ensembles historiques s'attache aux liens entre les objets entre eux, la possibilité de maintien *in situ* permet de préserver

[10] Étude d'impact 7 juill. 2015, 2.3.10. Mesure 44 : Ensembles historiques mobiliers et servitude de maintien dans les lieux (Art. 24, 7° et 10° ; art. L. 622-1-1, L. 622-1-2 et L. 622-4-1 du code du patrimoine).

[11] Art. L.622-1-1 du Code du patrimoine, al. 2 : « Cet ensemble ne peut être divisé ou aliéné par lot ou pièce sans autorisation de cette autorité ».

les liens entre les objets et le bâti qui les contient. Ainsi, la loi du 7 juillet 2016 a pris en considération les ensembles mixtes en instaurant une servitude de maintien dans les lieux d'objets entretenant des liens historiques ou artistiques remarquables avec l'immeuble de leur contexte[12]. Les deux mesures de protection peuvent intervenir ensemble[13].

Selon l'article L.622-1-2 du Code du patrimoine, cette servitude peut être mise en place : « Lorsque des objets mobiliers classés ou un ensemble historique mobilier classé sont attachés, par des liens historiques ou artistiques remarquables, à un immeuble classé et forment avec lui un ensemble d'une qualité et d'une cohérence dont la conservation dans son intégrité présente un intérêt public ». Le principal effet de ladite servitude est qu'elle empêche à la fois la dispersion de l'ensemble et le déplacement hors de l'immeuble classé à moins d'obtenir une autorisation administrative[14]. Contrairement à l'ensemble historique mobilier dont le classement peut être prononcé d'office, la servitude de maintien dans les lieux intervient nécessairement avec l'accord du propriétaire. La levée de la servitude se déroule dans les mêmes conditions. Si la levée de la servitude n'était pas autorisée, une indemnité pourrait être accordée au propriétaire[15]. La levée de la servitude reste suffisamment souple et équilibrée pour parer à des changements qui interviendraient dans la vie de l'ensemble mixte (par exemple : succession, difficultés économiques majeures) et éviter une atteinte trop forte aux droits des propriétaires privés. Ces deux nouvelles dispositions du Code du patrimoine prennent en considération les caractéristiques nécessaires à la protection de collections et d'ensembles mixtes : maintien de l'entité dans son intégrité et dans le meilleur des cas, dans son contexte. Compte tenu de leurs conséquences sur le droit de propriété, elles ont vocation à

---

[12] Cette nouvelle disposition rejoint les préoccupations de la recommandation n° R 98 (4) du Conseil de l'Europe pour les ensembles mixtes.

[13] Art. L.622-1-2 du Code du patrimoine, al. 3 : « La servitude de maintien dans les lieux peut être prononcée en même temps que la décision de classement des objets mobiliers ou de l'ensemble historique mobilier, ou postérieurement à celle-ci ».

[14] Art. L.622-1-2 du Code du patrimoine, al. 2 : « Le déplacement de cet objet mobilier ou de tout ou partie de cet ensemble historique mobilier classé est subordonné à une autorisation de l'autorité administrative ».

[15] Art. L.622-1-2 du Code du patrimoine, al. 3 : « Cette servitude peut être levée dans les mêmes conditions. En cas de refus de l'autorité administrative de lever la servitude, les sujétions anormales qui peuvent en résulter sont compensées par une indemnité. À défaut d'accord amiable, l'action en indemnité est portée devant le juge judiciaire ».

s'appliquer pour des ensembles exceptionnels. Là encore, la pratique administrative sera déterminante pour délimiter les contours de ces nouveaux régimes légaux de protection au titre des monuments historiques[16].

Donner une définition juridique générique de la collection privée est une tâche délicate. Il n'a été proposé ici que des pistes de réflexions dont il ressort que les critères constitutifs d'une collection semblent être de deux ordres. Soit l'on se place du côté de la création, la collection étant ainsi perçue comme une œuvre de l'esprit du collectionneur sous réserve qu'elle satisfasse aux critères de l'originalité. Soit l'on se place du côté du patrimoine culturel, la collection étant envisagée pour elle-même comme ayant une valeur artistique ou historique. Une troisième hypothèse consisterait à envisager la collection comme une entité nouvelle comparable à l'universalité de fait[17] . En résumé, et pour reprendre les termes du Professeur Lagarde, « la collection est un droit en construction »[18]. À suivre donc...

---

[16] À l'heure où est écrit ce texte, les articles L.622-1-1 et L.622-1-2 n'ont pas justifié un classement à notre connaissance.

[17] Éric Meillier, « L'universalité de fait », *RTD civ.*, 2012, p. 651

[18] Paul Lagarde, « Rapport général », *in La protection des biens culturels,* Journées polonaises, Travaux de l'Association Henri Capitant et des amis de la culture juridique française, Paris : Economica, 1989, p. 102.

The notion of private collection and its protection from an Italian perspective

Manlio FRIGO
Professor of International Law
Milan University of Counsel
BonelliErede

1. The Italian legislator's approach to art collections and collectors

The legislator's approach, at least in the past, has not been very sympathetic towards art collecting or private art collectors. In fact one could observe that the legislator has traditionally viewed collectors of artworks, manuscripts, coins and archaeological objects with undisguised mistrust – regarding them almost as the product of a selfish and bulimic instinct of wanting exclusive possession. The result has been that functions such as protecting, conserving and enhancing objects of artistic and cultural interest, which are strictly connected with art collecting, have been neglected. Indeed, protecting art collections – from art collectors – has frequently prevailed over encouraging and boosting the phenomenon of art collecting. This is quite paradoxical when one considers that gathering, protecting, conserving and preserving the unity of collected objects have been the basis for creating important art collections that are open to the public – some of which have even become part of important public collections.

Looking at the phenomenon from the above standpoint, it is unsurprising that some important definitions are included in the list of institutions and places of culture in Chapter II (Enjoyment and Enhancement of Cultural Property) of the Italian Landscape and Cultural Heritage Code[1] (Code): Museum is defined as "a permanent facility that acquires, conserves, arranges and exhibits cultural property for the purpose of education and studies"[2], library is defined as "a permanent facility that gathers and conserves an organised collection of books, materials and information, written or published on any kind of

[1] The Italian Legislative and Cultural Heritage was adopted by Legislative Decree No. 42 of 22 January 2004.
[2] See article 101.2.a) of the Code.

medium, and ensures consultation for the purposes of promoting reading and study"[3]; and archive is defined as "a permanent facility that collects, inventories and conserves original documents of historical interest and ensures consultation for purposes of study and research"[4]. Conversely, no definition whatsoever is provided for the word collection. One thus has to conclude that private collections take second place to the collector and that, consequently, the objective significance of each item of a collection, the sectoral relevance or the underlying philosophy of the collection is simply lacking or confined to the background.

2. Protection and enhancement of art collections

Purchasing vs loaning art collections, domestic vs international transfers of title, destination and enhancement are, for most art collectors, equally crucial issues as those of evaluation, due diligence, provenance, etc. Due to historical, cultural and, obviously, juridical reasons, each country's legislation takes a different approach to most of these issues. Some of the most significant differences between the Italian rules and those of France, Switzerland and the United Kingdom concern the tax implications and the protection, enhancement and the management and governance of collections (such as through foundations, business foundations, bank collections, Stiftung, and trusts).

With regard to protection, private collections and series of objects declared to be of cultural interest by the Ministry of Cultural Heritage, Activities and Tourism[5] benefit from a particular protection regime[6] if they are not the work of living authors or were produced less than 70 years ago. Two categories of objects are eligible to be declared of cultural interest:

[3] See article 101.2.b) of the Code.
[4] See article 101.2.c) of the Code.
[5] See article 13 of the Code. According to recent Italian caselaw, the criteria for an object to be declared of outstanding cultural interest used by the Ministry of Cultural Heritage, Activities and Tourism, entails a technical evaluation, which can be called into question by a court only if the evaluation is clearly incoherent, illogical, or insufficiently motivated; see Council of State, Division VI, Decision No. 556 of 1984 and Decision No. 3363 of 27 July 2016.
[6] See footnote 1.

- book collections of exceptional cultural interest that belong to private individuals[7]; and
- collections and series of objects (regardless of whom they belong to) that are of exceptional interest as a whole, due to their tradition, renown and particular environmental character, or due to their artistic, historic, numismatic or ethno-anthropological significance[8].

Other provisions concerning the protection of objects of cultural interest can be found here and there in the Code among the provisions on single cultural objects, whether or not they belong to collections. For example: (a) the requirement to obtain authorisation from the Ministry of Cultural Heritage, Activities and Tourism to break up collections and series[9], and to obtain authorisation to loan collections and series of objects (regardless of whom they belong to) that are of exceptional interest, as a whole, due to their tradition, renown and particular environmental character, or due to their artistic, historic, numismatic or ethno-anthropological significance[10]; and (b) the requirement to obtain authorisation for the temporary transfer of single objects (from a collection) declared to be of cultural interest[11]. The Code also sets out three legal regimes for the sale of single books from book collections that belong to private, non-profit associations or private collections[12].

3. International circulation

As to international circulation, even the merely temporary exit from the territory of the Republic of Italy is forbidden for "properties that constitute the principal collection of a determined and integral section of a museum, picture gallery, art gallery, archive or library, or any

[7] See article 10.3.c) of the Code.
[8] See article 10.3.e) of the Code.
[9] See article 21.1.c) of the Code.
[10] See article 48.1.c of the Code.
[11] See article 21.1.b) of the Code.
[12] The three legal regimes mentioned in the text are: a) free sale of cultural property of living authors or that which was produced more than 70 years ago; b) soft inalienability, for collections and book collections that belong to private, non-profit associations, whereby the sale is authorised if it does not prevent or jeopardise the conservation and enjoyment of the objects in question (see Articles 56.1, 56.2 and 56.4 of the Code); and c) free sale of cultural property of non-living authors or that which was produced more than 70 years ago, conditional on advance notification to the Ministry (see article 13 of the Code). In such a case, the Ministry has a pre-emption right on the object(s) in question if it has been declared of cultural interest.

artistic or bibliographical collection"[13]. Permanent exit is forbidden for collections (and for single objects within a collection) that have been declared to be of cultural interest by the Ministry of Cultural Heritage, Activities and Tourism. Conversely, temporary exit may be authorised for art events, exhibits and expositions of great cultural interest, on condition that the integrity and safety of the concerned objects are ensured[14].

Conclusively, the set of rules to protect the integrity of collections are not exempt from criticism – because they are not combined with adequate provisions to encourage and boost the phenomenon of private collections.

4. Art collections and the issue of generation transfer

Broadly speaking, the issue of generation transfer involves not only art collectors but also wealth managers, business people, art advisors and lawyers, to name but a few. And it is an important issue, as without a generation transfer plan, collections share the fate of any other asset within an estate: If no restrictions encumber the free disposal of the collection, it is the heirs and legatees who decide its fate – who may divide the collection in proportion to their respective shares of the estate. But even with a generation plan, the collection may be affected by factors out of the collector's or the heirs' control.

This is certainly so for collections produced more than 70 years ago (and for works of deceased authors), as they may be fully or partially declared of cultural interest by the Ministry of Cultural Heritage, Activities and Tourism[15]. Indeed, although such a declaration does not directly affect the right of ownership, it does entail significant consequences that should be borne in mind. These include, in the case of sale, the pre-emption right of the State or other territorial entities[16] and an absolute prohibition on its permanent export[17]. Even more important to bear in mind is that when a collection in its entirety is declared to be of cultural exceptional artistic, historical, archaeological,

[13] See article 66.2.b) of the Code.
[14] See article 66.1 of the Code.
[15] See articles 12 and 13 of the Code. The declaration provided for under article 12 must attest to the existence of the interest required under article 10, para. 3.
[16] See article 60 of the Code.
[17] See article 65 of the Code.

numismatic or ethno-anthropological interest, it may be sold or donated in Italy but not divided up without authorisation from the Ministry[18].

5. The generation transfer options under Italian law

Collectors and advisors to collectors who wish to ensure their collections remain united, conserved and enhanced have various options available, including if the collector has numerous heirs and beneficiaries. Besides the more traditional options – such as donation with a restriction on disposal, a trustee mandate and the establishment of a trust or foundation – collectors may also now establish a 'benefit company' (introduced in Italy by the 2016 Stability Law)[19].
As the first two are the least commonly used for the purpose of generation transfer, this article provides a brief comparison of the three other options and highlights the particular advantages of benefit companies.

5.1 Trusts

Although trusts are not envisaged in the Italian Civil Code, they may be established by selecting a foreign law as the governing law of the trust (often the law of Jersey is chosen). This was made possible by the Hague Convention of 1 July 1985 on the Law Applicable to Trusts and on their Recognition, to which Italy was the first civil law country to become a signatory party. Consequently, art collectors may transfer a collection to – and impose restrictions on – a trustee to administer it on trust for the benefit and in the interest of the heirs[20].

5.2 Foundations

As is well known, foundations, in their various forms, allow a set of assets to be tied up – generally perpetually – in order to achieve a goal. The versatility of foundations lies in the fact that a foundation enables the founder to carry out a philanthropic activity and manage the generation transfer, including of company assets. Foundations are

---

[18] See article 21.1.b) of the Code.

[19] See Law No. 208 of 28 December 2015, *Disposizioni per la formazione del bilancio annuale e pluriennale dello Stato*, published in the Official Journal (*Gazzetta Ufficiale*), No. 302 of 30 December 2015.

[20] Italy ratified the Hague Convention of 1 July 1985 with Law No. 364 of 16 October 1989, published in the Official Journal (*Gazzetta Ufficiale-Supplemento Ordinario*), No 261, of 8 November 1989.

certainly an option worth considering because they can ensure that an art collection is both conserved and enhanced (e.g., by granting public access and generating funding therefrom) In fact this is why they are popular in Italy.

Foundations may be established by: (a) a public unilateral deed (through which assets are allocated to the heirs or donated at certain conditions – usually charitable)[21]; (b) a will; or (c) transformation of a company into a foundation. Unlike in other countries, no minimum initial capital is required to establish a foundation in Italy. However, once established, the founder no longer has the power to dispose of the assets he/she contributed to the foundation. Furthermore, although foundations are non-profit organisations (and therefore may not distribute profits), they are allowed to operate as a business if the corporate purpose is altruistic. A business foundation (*fondazione d'impresa*) may also establish a holding foundation, i.e., a foundation to which it assigns the management and enhancement of the assets to achieve the goals of the business foundation[22].

5.3 Benefit companies

This corporate form was introduced in 2016[23] with the aim of increasing awareness of social and environmental issues and combining the pursuit of profit with the common benefit of shareholders. Consequently, unlike foundations, benefit companies may carry on a business that distributes profits – but this is balanced with the requirement to pursue a common benefit for people, communities, the environment, property and activities of a cultural or social interest, which must be set out in the company's corporate purpose. Companies (partnerships, limited partnerships, limited liability companies, joint-stock companies, etc.) established before this new corporate form was introduced may transform into a benefit company by amending their articles of association and adding the common benefit goals to their corporate purpose.

To ensure that benefit companies do indeed pursue a common benefit, they must submit their annual financial statements to an independent

---

[21] See article 14 and ff. of the Civil Code.

[22] See M. Minciullo, *Fostering Orientation to Performance in non-profit organizations through control and coordination: The Case of Corporate Foundations and Founder Firms*, in Gnan L., Hinna A., Monteduro A. (ed.), *Studies in Public and Non-Profit Governance*, vol. 5, 2016, pp. 207-232.

[23] See footnote 19.

auditing firm for assessment. If it is concluded that the benefit company is not pursuing a common benefit, the Italian Competition Authority may impose fines for misleading advertising.
Furthermore, although benefit companies can deduct costs from their income, no tax incentives are currently available to them. This is because, based on the spirit of the law, choosing to establish a benefit company should be led by the desire to work for the common good and aim to provide a model for other stakeholders in the relevant sector.

Given that the most frequent corporate purposes of benefit companies are to promote art and science and advance knowledge, they can serve as a viable option for generation transfer even though not expressly created for this purpose. This not only in terms of restrictions on use and stability of management, but also in terms of attracting additional capital from ethically-minded funds and investors.

Indeed, only 27 months on from being introduced, benefit companies are being viewed ever more favourably by the business world. Thanks to their distinctive features and increasingly positive reputation, the emphasis on social responsibility is proving to be a secret weapon for the success of benefit companies as an effective ‘tool’ for managing art collections. Collectors and their advisors would thus do well to investigate this option more closely.

La protection publique des collections privées

Marie Cornu
Directrice de recherche au CNRS

Un certain nombre de ressorts du droit public assurent la protection des collections privées, particulièrement la conservation des éléments qui les composent, tout autant que l'unité qu'elles forment. Plusieurs d'entre eux permettent de protéger des pièces isolées de collection. D'autres visent l'entité, prise comme telle. Laissant de côté les aspects purement institutionnels, je m'intéresserai ici au régime des collections à proprement parler, considérées comme ensemble de biens reliés par un même intérêt.
La notion de patrimoine telle qu'elle est définie à l'article 1 du Code du patrimoine désigne tout à la fois des biens privés et publics. Le texte le dit expressément. Elle a donc vocation à saisir les collections privées. En tant qu'universalités patrimoniales, elles appellent en renfort le droit public. Dans le Code du patrimoine, on peut isoler deux sortes de dispositifs pertinents, ceux qui ont pour objet d'encadrer l'affectation au public des collections et ceux qui ont pour finalité de préserver l'unité d'ensembles distingués pour leur caractère remarquable. Sur ces deux fronts, on le verra, la loi sur la liberté de création, l'architecture et le patrimoine du 7 juillet 2016 a introduit d'intéressants compléments et innovations[1].

1. L'affectation au public des collections privées

Le motif de protection tient dans ce cas au fait que certaines collections privées trouvent place dans des musées ou plutôt sont organisées et gérées sous forme de musées, et sont ainsi affectées au public. Pour ces institutions, le Code prévoit deux figures intéressantes, le label *Musée*

---

[1] Sur la genèse de la protection des ensembles : M. Roellinger, *La protection des collections et des ensembles mixtes, de 1913 au Code du patrimoine, une loi en évolution sur les monuments historiques*, (dir. J.-P. Bady, M. Cornu, J. Fromageau, J.-M. Leniaud et V. Négri), Paris, La Documentation française – Comité d'histoire du ministère de la Culture, 2018, p. 137 et s.

de France et le label *Fonds régional d'art contemporain*, nouvellement introduit par la loi de 2016.

1.1 Le label Musée de France

Toutes sortes de musées privés sont invisibles pour le droit public. Le terme « musée » n'étant pas, en soi, protégé, des personnes privées ont pu, tout à fait librement, prendre cet intitulé. Les travaux parlementaires autour de l'adoption de la loi du 4 janvier 2002 relative aux musées de France montrent bien qu'il ne s'agissait pas de contrôler l'usage de ce terme. Les modèles économiques de ces nombreux musées sont en réalité multiples, des musées d'art populaire aux véritables entreprises telles que le Musée des lettres et manuscrits, adossé à la société Aristophil, structure aujourd'hui disparue, la Pinacothèque de Paris ou encore le Musée Maillol. Tout au contraire, la dénomination « Musée de France » est protégée. Aux termes de l'article L. 442-5 du Code du patrimoine, « le fait, pour le fondateur ou le dirigeant, de droit ou de fait, d'une institution ne bénéficiant pas de l'appellation « Musée de France », d'utiliser ou de laisser utiliser cette appellation dans l'intérêt de cette institution est puni d'une amende de 15 000 euros ». Cette appellation peut être attribuée à des personnes privées dès lors qu'elles poursuivent un but non lucratif. Il peut s'agir de fondations ou d'associations mais non de sociétés civiles ou commerciales. Les musées privés représentent treize pour cent des musées de France. L'appellation « musée de France » est attribuée à la demande de la ou des personnes morales propriétaires des collections, par décision de l'autorité administrative après avis du Haut Conseil des musées de France.
Le Code du patrimoine définit ce que doit être un musée de France et les finalités qu'il doit poursuivre. L'article L410-1 dispose : « Est considéré comme musée, au sens du présent livre, toute collection permanente composée de biens dont la conservation et la présentation revêtent un intérêt public et organisée en vue de la connaissance, de l'éducation et du plaisir du public ». On aperçoit déjà, dans cette définition, les obligations qui dérivent de l'attribution de ce label : conservation du bien et présentation au public, étant entendu que la première est enchâssée dans des normes plus contraignantes et plus précises que la seconde. Dans le droit du patrimoine, c'est l'obligation de conservation qui vient en premier, dès les premiers textes, même si l'on peut bien soutenir que l'accès au public est une des missions

fondamentales de l'institution muséale. Ce versant apparaît plus nettement au travers des finalités auxquelles doit souscrire le musée, énoncées à l'article L. 441-2 du Code du patrimoine. Il s'agit notamment de « rendre les collections accessibles au public le plus large », de « concevoir et mettre en œuvre des actions d'éducation et de diffusion visant à assurer l'égal accès de tous à la culture », de « contribuer aux progrès de la connaissance et de la recherche ainsi qu'à leur diffusion. Mais le contenu juridique de ces finalités de mise à disposition du public n'est guère précisé. Sans doute l'obligation d'établissement d'un projet scientifique, rendu obligatoire par la loi du 7 juillet 2016 pourra leur donner une certaine consistance, mais elle restera modulable en fonction de la structure et du projet qu'elle met en avant. On peut encore citer les dispositions relatives au droit d'entrée qui doit être « fixé de manière à favoriser l'accès de ces musées au public le plus large »[2] et celles qui imposent aux musées de France de disposer "d'un service ayant en charge les actions d'accueil du public, de diffusion, d'animation et de médiation culturelles »[3], lequel peut être commun à plusieurs musées.

Si l'on se penche plus avant sur les sujétions que supporte le propriétaire privé d'une collection Musée de France, on identifie deux tendances marquant le statut des institutions privées. D'une part, le législateur a tenté de rapprocher le statut des collections privées de celui des collections publiques, sans pour autant qu'il y ait assimilation. Un certain nombre de règles sont communes aux deux institutions. La loi est indifférente à la qualité du propriétaire. Par exemple, tous les biens des musées de France sont imprescriptibles et insaisissables. Le secteur privé bénéficie alors de règles que connaît déjà le musée public et qu'il tire du régime de domanialité publique de ses collections. La loi étend par ailleurs le bénéfice du droit de préemption aux musées privés, pourtant levier régalien d'acquisition publique. Sans doute, sa mise en œuvre n'est pas tout à fait de même portée dès lors que l'État n'est pas tenu de préempter à leur demande. Mais il ne l'est pas non plus à la demande d'une commune. Les collections privées reçoivent également la qualification de trésor national. Elles sont en cela frappées d'une interdiction de sortie du territoire à titre définitif. Enfin, l'entrée en collection est soumise à l'avis d'une commission qui statue sur les

[2] Art. L442-6 du Code du patrimoine.
[3] Art. L442-7 du Code du patrimoine.

acquisitions tant publiques que privées et le contrôle scientifique et technique de l'État s'exerce pareillement, en principe, sur tous les musées de France.

Cela étant, l'assimilation du statut des biens n'est pas totale. En particulier, les biens des collections ne sont pas inaliénables. Le droit public du patrimoine culturel n'institue à aucun moment une telle règle d'indisponibilité, s'agissant des biens privés. La singularité de la collection privée se manifeste ainsi au travers d'un régime propre. C'est le deuxième mouvement. La loi exige notamment, lors de la sollicitation du label par une personne privée, qu'elle produise un « inventaire des biens composant les collections », qu'elle justifie « de l'absence de sûretés réelles grevant ces biens » et qu'elle introduise dans ses statuts une « clause prévoyant l'affectation irrévocable des biens acquis par dons et legs ou avec le concours de l'État ou d'une collectivité territoriale à la présentation au public »[4]. L'exigence d'un inventaire exprimée pour les seuls musées privés, dans la loi, trouve une explication dans le fait que la plupart des collections publiques ont reçu, de droit, le label « Musée de France » en 2002[5]. Le processus de demande d'attribution concernait en ce sens davantage les musées privés, justifiant alors l'imposition d'un inventaire précis avant d'entrer dans le cercle de ces musées. Mais, on aurait bien pu étendre la règle à tout musée sollicitant ce label. Quant à la preuve de l'absence de sûretés réelles, la règle s'imposait dès lors que la loi déclare les biens des collections insaisissables. Il ne fallait pas que le mécanisme puisse être neutralisé par l'invocation d'un droit antérieur à l'application du statut de Musée de France, par un créancier. Pour les musées publics, la question ne se posait pas, dès lors que les biens publics sont insaisissables. Enfin, le dernier ressort propre aux musées privés concernant l'affectation irrévocable de certains des biens de ces collections, en voisinage avec la règle d'inaliénabilité, s'en démarque cependant. Règle originale en ce qu'elle se concentre sur la préservation de l'affectation publique de ces biens. Au sens de l'article 451-10 du Code du patrimoine, « Les biens des collections des musées de France appartenant aux personnes morales de droit privé à but non lucratif acquis par dons et legs ou avec le concours de l'État ou d'une collectivité

---

[4] Art. L442-1 du Code du patrimoine.

[5] Ça a été le cas des musées nationaux, des musées classés et des musées contrôlés, soit plus de deux mille musées.

territoriale ne peuvent être cédés, à titre gratuit ou onéreux, qu'aux personnes publiques ou aux personnes morales de droit privé à but non lucratif qui se sont engagées, au préalable, à maintenir l'affectation de ces biens à un musée de France. La cession ne peut intervenir qu'après approbation de l'autorité administrative après avis du Haut Conseil des musées de France ».

1.2 Le label FRAC

Les fonds régionaux d'art contemporain (FRAC) ont été créés au début des années quatre-vingt sous une perspective particulière. Sur un modèle inspiré du Fonds national d'art contemporain (FNAC), ces institutions avaient pour vocation d'aider la création artistique sous toutes ses formes en région. Le mécanisme avait pour ambition de couvrir tous les champs et toutes les réalités de la création contemporaine, de la photographie aux nouvelles formes de création telles que les installations. Aider les artistes en achetant ses œuvres et en les diffusant au public. Telle était la feuille de route. Mais progressivement, ces institutions se sont rapprochées du modèle du musée. Ayant, avec le temps, rassemblé de véritables collections, les FRAC se sont posé la question du statut de ces biens, estimant, à tort, que ceux-ci étaient inaliénables en tant qu'ils relevaient de leur domaine public. En effet, ces institutions sont constituées en grande majorité sous la forme associative, à une époque où l'action administrative emprunte volontiers ce chemin pour exercer plus souplement certaines de ses missions. Or, la règle d'inaliénabilité attachée au régime de domanialité publique suppose, en amont, une propriété publique. Les biens doivent appartenir à une personne publique et ce n'était pas le cas pour les FRAC. Si l'on pouvait entendre l'affirmation d'inaliénabilité des collections comme une forme de déclaration de politique institutionnelle de la part des FRAC, l'on ne pouvait en déduire un statut juridique d'indisponibilité de ces biens. L'institution peut s'engager à ne pas disperser ces biens, en particulier, inscrire cette obligation dans ses statuts, ce qu'ont fait plusieurs de ces structures. Mais une telle formalisation crée simplement une obligation à la charge des responsables de l'institution qui peuvent, en cas de non-respect de la règle, engager leur responsabilité devant leurs membres. Elle n'institue pas les biens inaliénables. Certes, devant le juge, l'argument de l'association transparente ou parapublique pouvait mettre en cause l'institution/écran[6]. En ce sens, le Conseil d'État décide que « lorsqu'une personne privée est créée à l'initiative d'une personne publique qui en contrôle l'organisation et le fonctionnement et qui lui procure l'essentiel de ses ressources, cette personne privée doit être regardée comme « transparente »[7]. Dans cette appréciation, le juge a recours à la méthode du faisceau d'indices, prenant en compte l'objet de l'association et le fait qu'il représente un service public ou une activité d'intérêt général, l'étendue du contrôle de la collectivité publique, donc le degré d'autonomie de la structure et le fait que l'essentiel des ressources provienne de subventions publiques[8]. Ces critères cumulatifs se retrouvent en tout ou partie dans les FRAC. Ils sont financés par l'État et la Région, poursuivent une activité d'intérêt général qui consiste à aider les créateurs, comprennent dans leurs instances de nombreux élus régionaux et représentants de l'État. Cependant, aucun contentieux n'a mis en cause leur mode de constitution sous la forme associative, ce qui aurait pu, paradoxalement assurer la protection de leurs collections comme appartenant à la collectivité publique décisionnaire[9]. Du coup, la fragilité de la condition juridique des biens des FRAC s'est révélée de façon plus vive, en particulier au cours des discussions autour de l'adoption de la loi sur les musées de France et plus spécialement à propose de la portée du principe d'inaliénabilité. La consolidation de leur statut s'est imposée dans la loi du 7 juillet 2016, qui, sous cette perspective, s'inspire de la technique utilisée dans la loi sur les musées de France pour les collections privées. Un nouvel article 116 est introduit dans le livre premier du Code du patrimoine créant un nouveau label « Fonds régional contemporain » qui peut être attribué à des personnes morales de droit public ou de droit privé à but non lucratif. Cette intégration dans le droit du patrimoine et cette forme de mimétisme illustre ce mouvement de rapprochement de la logique muséale des FRAC. Tout en même temps, l'esprit qui a marqué la fondation des FRAC persiste. Cet entre-deux patrimoine/création est perceptible dans l'énoncé du dispositif. Les œuvres des collections des FRAC doivent être

---

[6] Cette technique est en effet très prisée par l'État dans cette période des années 80/90.

[7] C.E. Commune de Boulogne-Billancourt, 21 mars 2007.

[8] Critères dégagés notamment par C.E. Département de la Dordogne, 5 déc. 2005 et C.E. Commune de Boulogne-Billancourt, 21 mars 2007.

[9] La remise en cause de la structure associative n'aurait pas été tout à fait évidente dans la mesure du moins pour celles d'entre elles qui disposent d'une marge d'action et d'une autonomie relativement à leur tutelle.

« acquises, sauf exception, du vivant de l'artiste, avec des concours publics et sur proposition d'une instance composée de personnalités qualifiées dans le domaine de l'art contemporain ou par dons et legs ». En principe, les artistes sont vivants, mais le texte admet par exception les acquisitions post mortem ainsi que les entrées par dons et legs. Elles doivent être « représentatives de la création contemporaine française et étrangère dans le domaine des arts graphiques et plastiques ainsi que des arts appliqués ». On est ici pleinement dans le schéma initial comme avec l'exigence que ces œuvres soient « destinées à la présentation au public dans et hors les murs ». La mention selon laquelle elles peuvent être montrées « en des lieux non dédiés à l'art » est typiquement dans l'air de ce temps de la loi de 2016[10]. Pour les collections publiques, le label n'a, en principe guère de prise sur le statut des biens de leurs collections, dans la mesure où ils sont soumis, au regard de leur intérêt culturel, aux règles de la domanialité publique[11]. Cela étant, elles devront, comme les structures de droit privé, élaborer un projet artistique et culturel précisant « la stratégie d'enrichissement, de conservation, d'étude scientifique et de mise en valeur de la collection » et satisfaire à un certain nombre d'obligations et risque le retrait du label en cas de non-respect des obligations liées à l'attribution du label[12]. En ce qui concerne le statut des biens, la mise en place est quelque peu différente pour les personnes morales de droit privé. L'article 116-2 du Code du patrimoine reprend en substance le régime des collections privées sous dénomination musée de France, imposant que les FRAC constitués sous la forme d'une personne morale de droit privé inscrivent dans leurs statuts une clause d'« affectation irrévocable des biens acquis par dons et legs ou avec le concours de l'État ou d'une collectivité territoriale à la présentation au public. Ces biens ne peuvent être cédés, à titre gratuit ou onéreux, qu'aux personnes publiques ou aux personnes morales de droit privé à but non lucratif qui se sont engagées, au

[10] Aux termes de l'article L 116-1, elles doivent également faire l'objet d'actions de médiation et d'éducation artistique et culturelle en direction des publics et être portées sur un inventaire.

[11] Art. L. 2112-1 du CGPPP.

[12] En application du décret n° 2017-432 du 28 mars 2017 relatif aux labels et au conventionnement dans les domaines du spectacle vivant et des arts plastique, retrait qui impose que soient définies les conditions ultérieures de dévolution de propriété, de conservation et de gestion des biens de la collection acquis par dons et legs ou avec le concours de l'État ou d'une collectivité publique. Ces mentions devraient trouver une application différente selon la qualité de la personne instituée en FRAC.

préalable, à maintenir l'affectation de ces biens à la présentation au public. La cession ne peut intervenir qu'après approbation de l'autorité administrative après avis de la Commission scientifique nationale des collections ».
La loi du 7 juillet 2016 prévoit en outre de nouvelles servitudes sur les ensembles patrimoniaux.

2. La protection d'ensembles remarquables

Jusqu'à la loi de 2016, le droit et plus spécialement le code du patrimoine était peu outillé lorsqu'il s'agissait de préserver l'unité des collections. Patrick Michel évoquait le statut symbole de la collection. Elle est assurément une valeur en soi, notamment une forme de « mise en valeur économique du passé » comme le démontrent Luc Boltanski et Arnaud Lesquerre[13]. Mais cette réalité sociale ne trouvait que des assises ponctuelles dans les ressorts du droit (**2.1.**). Les ensembles apparaissent véritablement comme objets de protection pris comme universalités patrimoniales dans la loi de 2016 (**2.2.**).

2.1. Les assises ponctuelles d'un droit des collections

C'est avant tout au travers des règles de circulation des biens culturels que le droit du patrimoine assure une protection aux collections même si celle-ci se révèle somme toute relative. La loi du 17 juillet 1909, dont les termes sont repris dans la loi du 31 décembre 1913 prévoit déjà une interdiction de sortie du territoire des objets mobiliers et immeubles par destination classés au titre des monuments historiques. L'actualité en renforce la nécessité à cette époque. Dès la fin du XIXe siècle, « se constituent, en particulier aux États-Unis, de grandes collections d'œuvres d'art et de vestiges monumentaux »[14] importées d'Europe. Le dispositif s'est étoffé au fil du temps. Outre la protection au titre des

---

[13] Luc Boltanski et Arnaud Lesquerre, « La collection, une forme neuve du capitalisme, la mise en valeur économique du passé et ses effets » et l'enrichissement, ref.

[14] J. Kagan, *Préservation du patrimoine : l'apport de la loi du 31 décembre 1913 vu à travers l'action administrative, 1913, genèse d'une loi sur les monuments historiques* (dir. J.-P. Bady, M. Cornu, J. Fromageau, J.-M. Leniaud, V. Négri), la documentation française, le comité d'histoire du ministère de la culture, 2013, ouvrage qui traite plus généralement de cette période de l'histoire législative de la protection des monuments historiques.

monuments historiques, plusieurs dispositifs se sont saisis de la question du contrôle de circulation des biens culturels, entre autres la loi du 27 septembre 1941 et, après la création du marché unique, la loi du 31 décembre 1992 aujourd'hui codifiée. Le système assure le maintien sur le territoire des éléments majeurs du patrimoine national, qualifiés de trésors nationaux. L'article L.111-1 en donne une définition. Sont des trésors nationaux au sens du Code du patrimoine, les collections des musées de France, les archives publiques, les archives historiques classées, les objets mobiliers classés au titre des monuments historiques et tout bien faisant partie du domaine public mobilier. Ce dernier se définit en effet par référence à la présence d'un intérêt public d'histoire, d'art, d'archéologie, de science ou de technique. Cette première série désigne les biens qui ont reçu une protection du côté soit du Code du patrimoine, soit du régime de domanialité publique. Mais cette enveloppe est plus largement entendue et concerne aussi des biens qui ne sont pas encore protégés et mériteraient de l'être en raison de leur intérêt majeur pour le patrimoine national. Un certain nombre de biens culturels sont en effet conservés dans des patrimoines privés, sans que l'on ait eu conscience ou connaissance de leur valeur. Ils paraissent au grand jour à la faveur d'une mise sur le marché ou d'une demande d'exportation, les deux événements étant le plus souvent liés. Le droit déploie alors des outils pour, le cas échéant, leur assurer un statut patrimonial de trésor national. Sans entrer dans le détail du dispositif, nous mentionnerons simplement la veille assurée sur les demandes de sortie du territoire qui, depuis 1992, se réalise sur des catégories spécifiées de biens culturels, qui au vu de leur valeur économique et/ou leur datation, pourraient aussi avoir une valeur culturelle. Le Code du patrimoine impose, pour les biens culturels qui atteignent ces seuils et qui sont destinés à circuler en dehors du territoire, qu'ils soient dotés d'un certificat de libre circulation et le cas échéant d'une autorisation de sortie[15]. Parmi ces catégories, figurent les collections dont la valeur d'ensemble est estimée globalement. Lorsqu'une collection atteint le seuil de 50 000 euros, elle est soumise à l'exigence des formalités de sortie, alors même que les éléments qui la composent, s'ils étaient pris isolément pourraient circuler librement. L'identification de cette notion de collection permet ainsi d'actionner un seuil de valeur sur l'ensemble

[15] Formalité qui s'impose lorsque le bien circule en dehors du territoire douanier de l'union, vers les pays tiers.

constitué beaucoup moins élevé que s'il avait fallu raisonner pièce à pièce. Le droit français contient une définition intéressante de cette notion de collection. En vertu de l'article R.111-3 du Code du patrimoine, « constitue une collection, un ensemble d'objets, d'œuvres et de documents dont les différents éléments ne peuvent être dissociés sans porter atteinte à sa cohérence et dont la valeur est supérieure à la somme des valeurs individuelles des éléments qui le composent. La valeur et la cohérence de la collection s'apprécient en fonction de son intérêt pour l'histoire ou pour l'histoire de l'art, des civilisations, des sciences et des techniques ». Cette définition introduite en 2001 est la première expression juridique de la notion de collection dans le champ du droit du patrimoine qui, très justement fait valoir la valeur tirée de l'ensemble.
Cette nouvelle figure permet d'immobiliser des ensembles historiques ou artistiques de grand intérêt. Mais, en dépit de son intérêt, elle n'en garantit cependant pas pour autant la non-dispersion juridique et matérielle des éléments, quand bien même la collection serait classée ou entrerait dans un musée privé ou public protégé au titre du Code du patrimoine. Le propriétaire privé peut bien vendre certains éléments de collection, ou encore l'entreposer en plusieurs lieux sans que le droit et les servitudes du Code du patrimoine ne puissent s'y opposer. Quant au propriétaire public, s'il est tenu par la règle d'inaliénabilité, il n'est pas obligé de maintenir en un lieu les collections qu'il possède. C'est précisément cette question que résout la loi du 7 juillet 2016 avec l'introduction de règles de protection d'ensembles historiques ou artistiques.

2.2. La protection des ensembles au titre des monuments historiques

La loi du 7 juillet 2016 introduit un double de dispositif de protection des ensembles au titre des monuments historiques. Sont concernés d'une part les collections d'objets mobiliers, d'autre part les ensembles dits mixtes, associant des éléments mobiliers et immobiliers. En effet certains de ces ensembles « composés d'éléments souvent hétérogènes » sont « indissociables de leur environnement architectural » en ce qu'ils font partie intime de l'histoire des lieux[16].

[16] Judith Kagan, Dominique Séréna-Allier et Anne Tricaud, *Ensembles mobiliers, industriels, techniques. Connaissance, protection, conservation, présentation au*

En forme de reconnaissance de la doctrine du maintien *in situ* portée par Quatremère de Quincy, le droit français jusqu'alors peu ouvert à cette question évolue opportunément. Pour ces deux séries de biens culturels complexes, le législateur institue une possibilité de classement au titre des monuments historiques[17]. On travaille ici sur des collections dont la valeur exceptionnelle est appréciée distinctement de la valeur des biens pris isolément. C'est précisément parce que l'ensemble dégage une valeur propre, que l'effet principal attaché à cette qualification est la non-division de l'ensemble, l'assignation à résidence pour les ensembles mixtes. Ceux-là sont alors assujettis à une double servitude d'indivisibilité et de maintien *in situ*. La charge est assez lourde par conséquent. Il s'agit là d'une règle nouvelle, mais en réalité, le débat est ancien. Mathilde Roellinger a pu évoquer cette histoire, car elle s'est intéressée à la genèse des premiers projets de protection des ensembles mobiliers dans le cadre du programme de recherches *mémoloi*[18]. Le premier projet date en effet du début du vingtième siècle. Plus récemment, l'affaire dite des châteaux japonais avait ému quelques parlementaires. Il s'agissait d'immeubles classés au titre des monuments historiques que les propriétaires avaient dépouillés de leur mobilier, lequel avait été dispersé à la faveur de ventes publiques. L'Assemblée nationale a adopté en première lecture un texte en ce sens en 2001, proposition de loi portée par M. Lequiller, mais qui n'a jamais été examiné devant le Sénat. Une autre proposition de loi sur le patrimoine a repris ce chantier en 2007 mais à nouveau sans succès. Il peut être intéressant de se pencher sur les raisons de ces échecs successifs. Le législateur a dû affronter deux séries de difficultés. La première est celle de l'équilibre à trouver entre la charge, lourde en l'espèce, et les contreparties possibles. Évidemment, s'invite dans ce débat la question du consentement du propriétaire, mais la mise en place est plus complexe. Les questions liées à la transmission successorale sont un autre des défis, notamment dans les hypothèses où plusieurs héritiers viennent à la succession et où le patrimoine du défunt tient pour l'essentiel dans sa collection. La loi crée une possible situation d'indivision ou de propriété multiple sur les éléments d'une collection

---

public, In Situ (en ligne), 29/2016, mis en ligne le 28 août 2017. URL : http://insitu.revues.org/13500.

[17] *Ibid.*, sur cette illustration de ces ensembles et les nombreuses formes qu'ils peuvent prendre.

[18] De 1913 au Code du patrimoine, une loi en évolution sur les monuments historiques, *op. cit.*, p.137 et s.

dont on impose l'indivisibilité et le cas échéant l'immobilisation. Les objets ou les lieux ne seront pas nécessairement dans les mêmes mains, par conséquent certains héritiers pourront être privés de la jouissance de leur bien, situations qui peuvent être potentiellement inextricables. Ce sont ces questions qui font échouer jusque-là les propositions de loi et auxquelles répond le législateur en 2016. Aux termes de l'article L622-1-1 « Un ensemble ou une collection d'objets mobiliers dont la conservation dans son intégrité et sa cohérence présente un intérêt public au point de vue de l'histoire, de l'art, de l'architecture, de l'archéologie, de l'ethnologie, de la science ou de la technique peut être classé au titre des monuments historiques comme ensemble historique mobilier par décision de l'autorité administrative, après avis de la Commission nationale du patrimoine et de l'architecture ». L'effet principal est que « cet ensemble ne peut être divisé ou aliéné par lot ou pièce sans autorisation de cette autorité ». L'article L622-1-2 du Code du patrimoine concerne quant à lui « les objets mobiliers classés ou un ensemble historique mobilier classé (…) attachés, par des liens historiques ou artistiques remarquables, à un immeuble classé (qui) forment avec lui un ensemble d'une qualité et d'une cohérence dont la conservation dans son intégrité présente un intérêt public ». Ces éléments « peuvent être grevés d'une servitude de maintien dans les lieux par décision de l'autorité administrative, après avis de la Commission nationale du patrimoine et de l'architecture et accord du propriétaire ».

Au vu de l'ampleur de la charge, dans le système de protection des monuments historiques, si en principe le classement requiert le consentement du propriétaire, la loi prévoit dès l'origine en matière immobilière et à partir de 1924 dans le domaine des objets mobiliers, le classement d'office. Il est possible sous réserve de l'allocation d'une indemnité du moins si le propriétaire démontre qu'il subit un préjudice direct et certain du fait de la protection. Le principe d'indemnisation ne joue que si le propriétaire n'est pas d'accord avec la protection. Dans le nouveau dispositif, les solutions ne sont pas du même ordre pour la protection des collections mobilières et pour celles des ensembles mixtes. Dans le premier cas, le classement d'office est possible à défaut de consentement du propriétaire qui, dans ce cas, peut recevoir une indemnité. À propos d'un recours pour excès de pouvoir d'une décision de classement au titre des monuments historiques d'un ensemble d'objets mobiliers conservés au château de Craon à Haroué, les propriétaires faisaient notamment valoir l'atteinte excessive au droit de

propriété et le fait qu'ils avaient auparavant obtenu la délivrance de certificats d'exportation. Mais le juge, négligeant ce dernier argument estime que les limitations prévues sont justifiées par l'objectif d'intérêt général de conservation du patrimoine et qu'en outre, ces limitations pourront donner lieu au paiement d'une indemnité représentative du préjudice résultant de la servitude de classement[19].
En revanche, le classement d'un ensemble mixte entraînant une servitude de maintien *in situ* requiert nécessairement le consentement du propriétaire.
Sur la question des successions et de la possible complexification des situations, plusieurs règles sont intéressantes. Pour les ensembles, la division ou l'aliénation d'un lot ou d'une pièce n'est pas exclue ; simplement elle ne peut se faire sans l'aval de l'autorité administrative. Pour les objets attachés par des liens historiques ou artistiques à un immeuble, la servitude peut être levée et en cas de refus de l'autorité administrative, « les sujétions anormales qui peuvent en résulter sont compensées par une indemnité ». Par ailleurs, le déplacement des objets protégés peut être autorisé par l'autorité administrative. La loi de 2016 a aussi introduit une autre figure de protection des ensembles en matière archéologique pour lesquels apparaît une servitude nouvelle. L'article L541-6 du Code du patrimoine crée en effet une servitude d'un genre inédit lorsque « les biens archéologiques mobiliers mis au jour constituent un ensemble cohérent dont l'intérêt scientifique justifie la conservation dans son intégrité », ils reçoivent un régime, particulier dès lors que l'autorité les reconnaît comme tels. L'aliénation des biens qui en relèvent ainsi que la division par lot ou pièce de l'ensemble sont soumises à une formalité de « déclaration préalable auprès des services de l'État chargés de l'archéologie ».

L'histoire des collections est pleine de ces dispersions des ensembles. Les pertes sont nombreuses comme le rappellent Judith Kagan, Dominique Séréna-Allier et Anne Tricaud, qui citent à ce propos l'exemple de la « pharmacie néo-égyptienne de Clermont-Ferrand, cas emblématique de la difficulté de pérenniser un ensemble lié à une fonction commerciale » ou encore celui d'un ensemble scientifique (…) conservé à l'observatoire Camille Flammarion du fait de la multiplicité des acteurs »[20]. Ces nouveaux outils manquaient dans le paysage des

[19] Conseil d'État, 6 avr. 2018, n° s 402065, 415575 ; CE 7 juin 2019, n° 419856.
[20] *Op. cit.*, n° 39.

servitudes patrimoniales. Le droit positif investissant cette notion d'ensemble dans plusieurs des champs patrimoniaux, sera de nature à faire avancer cette cause patrimoniale. Nous aurions bien pu aussi évoquer le cas des fonds d'archives que la loi de 2016 préserve plus nettement des risques de division et de dispersion. Il reste que la question du consentement du propriétaire continuera de brider quelque peu le dispositif.

III

Mises en valeur et accessibilité des collections

Sous la présidence de Manlio Frigo

L'accessibilité publique des collections privées

Marc-André RENOLD[1]
Professeur à l'Université de Genève
Chaire UNESCO en droit international de la protection des biens culturels
Directeur du Centre du droit de l'art

« Il y a deux sortes de collectionneurs,
celui qui cache ses trésors et celui qui les montre,
on est placard ou bien vitrine. »
Sacha Guitry

Introduction

Les collections privées recèlent souvent des joyaux. Nombreuses sont celles qui finissent, un jour ou l'autre, sur les cimaises de musées et peuvent ainsi être admirées de tous. Toutefois, elles peuvent aussi rester entre les quatre murs des collectionneurs et ne jamais être montrées ou, pire encore, entre ceux de coffres ou de dépôts. La présente contribution vise à déterminer comment de telles situations peuvent être évitées en permettant la diffusion de la culture pour le bienfait du plus grand nombre.
Nous commencerons par examiner les modes d'accessibilité publique d'une collection privée, en partant de la création d'une structure particulière (fondation ou trust, par exemple) pour continuer avec la transmission par legs, donation, dation en paiement, prêt ou encore par certaines formes de partenariats (**I**). Nous verrons ensuite comment favoriser l'accessibilité publique des collections par décision populaire - c'est l'exemple du Canton de Bâle - ou par décision politique, tel l'encouragement par l'octroi de licences particulières ou l'adoption de mesures fiscales (**II**). Nous verrons enfin qu'il existe divers freins possibles à l'accessibilité publique et tenterons de déterminer comment en diminuer l'impact (**III**).

---

[1] L'auteur tient à remercier Mme Vanessa Vuille, assistante au Centre du droit de l'art de l'Université de Genève, pour son aide dans la finalisation du présent article.

I. Les différents modes d'accessibilité publique des collections privées

Souvent, le collectionneur voudra pérenniser sa collection de son vivant en la mettant à l'abri d'une structure juridique particulière. Nous examinerons en premier lieu la fondation (**A**), avant d'étudier le trust (**B**) et d'autres mécanismes envisageables (**C**).

A. La fondation

La fondation est un outil fréquemment utilisé en droit comparé pour permettre la pérennité d'une collection et, à terme, son accessibilité publique[2]. Nous nous concentrerons sur le droit suisse qui est particulièrement favorable à l'utilisation de cette institution, notamment dans le domaine culturel[3]. C'est ainsi qu'en 2013, l'association *Swissfoundation* faisait état de 113 fondations de droit suisse ayant un but en rapport avec l'art[4]. En droit suisse, la fondation est prévue aux articles 80 ss du Code civil suisse (CCS). Une fondation se définit par l'affectation de biens en faveur d'un but spécial (art. 80 CCS). Les buts d'une fondation peuvent être variés, mais ils sont souvent philanthropiques.

La fondation est sous le contrôle d'une autorité de surveillance, cantonale pour les fondations dont les activités sont à petite échelle, fédérale pour les fondations dont les activités dépassent les frontières d'un canton ou de la Suisse (art. 84 CCS)[5]. Les autorités de surveillance

---

[2] Parisima Vez, *Commentaire romand du Code civil, Art. 80, in* Pascal Pichonnaz, Bénédict Foëx (éd.), Commentaire romand du Code civil, Bâle (Helbing Lichtenhahn) 2016, p. 564, NN 6-8 ; voir également Marie Cornu, Jérôme Fromageau (éd.), *Fondation et trust dans la protection du patrimoine*, Paris, L'Harmattan, 1999.

[3] Avec presque 20 000 fondations, la Suisse occupe le deuxième rang des pays européens en termes de nombre de fondations par habitants, juste après le Liechtenstein (Parisima Vez, Commentaire romand du Code civil, Art. 80, *in* Pascal Pichonnaz, Bénédict Foëx (éd.), Commentaire romand du Code civil, Bâle (Helbing Lichtenhahn) 2016, p. 563-564, NN 4-5).

[4] CEPS Forschung und Praxis, Rapport sur les fondations en Suisse 2017, vol. 17, p. 10, (en ligne : http://www.swissfoundations.ch/fr/rapportsurlesfondationsensuisse) (10.05.2018).

[5] Pour la Suisse, voir Département fédéral de l'intérieur, Autorité fédérale de surveillance des fondations (en ligne : https://www.edi.admin.ch/edi/fr/home/das-edi/organisation/services-specialises/autorite-federale-de-surveillance-des-fondations.html) (10.05.2018).

effectuent un contrôle étroit des fondations, notamment de leur comptabilité, et n'autorisent le changement de statuts que de manière très limitée.
Une fois créée, la fondation peut demander la reconnaissance de son affectation à un but d'utilité publique, ce qui lui permettra de bénéficier d'une exonération fiscale, totale ou partielle, sur un plan fédéral ou cantonal[6].
La Fondation Martin Bodmer offre un très bon exemple d'une fondation suisse qui a permis l'ouverture au plus grand nombre d'une collection unique de manuscrits. En effet, Martin Bodmer collectionna toute sa vie, mais sa collection n'était que d'un accès public très restreint jusqu'à ce qu'il crée une fondation. Dans un premier temps, l'accès à la collection de cette fondation était limité, mais rapidement, au vu de l'intérêt qu'elle suscitait, la collection fut transformée en musée, en particulier grâce à la vente d'une pièce unique (un dessin de Michel-Ange) qui finança à lui seul la construction d'un musée qui est maintenant quotidiennement ouvert au public[7].
Un autre exemple intéressant est le Musée d'art moderne et contemporain de Genève, constitué tout d'abord d'une fondation de droit privé, mais complété par la suite par une fondation de droit public, autrement dit, une fondation créée par un acte législatif, qui vient chapeauter la collection privée et permet un financement public du Musée d'art moderne et contemporain[8].

B. Le trust

Le trust est une institution connue essentiellement en droit anglo-américain. Elle permet une dissociation de la propriété juridique et de la propriété économique, le trustee étant propriétaire juridique des biens du trust qu'il gère en faveur du bénéficiaire du trust, qui en est le propriétaire économique[9]. Le trust est utilisé pour la création de musées

---

[6] Parisima Vez, *Commentaire romand du Code civil, Art. 80*, *in* Pascal Pichonnaz, Bénédict Foëx (éd.), Commentaire romand du Code civil, Bâle (Helbing Lichtenhahn) 2016, p. 564, N 8.
[7] Fondation Bodmer, Page d'accueil (en ligne : www. fondationbodmer.ch) (14.05.2018).
[8] Sur la fondation de droit public, voir Parisima Vez, Art. 80, *in* Pascal Pichonnaz, Bénédict Foëx (éd.), *Commentaire romand du Code civil*, Bâle (Helbing Lichtenhahn) 2016, p. 566, N 17.
[9] Claude Lambrechts, *Le trust et la protection de la nature aux États-Unis*, *in* Marie

privés, surtout aux États-Unis, et de musées publics, en particulier en Grande-Bretagne. Tout comme la fondation, il est placé sous le contrôle de l'autorité. Aux États-Unis, il s'agit souvent du Procureur général de l'État où est situé le trust.

Il arrive que le créateur d'un trust le soumette à des conditions qui peuvent mettre les trustees dans l'embarras. Ainsi en est-il allé du Trust Barnes à Philadelphie, le créateur du trust ayant opté pour un maintien strict des collections dans leur lieu d'origine (banlieue de Philadelphie) et selon l'accrochage voulu par le propriétaire originel et créateur du trust, sans qu'aucun changement ou déplacement ne puisse lui être apporté. Plus personne ne venant visiter le trust, celui était voué à une mort certaine, sauf que le Procureur général autorisa finalement le déplacement de la collection au centre de la ville de Philadelphie dans un magnifique bâtiment moderne qui permit au grand public d'accéder aux collections (qui durent cependant respecter intégralement l'accrochage d'origine)[10].

C. Autres mécanismes

Le droit prévoit également plusieurs mécanismes par lesquels un particulier peut transférer la possession ou la propriété de biens, notamment d'œuvres d'art.

Le premier de ces outils est le legs (voir par exemple les articles 485 ss du Code civil suisse). Dans son testament, le disposant peut prévoir le legs de biens déterminés, telle une sculpture ou une collection d'œuvres d'art, à un légataire. Le disposant doit cependant veiller au respect des dispositions légales spéciales, en particulier celles qui réservent une partie de la succession aux héritiers légaux.

Le cas du Musée Oskar Reinhart, dans le canton de Zurich, en Suisse, est intéressant en ce qu'il réunit deux des mécanismes présentés ci-dessus : la création d'une fondation et le legs. Homme d'affaires et collectionneur d'art, Oskar Reinhart crée en 1940 la Fondation Oskar Reinhart pour la Ville de Winthertour afin de mettre son patrimoine artistique au service de la cause publique[11]. Il cède à la Fondation une

---

Cornu, Jérôme Fromageau (éd.), Fondation et trust dans la protection du patrimoine, Paris (L'Harmattan) 1999, p. 161-170, p. 161.

[10] Barnes Foundation, Page d'accueil (en ligne : www.barnesfoundation.org) (14.05.2018).

[11] Dictionnaire historique de la Suisse, Reinhart Oskar, 04.05.2012 (en ligne : http://www.hls-dhs-dss.ch/textes/f/F27755.php) (09.05.2018).

partie de sa riche collection, soit les œuvres de peintres suisses, autrichiens et allemands. Ces tableaux composent l'actuel Kunst Museum Winterthur Reinhart am Stadtgarten de Winterthur[12]. En 1958, quelques années avant sa mort, Oskar Reinhart lègue l'autre partie de sa collection, soit 200 œuvres de peintres français, ainsi que sa résidence dite « Am Römerholz » à la Confédération suisse[13]. Cette dernière ouvre le Musée Oskar Reinhart « Am Römerholz » au public en 1970.

Il convient de préciser que même si le legs entraîne le transfert de la propriété des biens, il peut être grevé de charges qui limitent le pouvoir de disposer des biens (art. 485 al. 1 CCS). Dans le domaine de l'art, il est courant qu'un disposant lègue sa collection à un légataire, à charge pour lui ne de pas aliéner ladite collection. Une telle charge peut se révéler problématique lorsque le légataire doit faire face à une demande de restitution, comme l'illustre la récente affaire du tableau *La Vallée de la Stour*, dans le canton de Neuchâtel, en Suisse[14].

Similaire au legs, le deuxième mode permettant de transférer la propriété d'un bien culturel afin de lui offrir une meilleure visibilité est la donation. La donation entre vifs est, au sens du Code des obligations suisses (COS), la disposition par laquelle une personne cède tout ou partie de ses biens à une autre sans contre-prestation correspondante (art. 239 COS)[15]. Comme le legs, la donation peut être grevée de conditions ou de charges (art. 245 al. 1 et s. COS)[16].

---

[12] Kunst Museum Wintertuhr Reinhart am Stadtgarten (en ligne : https://www.kmw.ch/museum/portrait-reinhart-am-stadtgarten/) (09.05.2018) ; Étienne Dumont, « Le Museum Oskar Reinhart poursuit son grand chambardement », *in* Bilan, 09.03.2017 (en ligne : http://www.bilan.ch/etienne-dumont/courants-dart/winterthourle-museum-oskar-reinhart-poursuit-chambardement) (09.05.2018).

[13] Collection Oskar Reinhart am Römerholz (en ligne : http://www.bundesmuseen.ch/roemerholz/index. html?lang=fr); Collection Oskar Reinhart am Römerholz Musée, Le collectionneur (en ligne : http://www.bundesmuseen.ch/roemerholz/00440/00652/index.html?lang=fr) (09.05.2018).

[14] Sur cette affaire, voir notamment Anne Laure Bandle, Vanessa Vuille, Marc-André Renold, « Affaire Vallée de la Stour – Héritiers Jaffé et La Chaux-de-Fonds », Plateforme ArThemis (http://unige.ch/art-adr), Centre du droit de l'art, Université de Genève, mars 2018 (en ligne : https://plone.unige.ch/art-adr/cases-affaires/vallee-de-la-stour-2013-heritiers-jaffe-et-la-chaux-de-fonds) (09.05.2018).

[15] Sur la donation, voir notamment Margareta Baddeley, Art. 239, *in* Luc Thévenoz et al. (éd.), Commentaire romand du Code des obligations, 2e éd., Bâle (Helbing Lichtenhahn) 2017, p. 1604 et s.

[16] Sur les conséquences de l'inexécution d'une charge et la possibilité de révoquer la

Qu'il s'agisse de la donation d'une œuvre ou de celle d'une collection entière, que le donateur soit un particulier ou une fondation, les cas de donation d'œuvres d'art à des musées sont nombreux. Mentionnons à titre d'exemple les Américains Marlene et Spencer Hays, qui, en 2016, ont fait don au Musée d'Orsay de leur collection de 600 œuvres d'une valeur de 350 millions d'euros[17]. Au Royaume-Uni, les donations ont permis l'entrée de 44 œuvres majeures dans les collections publiques durant l'année 2017, ces œuvres étant estimées à 39 millions de livres sterling[18].

Le troisième moyen dont dispose un particulier pour transférer la propriété de sa collection d'œuvres d'art en vue de la rendre accessible au public est la dation en paiement. La dation en paiement se définit comme la convention par laquelle le débiteur et le créancier conviennent que la dette sera exécutée par la remise ou la cession d'un bien autre que celui qui avait été originellement convenu[19]. Plus particulièrement, la dation permet au contribuable de payer les droits relatifs aux successions, donations et mutations non pas en monnaie, mais par le biais d'une œuvre d'art ou d'un bien culturel présentant une valeur exceptionnelle[20]. Elle a pour avantage de faire entrer dans les collections muséales publiques des œuvres qui, autrement, ne leur seraient pas accessibles, faute de moyens financiers suffisants. Elle permet également d'éviter la dispersion d'une collection[21].

Introduite au Royaume-Uni en 1894, puis reprise en France par la Loi Malraux de 1968 en vue de la succession imminente de Pablo Picasso[22],

---

donation d'un tableau, voir l'arrêt Hoirs Varenne et consorts contre Ville de Genève, 4A_28/2007 du 30.05.2007.

[17]Martine Robert, « Art : les collections publiques toujours plus dépendantes du privé », *in Les Échos*, 28.10.2016 (en ligne : https://www.lesechos.fr/28/10/2016/LesEchos/22308-024-ECH_art-les-collections-publiques-toujours-plus-dependantes-du-prive.htm).

[18] Arts Council England, Cultural Gifts Scheme & Acceptance *in* Lieu, Report 2017, Manchester, november 2017, p. 5.

[19] Arrêt 4A_407/2010 ; Pierre Tercier, Pascal Pichonnaz, *Le droit des obligations*, 5e éd., Genève (Schulthess) 2012, p. 229, N 1016.

[20] Le type d'impôts pouvant être acquittés par dation varie quelque peu selon les États, mais reste lié aux questions de succession (Ignace Claeys Bouuaert, *La dation en paiement : éléments de droit comparé, in* Quentin Byrne-Sutton, Fabienne Mariéthoz, Marc-André Renold, *La dation d'œuvres d'art en paiement d'impôts, Études en droit de l'art,* vol. 8, Zurich (Schulthess) 1996, p. 11-21, p. 12).

[21] Viviane Milgrim, *La dation en paiement d'œuvres d'art en Europe*, École du Louvre, mars 2005, p. 4.

[22] Loi n° 68-1251 du 31.12.1968 tendant à favoriser la conservation du patrimoine

cette institution fiscale a depuis été intégrée à plusieurs droits nationaux notamment en Italie, en Belgique ainsi que dans divers cantons romands en Suisse[23]. En dépit des particularités nationales, la dation est toujours soumise à une procédure d'agrément entre le contribuable et l'État. Celle-ci se compose de trois phases : l'offre de dation du contribuable, un examen administratif (comprenant notamment la détermination de la valeur des biens) et l'agrément final. Cette procédure peut se révéler longue et contraignante pour les héritiers, ce qui explique sans doute que le recours à la dation en paiement soit relativement rare à l'heure actuelle[24].

Le cas le plus emblématique de la dation en paiement est probablement celui du Musée Picasso de Paris. Suite au décès de Pablo Picasso en avril 1973 dans le sud de la France, ses héritiers recourent à la dation en paiement prévue par la Loi Malraux pour payer les droits de succession d'un héritage estimé à plus d'un milliard de francs français[25]. Après cinq ans de pourparlers avec la Commission d'agrément pour la conservation du patrimoine national, la propriété de plusieurs milliers de peintures, sculptures, dessins, céramiques et gravures passe à l'État français. Cette importante dation a permis de garder réunies un nombre important d'œuvres de Picasso et de créer le

---

artistique national ; Musée Picasso Paris, La Collection (en ligne : http://www.museepicassoparis.fr/presentation/) (09.05.2018).

[23] Viviane Milgram, *La dation en paiement d'œuvres d'art en Europe*, École du Louvre, mars 1995, p. 1. En Suisse, il s'agit des cantons de Fribourg, de Vaud, du Valais, de Genève et du Jura (Administration fédérale des contributions, Les impôts sur les successions et les donations. État de la législation au 1er janv. 2017, Berne 2016, p. 45).

[24] Ignace Claeys Bouuaert, *La dation en paiement : éléments de droit comparé*, *in* Quentin Byrne-Sutton, Fabienne Mariéthoz, Marc-André Renold, *La dation d'œuvres d'art en paiement d'impôts*, *Études en droit de l'art,* vol. 8, Zurich (Schulthess) 1996, p. 11-21, p. 12 ; ATS, « Elle paie l'impôt sur les successions avec la peinture d'une Genevoise », *in* Tribune de Genève, 03.06.2014 (en ligne : https://www.tdg.ch/suisse/Elle-paie-l-impot-sur-les-succession-avec-une-peinture/story/29357821) (09.05.2018) ; Simon Corthay, « Quand les impôts de successions sont payés en œuvres d'art », *in* RTS, 18.01.2017 (en ligne : https://www.rts.ch/info/culture/arts-visuels/8319146-quand-les-impots-de-succession-sont-payes-en-uvres-d-art.html) (09.05.2018).

[25] Succession Picasso, La dation Picasso : Conserver les œuvres sur le territoire national (en ligne : https://www.picasso.fr/details/ojo-les-archives-novembre-2014-ojo-27-a-lire-la-legende-picasso-et-son-musee-la-dation-picasso-conserver-les-oeuvres-sur-le-territoire-national) (09.05.2018).

Musée national Picasso, lequel a ouvert ses portes en 1985[26]. Il a été enrichi depuis par la dation de Jacqueline Picasso, dernière épouse du peintre, en 1990 ainsi que par plusieurs donations[27].

À un niveau plus modeste, le Musée cantonal des beaux-arts de Lausanne, en Suisse, a également enrichi sa collection en janvier 2017 grâce à la dation de sept cahiers de l'artiste vaudoise schizophrène Aloïse Corbaz[28]. Il s'agit de la seconde dation en paiement effectuée sur la base de la loi vaudoise sur la dation en paiement depuis son entrée en vigueur en 2006[29].

Le quatrième procédé légal présenté consiste en un prêt, soit le transfert de possession d'un bien, en général à long terme, mais non de sa propriété. Le prêt à usage se définit en droit suisse comme un contrat par lequel le prêteur s'oblige à céder gratuitement l'usage d'une chose que l'emprunteur s'engage à lui rendre après s'en être servi (art. 305 COS). Ainsi, le prêt est gratuit et limité dans le temps, et il bénéficie en général à l'emprunteur. De par sa nature temporaire, le prêt offre une grande mobilité aux œuvres et permet au collectionneur de rendre accessible sa collection de manière ponctuelle. En 2009, la Fondation de l'Hermitage, à Lausanne, réussit le pari de monter une exposition dédiée à Cézanne et Rothko grâce aux prêts de collectionneurs privés suisses[30]. Ce cas démontre le double rôle des musées, qui sont à la fois des lieux d'expositions et des interlocuteurs privilégiés des collectionneurs. Mais ce privilège peut aussi représenter une

---

[26] Musée Picasso Paris, Histoire (en ligne : http://www.museepicassoparis.fr/histoire/) (09.05.2018).

[27] Musée Picasso Paris, La collection (en ligne : http://www.museepicassoparis.fr/presentation/) (09.05.2018).

[28] Musée cantonal des beaux-arts de Lausanne, Le mcb-a enrichit son fonds Aloïse avec 8 nouveaux cahiers, Newsletter nº 30, 17.01.2017 (en ligne : http://www.emailing.vd.ch/wb.php?p=1nj/1ef/rs/1jd/tp/rs#) (10.05.2018).

[29] Loi sur la dation en paiement d'impôts sur les successions et donations (LDSD), 648.21 ; Musée cantonal des beaux-arts de Lausanne, Le mcb-a enrichit son fonds Aloïse avec 8 nouveaux cahiers, Newsletter nº 30, 17 janv. 2017 (en ligne : http://www.emailing.vd.ch/wb.php?p=1nj/1ef/rs/1jd/tp/rs#); ATS, « Elle paie l'impôt sur les successions avec la peinture d'une Genevoise », in Tribune de Genève, 03.06.2014 (en ligne : https://www.tdg.ch/suisse/Elle-paie-l-impot-sur-les-succession-avec-une-peinture/story/29357821) (10.05.2018).

[30] Fondation de l'Hermitage, Passions partagée. De Cézanne à Rothko, chefs-d'œuvre du XXᵉ siècle dans les collections privées suisses, 26.06-25.10.2009, Lausanne (en ligne : https://www.fondation-hermitage.ch/index.php?id=147&selected=4&tx_ttnews[tt_news]=17&L=) (10.05.2018).

responsabilité, celle d'encourager les collectionneurs à partager leurs œuvres avec le public.
L'Association des musées suisses a par ailleurs établi un contrat-cadre de prêt afin de faciliter la conclusion de contrats de prêt et d'attirer l'attention des parties sur certaines problématiques qui peuvent se poser comme le transport des biens, les assurances et les droits de reproduction des œuvres[31].
En pratique, les prêts peuvent être le prélude à une donation. Trois ans déjà avant d'effectuer la donation de leur collection privée au Musée d'Orsay en 2016, Marlene et Spencer Hays avaient déjà prêté quelque 200 œuvres au musée[32]. Dans une affaire portant sur une demande de restitution qui opposait des héritiers français au Musée d'art et d'histoire de Genève, le prêt d'une durée de six mois a été renouvelé une douzaine de fois avant d'être finalement transformé en donation[33].
Il convient enfin de noter que le prêt se distingue du dépôt (art. 472 et s. COS) sur au moins quatre aspects. À la différence du contrat de prêt, le contrat de dépôt profite au déposant. Le dépositaire ne peut se servir de la chose sans la permission du déposant (art. 474 al. 1 COS) et ne peut exiger une rémunération que si elle a été expressément prévue dans le contrat ou si, eu égard aux circonstances, il devait s'attendre à être rémunéré (art. 472 al. 2 COS). Enfin, c'est le déposant qui assume les dépenses nécessaires à l'exécution du contrat de dépôt (art. 473 al. 1 COS).
Le cinquième moyen de rendre accessible une collection privée n'est pas expressément prévu par la loi, mais relève de la liberté contractuelle des parties : le partenariat public-privé offre une multitude de possibilités de rendre une collection privée accessible. Outre le cas de la Fondation Gandur pour l'art et le Musée d'art et d'histoire de Genève

---

[31] Association suisse des musées, Système de prêt. Contrat-cadre, 2012 (en ligne : https://www.museums.ch/fr/publications/standards/syst%C3%A8me-de-pr%C3%AAt.html) (10.05.2018).
[32] Artprice, « En bref : Donation Hays », *in* Artprice, 04.11.2016 (en ligne : https://fr.artprice.com/artmarketinsight/en-bref-donation-hays-emmanuel-perrotin-jean-dubuffet-au-lam-maurizio-cattelan) ; Sarah Hugouneng, « Retour sur les coulisses de la donation Hays au musée d'Orsay », *in* Le Quotidien de l'Art, 25.10.2016 (en ligne : https://www.lequotidiendelart.com/articles/9826-retour-sur-les-coulisses-de-la-donation-hays-au-musee-d-orsay.html) (10.05.2018).
[33] Raphael Contel, Anne Laure Bandle, Marc-André Renold, « Affaire Fresques de Casenoves – Musée d'Art et d'Histoire de la Ville de Genève et la France », Plateforme ArThemis (http://unige.ch/art-adr), Centre du droit de l'art, Université de Genève.

qui sera détaillé plus loin, on peut mentionner l'exemple du Musée d'art moderne et contemporain, à Genève, le MAMCO, créé sous la forme d'une fondation de droit privé, à laquelle se joint une fondation de droit public, la FONDAMCO, qui permet un financement public en plus du financement privé d'origine[34].

Ainsi, plusieurs moyens légaux permettent de rendre une collection privée accessible au public, cette accessibilité pouvant découler de la création d'une entité juridique, d'un transfert de propriété ou de possession, ou encore d'une autre forme, selon la créativité des partenaires.

II. L'encouragement à l'accessibilité publique

Sacha Guitry distinguait les collectionneurs placards des collectionneurs vitrines, les premiers cachant jalousement leurs biens du regard de tout public, les seconds ne pouvant s'empêcher d'exhiber leurs richesses. Les motivations de ces collectionneurs vitrines peuvent être diverses : partage d'une passion, volonté de participation à l'éducation culturelle, acte de patriotisme ou d'utilité publique, envie de voir son nom célébré ou encore, plus rationnellement, souhait de bénéficier d'avantages fiscaux[35].

Il existe cependant des mesures permettant d'inciter les collectionneurs à ouvrir les portes de leurs coffres. Nous en présenterons trois exemples.

A. Par décision populaire (le cas du Canton de Bâle)

Le cas du canton de Bâle constitue un cas très particulier de mobilisation citoyenne en faveur de l'art.

En 1967, lors d'un épisode baptisé « le miracle Picasso de Bâle », la population bâloise s'est largement mobilisée afin d'acquérir deux tableaux de Pablo Picasso, « Les deux frères » et « Arlequin assis »[36].

Ces œuvres ont été prêtées par la famille Staechlin au Kunstmuseum de

---

[34] Voir la loi genevoise relative à la création de la Fondation de droit public du Musée d'art moderne et contemporain - FONDAMCO du 18.12.2004 (10.05.2018).

[35] Véronique Long, « Les collectionneurs d'œuvres d'art et la donation au musée à la fin du XIXe siècle : l'exemple du Musée du Louvre », *in Romantisme. Revue du dix-neuvième siècle*, vol. 112, 2001, p. 45-54, p. 52-53.

[36] Sur cet épisode, voir notamment Denise Chervet, « Das Picasso-Wunder von Basel », *in* SRF, 17.12.17 (en ligne : https://www.srf.ch/kultur/kunst/legendaerer-volksentscheid-das-picasso-wunder-von-basel) (09.05.2018).

Bâle, où elles sont depuis une vingtaine d'années. Or, en raison de difficultés financières, l'héritier Peter Staechelin est contraint de vendre certaines de ces œuvres. À l'annonce de la mise en vente de deux Picasso, la commission du musée réunit immédiatement la Fondation Staechelin et le gouvernement de Bâle-Ville afin d'éviter que les œuvres ne soient plus accessibles au public. Un accord est rapidement trouvé : la Fondation vend les tableaux à l'État pour un total de 8,4 millions de francs suisses, dont 6 à la charge de l'État et 2,4 à la charge de donateurs privés. Le Parlement approuve le crédit et la ville lance une campagne de récolte de dons. Les citoyens bâlois et l'industrie pharmaceutique locale répondent largement présents, de même que des cantons voisins comme Saint-Gall et Bâle-Campagne. Près de 2,5 millions de francs sont récoltés.
Mais un référendum est déposé contre le crédit adopté par le Parlement, et le peuple bâlois est appelé à voter. Le 17 décembre 1967, après une campagne virulente opposant une jeunesse essentiellement favorable à l'achat des tableaux à une population plus âgée peu enthousiaste, le crédit est approuvé à 32 000 voix contre 27 000. Touché par cette mobilisation citoyenne en faveur de l'art, Pablo Picasso offre alors « à la jeunesse bâloise » trois de ses peintures ainsi qu'une esquisse. Depuis, les deux tableaux achetés ainsi que les quatre œuvres reçues sont exposés au Kunstmuseum. Pour fêter les 50 ans de cette donation, le musée organise d'ailleurs une exposition rétrospective jusqu'au 12 août 2018[37].

B. Par décret législatif (le cas de la Jordanie)

L'accessibilité publique des collections privées peut également être initiée par le législateur. Dans le cadre de la révision de sa loi sur les antiquités, la Jordanie a souhaité ajouter des dispositions relatives aux collections privées. La Jordanie est un pays dit source, c'est-à-dire un pays dont proviennent nombre de biens archéologiques qui sont ensuite vendus illégalement sur le marché de l'art. En effet, comme la plupart des législations des pays sources, la loi jordanienne prohibe toute vente de bien archéologique jordanien. Malgré cette interdiction stricte, certains particuliers jordaniens ont acquis nombre de biens

[37] Pour plus d'informations, voir Kunstmuseum Basel, Art. Argent. Musée. 50 ans de Picasso-Story (en ligne : https://kunstmuseumbasel.ch/fr/expositions/2018/picasso-50-ans) (09.05.2018).

archéologiques sur le marché noir et possèdent désormais des collections extrêmement riches.
Conscient de cette réalité et soucieux de renforcer l'identité nationale en permettant au public d'admirer ces collections, le législateur jordanien envisage d'introduire dans sa nouvelle loi sur les antiquités un chapitre spécifiquement dédié aux collections archéologiques privées. Le Ministère du tourisme et des antiquités serait compétent pour délivrer des licences permettant d'établir des musées privés, à condition que ces musées poursuivent un but conforme à l'ordre public jordanien et participent au renforcement de l'identité nationale, à la sensibilisation en matière archéologique et à la promotion de la culture jordanienne[38].

C. Par l'incitation fiscale

L'outil fiscal est une mesure souvent privilégiée par les États pour encourager les particuliers à faire don de leurs collections à des collectivités publiques. L'exemple des États-Unis est fréquemment cité, mais d'autres droits permettent aussi de faire des donations déductibles fiscalement. C'est ainsi qu'en 2017 on recense la donation de 44 œuvres et objets d'art par des procédures de défiscalisation au Royaume-Uni[39].
Comme l'indiquent deux spécialistes du droit de l'art aux États-Unis : "The lifetime transfer of a collection to a charitable organization saves the donor income taxes because of the allowable income tax deduction; at the same time, the lifetime transfer relieves the donor of the expense and the worry connected with the maintenance of a valuable collection[40]".
Et pour ce qui concerne une donation par la voie testamentaire, les mêmes auteurs précisent que : "A testamentary transfer of a collection to a charitable organization saves the decedent's estate a great amount of estate taxes, because of the allowable estate tax deduction and, at the same time, relieves the estate of the problem of raising the cash

---

[38] Projet de loi sur les antiquités, non publié.
[39] Le Journal des Arts, 44 œuvres sont entrées en 2017 dans les collections publiques britanniques via les dispositifs de défiscalisation, *in* Le Journal des Arts, 14.12.2017 (en ligne : https://www.lejournaldesarts.fr/44-oeuvres-sont-entrees-en-2017-dans-les-collections-publiques-britanniques-les-dispositifs-de) (15.05.2018).
[40] Ralph Lerner/ Judith Bresler, *Art Law - The Guide for Collectors, Investors, Dealers and Artists*, vol. III, 2005, p. 1554.

necessary to pay the estate tax on a potentially nonliquid asset[41]".
En droit fiscal comparé, l'on constate que l'outil de la déduction fiscale des donations à des musées ou autres institutions culturelles est de plus en plus utilisé, que ce soit pour l'imposition de la fortune ou du revenu[42].
Un outil intéressant concernant l'accessibilité au public est celui qui est prévu en droit anglais : selon le "Conditional Exemption Tax Incentive Scheme" l'acquéreur d'un bien culturel d'intérêt scientifique, historique ou artistique national peut être exonéré des droits de succession ou du "capital gains tax" s'il accepte que l'objet reste au Royaume-Uni et de le montrer "raisonnablement" au public[43].

III. Les freins à l'accessibilité publique

Les situations présentées ci-dessus couvrent les cas dans lesquels l'État ou la population cherchent à encourager les collectionneurs privés à rendre leurs collections accessibles. Ces incitations partent toutes d'un même postulat : les collectionneurs doivent être incités, par différentes mesures, à ouvrir les portes de leurs collections afin d'en faire profiter le plus grand nombre.
Cependant, il arrive que la situation inverse se produise : soit le collectionneur propose de rendre sa collection publique, et c'est l'État ou la population qui refuse cette offre, soit, pour des raisons éthiques, il est jugé préférable de ne pas montrer certains objets, aussi beaux et intéressants soient-ils. C'est notamment le cas des biens qui proviennent du trafic illicite et de spoliations.

A. Les exigences du collectionneur

Le cas du Musée d'art et d'histoire de Genève est emblématique du dilemme auquel un musée peut être confronté lorsqu'un collectionneur offre d'exposer sa collection, mais à des conditions jugées trop élevées. Au regard de la vétusté du bâtiment, le Conseil municipal de la Ville de Genève vote en mai 2012 un crédit de CHF 132 millions afin de rénover

---

[41] *Idem*, p. 1554-1555.
[42] Gouvernement du Royaume-Uni, Capital taxation and tax-exempt heritage assets, 15.11.2017 (en ligne : https://www.gov.uk/government/publications/capital-taxation-and-tax-exempt-heritage-assets) (15.05.2018).
[43] Capital Taxation and The National Heritage, 15.11.2017, p. 132 et s. (en ligne : https://assets.publishing.service.gov.uk/government/uploads/system/uploads/attachment_data/file/65902 8/Capital_Taxation_National_Heritage.pdf) (15.05.2018).

et d'agrandir le Musée d'art et d'histoire, la moitié de cette somme devant provenir de donateurs[44]. Dans ce contexte, la proposition de partenariat public-privé entre la Ville et la Fondation Gandur pour l'Art, du nom de l'homme d'affaires et grand collectionneur genevois Jean Claude Gandur, cristallise rapidement l'attention.
En 2010 déjà, la Ville et la Fondation ont signé une convention liant mécénat et prêt. Suite au vote de 2015, les termes de la convention sont partiellement renégociés et précisés. Pour l'essentiel, la convention révisée[45] prévoit que la Fondation verse jusqu'à 40 millions de francs suisses pour le projet de rénovation et d'agrandissement du Musée et qu'elle prête une partie de son importante collection d'œuvres d'art et d'antiquités[46], afin que celle-ci soit exposée au Musée pour une durée de 99 ans. La convention prévoit également un droit de regard de la Fondation sur certaines activités du Musée, ainsi que la prise en charge par ce dernier d'un certain nombre de frais.
Un référendum est demandé. Tandis que les partisans du projet invoquent une opportunité en or d'avoir accès à une collection extrêmement riche et de renouveler l'écrin dans lequel les œuvres seront exposées, les opposants au projet dénoncent la « privatisation d'un patrimoine public » en raison de conditions trop favorables à la Fondation Gandur pour l'Art et, plus généralement, un projet "mal ficelé"[47]. À l'issue d'une campagne particulièrement virulente, la population genevoise rejette à 54% des voix le projet de rénovation et d'agrandissement. Immédiatement après et en toute logique, la Fondation dénonce la convention. L'avenir dira comment le peuple genevois trouvera comment rénover son musée, sans apport de fonds de la Fondation Gandur et surtout sans sa collection.

---

[44] ATS, La rénovation du Musée d'art et d'histoire est acceptée à Genève, *in* RTS, RTS, 20.05.2015 (en ligne : http://www.rts.ch/info/regions/geneve/6798547-la-renovation-du-musee-d-art-et-d-histoire-est-acceptee-a-geneve.html) (09.05.2018).

[45] Convention entre la Ville de Genève et la Fondation Gandur pour l'Art (en ligne : files.newsnetz.ch/upload//7/0/70307.pdf) (09.05.2018).

[46] Alexandre Demidoff, « Au royaume des dieux avec Jean Claude Gandur », *in* Le Temps, 12.02.2016 (en ligne : https://www.letemps.ch/culture/royaume-dieux-jean-claude-gandur) (09.05.2018).

[47] Ville de Genève, Brochure sur la votation communale du 28 février 2016, p. 11-12 (en ligne : https://www.ge.ch/votations/20160228/doc/brochure-communale.pdf) ; voir également la critique cinglante d'Anna Vaucher contre l'ensemble du projet dans « Le peuple a refusé le projet Nouvel. Que va-t-il se passer ? », *in* Tribune de Genève, 28.02.2016 (en ligne : https://www.tdg.ch/geneve/actu-genevoise/peuple-refuse-projet-nouvel-vatil-passer/story/26264287).

Il convient de rappeler que dans cette affaire, les conditions posées par le collectionneur n'étaient qu'un aspect du projet plus global de rénovation et d'agrandissement du Musée d'art et d'histoire, qui, à lui seul, suscitait certaines critiques. Il est par conséquent difficile de juger dans quelle mesure les exigences du collectionneur ont véritablement influencé le vote des Genevois.
La Fondation Gandur pour l'art, de son côté, poursuit des projets de partenariat avec d'autres institutions muséales, hors de Suisse notamment[48]. Dans ce contexte, se pose la question de la fuite des collections privées et des moyens d'éviter un tel départ de leur pays d'origine.

B. Le trafic illicite

Il arrive également que, pour des raisons éthiques, il soit jugé préférable de ne pas montrer certains objets.
Le premier cas est celui des biens issus du trafic illicite. En raison de l'augmentation des prix des œuvres et de la difficulté à identifier la provenance de certains biens, le marché de l'art et des biens culturels est particulièrement exposé au trafic illicite.
Un collectionneur qui sait ou soupçonne que certains des biens qu'il possède proviennent du trafic illicite ne les exposera vraisemblablement pas au public, et ce quelle que soit la valeur artistique, historique ou éducative des biens en cause. Les raisons semblent évidentes : du point de vue légal, le collectionneur peut être tenu pour responsable. Du point de vue de la réputation, il risque de perdre sa crédibilité vis-à-vis des autres acteurs du marché de l'art ainsi que leur confiance. Du point de vue éthique enfin, un collectionneur pourra craindre qu'en exposant des biens issus du trafic illicite, il encourage ce même trafic.
En 2017, le Musée d'art et d'histoire de Genève est placé face à un dilemme : doit-il montrer neuf objets archéologiques confisqués par le Ministère public aux Ports francs, alors que ces biens proviennent de fouilles illicites au Yémen, en Syrie et en Libye et qu'ils sont le fruit du trafic illicite[49] ? En accord avec le Ministère public, le Musée accepte de montrer et de conserver ces biens, en attendant leur restitution aux

---

[48] Sylvain Besson, « Où va aller la collection Gandur ? », *in Le Temps*, 28.02.2016 (en ligne : https://www.letemps.ch/suisse/va-aller-collection-gandur) (09.05.2018).
[49] Musée d'art et d'histoire de Genève, Dossier de presse « Trafic illicite de biens culturels », 04.03.2017.

États d'origine. Afin d'éviter toute assimilation avec les pilleurs et les receleurs, le Musée se montre particulièrement prudent : il ne s'agit pas d'une exposition, mais d'une « présentation » transparente et à but éducatif. En somme, l'événement doit être un acte de militantisme et de sensibilisation à la lutte contre le trafic illicite, et non un acte de complicité[50].

C. Les spoliations

Le second cas concerne les biens spoliés à l'époque de la Seconde Guerre mondiale qui, comme les biens issus du trafic illicite, soulèvent d'importantes questions juridiques et éthiques, y compris s'agissant de leur exposition.

Ces questions se sont posées au *Kunstmuseum* de Berne au printemps 2014, lorsque le Musée découvre que le collectionneur d'art allemand Cornelius Gurlitt lui a légué l'ensemble de sa riche collection de dessins et de peintures. Or, sur les 1400 œuvres, un certain nombre auraient été spoliées ou acquises à des prix dérisoires par son père, Hildebrand Gurlitt, marchand d'art proche d'Hitler. Après avoir longuement hésité à accepter ce « cadeau empoisonné », le *Kunstmuseum* consent au legs, à condition que seules les œuvres acquises licitement franchissent ses portes[51]. Depuis, une *task force* effectue en Allemagne une recherche de provenance sur chacune des œuvres et plusieurs ont été restituées à leurs ayants droit[52]. Dès novembre 2017, le *Kunstmuseum* de Berne et la *Bundeskunsthalle* de Bonn organisent conjointement deux expositions

---

[50] Pascale Zimmermann, Le MAH milite contre le trafic illicite en exposant des objets confisqués, *in* Tribuna de Genève, 14.03.2017 (en ligne : https://www.tdg.ch/culture/trafic-illicite-mah-expose-objets-art-confisques/story/15868016) (10.05.2018). Pour une approche plus critique, voir Étienne Dumont, Le MAH montre neuf objets archéologiques issus du Port franc, *in* Bilan, 16.03.2017 (en ligne : http://www.bilan.ch/etienne-dumont/courants-dart/genevele-mah-montre-neuf-objets-archeologiques-issus-port-franc) (10.05.2018).

[51] Kunst Frédéric Burnand, « Collection Gurlitt : un sac de nœuds pour la Suisse », *in* Swissinfo, 08.05.2014 (en ligne : https://www.swissinfo.ch/fre/art-spoli%C3%A9_collection-gurlitt--un-sac-de-n%C5%93uds-pour-la-suisse/38540830) (10.05.2018).

[52] Petra Krimphove, « La collection Gurlitt sous la loupe des détectives », *in* Swissinfo, 28.11.2014 (en ligne : https://www.swissinfo.ch/fre/art-spoli%C3%A9-par-les-nazis_la-collection-gurlitt-sous-la-loupe-des-d%C3%A9tectives/41139240). (10.05.2018).

de la Collection Gurlitt autour de la thématique de l'art dégénéré et des spoliations nazies[53].

Les cas du Musée d'art et d'histoire et celui du *Kunstmuseum* de Berne démontrent le poids de l'éthique dans la décision des musées d'exposer – ou non – certaines œuvres. Car outre le droit, les musées se doivent de respecter une déontologie sans faille dans le choix des objets qu'ils présentent, dont les standards sont codifiés dans le Code de déontologie de l'ICOM[54].

Conclusion

L'accessibilité des collections privées au public est une bonne chose qui doit être encouragée. Le droit nous donne plusieurs outils permettant d'y parvenir. C'est d'ailleurs, au vu de l'intérêt public évident qui justifie une telle accessibilité, l'affaire de tous, qu'il s'agisse de la population au sens large, du législateur, des autorités publiques et des musées, qui sont à la fois le lieu d'exposition par définition et l'interlocuteur privilégié des collectionneurs.

Les musées, soutenus en cela par les collectivités publiques, se doivent d'avoir une attitude proactive et transparente envers les collectionneurs privés. Car finalement ils dépendent d'eux. Comme le dit Guillaume Cerutti, Président de Christie's pour l'Europe et le Moyen-Orient « Plus que jamais, l'avenir des collections publiques passe par le développement des collections privées. »[55]

Mais cette interaction, quelque positive et enrichissante qu'elle soit, doit se faire dans la légalité et le respect de la déontologie, en particulier d'agissant de biens issus du trafic illicite ou de spoliations.

---

[53] Kunstmuseum Bern, Collection Gurlitt, état des lieux « L'art dégénéré » – confisqué et vendu » (en ligne : https://www.kunstmuseumbern.ch/fr/voir/aujourdhui/688-collection-gurlitt-etat-des-lieux-120.html) (10.05.2018) ; Kunstmuseum Bern, Collection Gurlitt, état des lieux 2e partie. « Les spoliations nazies et leurs conséquences » (en ligne : https://www.kunstmuseumbern.ch/fr/see/today/738-gurlitt-status-report-120.html) (10.05.2018).

[54] ICOM, Code de déontologie, 08.10.2004 (en ligne : http://icom.museum/la-vision/code-de-deontologie//L/2/). (10.05.2018).

[55]Martine Robert, « Art : les collections publiques toujours plus dépendantes du privé » *in* *Les Échos*, 28.10.2016 (en ligne : https://www.lesechos.fr/28/10/2016/LesEchos/22308-024-ECH_art-les-collections-publiques-toujours-plus-dependantes-du-prive.htm) (10.05.2018).

Interactions entre collections privées et secteur privé Approche de droit français

Géraldine GOFFAUX CALLEBAUT
Professeur à l'Université d'Orléans
Membre du Centre de recherche juridique Pothier (EA 1212)

Les fondations présentant au public des collections privées sont de plus en plus nombreuses, participant ainsi à un mouvement de privatisation de la culture, sous l'influence du monde anglo-saxon. À Paris, la Fondation Cartier pour l'art contemporain présente notamment les collections de la société ; la Fondation Louis Vuitton permet d'exposer les collections du groupe dirigé par Bernard Arnaud et d'autres collectionneurs privés ; François Pinault envisage d'installer une partie de ses collections à la Bourse du commerce et Laurent Dumas, président d'Emerige, expose ses collections dans un hôtel particulier du 16e arrondissement, avant de pouvoir le faire sur l'Ile Seguin[1] (où François Pinault avait envisagé un temps de se poser avant de partir à Venise). En province, Hélène et Edouard Leclerc ont ouvert son fonds de dotation à Landernau et Bernard Magrez, un propriétaire de vignobles, a créé un fonds de dotation à Bordeaux pour exposer sa collection. Si le phénomène présente une certaine actualité, il n'est pourtant pas nouveau. Dès 1967, Renault a commencé à constituer sa collection, avec pour démarche de collaborer avec les artistes de l'époque en leur fournissant des matériaux ou un soutien logistique. Ainsi, le constructeur a-t-il fourni des pièces automobiles pour les compressions de César, des matériaux innovants à Dubuffet pour la création de l'Hourloupe ou des pièces détachées pour les mobiles de Tinguely. De façon générale, les entreprises détiennent deux grands types de collections : des collections patrimoniales, reposant sur l'histoire de la marque, et des collections artistiques. À cet égard, la collection d'art contemporain de la Société générale est emblématique des liens entre secteur privé et collections privées[2].

---

[1] https://www.lesechos.fr/30/01/2017/lesechos.fr/0211748468117_le-projet-culturel-sur-l-ile-seguin-enfin-devoile.htm [dernière visite le 6 déc. 2017]
[2] http://www.collectionsocietegenerale.com/fr/

Au-delà de ces exemples, la question des interactions des collections privées avec le secteur privé n'appelle pas de réponse évidente. On peut d'abord noter que si le Code du patrimoine[3] a pu définir ce qu'est une collection comme « un ensemble d'objets, d'œuvres et de documents dont les différents éléments ne peuvent être dissociés sans porter atteinte à sa cohérence et dont la valeur est supérieure à la somme des valeurs individuelles des éléments qui le composent », sachant que « la valeur et la cohérence de la collection s'apprécient en fonction de son intérêt pour l'histoire ou pour l'histoire de l'art, des civilisations, des sciences et des techniques », rien n'est précisé quant aux éventuelles spécificités des collections privées. À cet égard, on peut ajouter que le Code civil ne définit pas plus ces collections privées. Quant au secteur privé, il est défini comme la partie de l'économie où l'État n'intervient pas ou peu. On y retrouve les entreprises privées, les banques à capitaux privés, l'économie sociale et solidaire et les organisations non gouvernementales.

Une étude économique menée par une collègue de l'Université de Montpellier et financée par Axa Art[4], *Collections et entreprises : liaisons interdites ou mariage de raison ?*, dresse un tableau particulièrement intéressant par rapport au secteur privé. Ainsi, parmi les chiffres clés, on peut relever que les collections d'entreprises appartiennent pour 48,5% à des PME, 26,5% à des entreprises de taille intermédiaire, 19,1% à des grandes sociétés et 5,9% à des micro-entreprises. S'agissant des secteurs d'activité, 22% des collections d'entreprises sont détenues par des banques, 16% sont dans le secteur immobilier et 10% dans le secteur du luxe. De façon générale, seule une petite majorité des entreprises bénéficient des avantages fiscaux, alors qu'on pourrait penser qu'une des principales motivations est d'ordre fiscal. S'agissant de la période de création, 60% de ces collections ont été créées après 2000, plus de 20% après 2010. Enfin, s'agissant de la propriété, 25% appartiennent au chef d'entreprise et 10% sont constituées en fondations ou en fonds de dotation, ce qui signifie que dans 65% des cas, l'entreprise appartient en propre à la société.
Que les collections appartiennent au chef d'entreprise ou à la société, le

---

[3] Anc. art. R. 113-1 C. patr., issu du décr. n° 93-124 du 29 janv. 1993, art. 1er, al. 2.
[4] N. Moureau, *Collections et entreprises : liaisons interdites ou mariage de raison ?*, 2016, en ligne : https://axa-art.cdn.axa-contento-118412.eu/axa-art%2F8a5e6636-2efc-415e-bc0c-be502303931c_rapport+complet+-+collections+d%27entreprise.pdf

risque tient à ce que ces collections constituent des actifs qui peuvent répondre de toutes les dettes du propriétaire, ce qui met potentiellement en danger la collection en cas de difficultés financières. La pérennité de la collection peut alors être en cause. En outre, en cas de changement de direction de la personne morale ou en cas de décès de la personne physique, le risque d'aliénation ou de dispersion de la collection est important.

Par ailleurs, dans le cadre d'une société, l'acquisition d'une collection pose la question de la conformité à l'objet social des achats d'œuvres d'art ou d'objets de collection. Les risques pour le dirigeant d'entreprise sont d'ordre civil puisque sa responsabilité pourra être mise en œuvre par les associés par une action sociale exercée *ut singuli* et il pourra être révoqué pour juste motif[5]. Par ailleurs, dans le cadre d'une société à responsabilité limitée ou d'une société par actions, le risque peut être pénal puisque ces acquisitions peuvent être qualifiées d'abus de biens sociaux[6] pour les dirigeants qui font, de mauvaise foi, des biens ou du crédit de la société, un usage qu'ils savent contraire à l'intérêt de celle-ci, à des fins personnelles ou pour favoriser une autre société ou entreprise dans laquelle ils sont intéressés directement ou indirectement. Ceci étant, ce risque d'abus de biens sociaux se comprend bien lorsque la « danseuse du président » ne profite qu'à ce dernier. Mais aujourd'hui, le risque semble réduit dans la mesure où les collections d'entreprises sont vues comme des outils de communication, de lien social et surtout des sources d'avantages fiscaux. En effet, le Code général des impôts permet de déduire fiscalement l'acquisition dans certaines limites, notamment celle de l'exposition publique de la collection[7], validant ainsi – en quelque sorte – ce type d'acte.

Se pose alors la question de l'intérêt de fonder une fondation ou un fonds de dotation pour abriter la collection. Sans doute, l'intérêt de constituer une structure tient d'abord à la possibilité de donner une unité formelle à la collection. Il tient ensuite à la possibilité de renforcer le

[5] Notamment art. L. 223-25 C. com. (SARL), art. L. 225-55 C. com. (SA monistes).
[6] Art. L. 241-3, 4° (SARL) et L. 242-6, 3° (SA) du Code de commerce. Les peines sont de 5 ans d'emprisonnement et 375 000 euros d'amende.
[7] Déduction de l'acquisition dans la limite de 5 pour mille, sur une durée de 5 années. Art. 238 bis AB du CGI. *Cf. infra.*

degré d'inaliénabilité de la collection privée par le rattachement de la structure à l'intérêt général (à développer). Enfin, la fondation ou le fonds de dotation permettent, dans une moindre mesure de financer la conservation et le développement de la collection.

Au-delà de cet intérêt, deux questions doivent être envisagées. En premier lieu, si l'on s'intéresse aux 10% de collections qui sont organisées sous couvert d'une fondation ou d'un fonds de dotation, il faut s'intéresser aux types de structures utilisées. En second lieu, puisque 65% des collections ne sont pas détenus par la société, cela amène à se demander comment adapter le droit français aux spécificités de l'objet de la détention de ces collections.

I. La variété des structures utilisées pour accueillir les collections

La variété des structures utilisées s'explique notamment par le développement de l'offre législative française. Dans un premier temps, le choix s'est porté sur les fondations puis, dans un second temps, plus récent, le choix des collectionneurs tend plutôt vers les fonds de dotation.

A. Le choix premier des fondations

Les collections privées sont, en pratique, affectées à tous les types de fondations au sens classique du terme, selon les volontés particulières de l'affectataire. Ainsi, on trouve des fondations d'entreprise, mais aussi des fondations abritées et des fondations reconnues d'utilité publique.

Les fondations d'entreprise ont été créées en France par la loi du 4 juillet 1990[8]. Dans le domaine des arts et de la culture, on en recense 112 sur le site du Centre français des fonds et fondations[9], parmi lesquelles la Fondation Ricard pour l'art contemporain, la Fondation

---

[8] Loi n° 90-559 du 4 juill. 1990 créant les fondations d'entreprise et modifiant les dispositions de la loi n° 87-571 du 23 juill. 1987 sur le développement du mécénat, relatives aux fondations.

[9] V. l'annuaire du Centre français des fonds et fondations, en ligne : https://www.centre-francais-fondations.org/cercles-themes/les-domaines-dengagement/culture/annuaire/annuaire-des-fondations-culturelles [dernière visite 15 mai 2018]

Louis Vuitton ou la Fondation Carmignac, mais ces 112 fondations d'entreprise ne sont pas toutes propriétaires d'une collection. De façon générale, la fondation d'entreprise est une personne morale privée à but non lucratif créée soit par des sociétés civiles ou commerciales, soit par des établissements publics industriels et commerciaux, soit par des coopératives ou des mutuelles. Comme toutes les fondations, les fondations d'entreprise ont pour objet la réalisation d'une œuvre d'intérêt général. La différence réside dans le fait qu'elles bénéficient d'un régime juridique plus souple que les fondations reconnues d'utilité publique, et ce à plusieurs égards. Toutefois, les fondations d'entreprise ont nécessairement une durée de vie limitée dans la mesure où elles servent des actions temporaires de mécénat. La durée initiale ne peut être inférieure à 5 ans et peut être prorogée pour au moins 3 ans. Il s'agissait par cette création, de répondre à certaines critiques faites au droit des fondations reconnues d'utilité publique mais également à la pratique. Au moment de l'adoption de la loi du 23 juillet 1987[10], le ministre de l'Intérieur, Charles Pasqua, avait d'ailleurs stigmatisé des structures dont l'appellation de fondation n'avait d'autre vocation que publicitaire, pour relever que « les fausses fondations préjudicient à l'intérêt général en provoquant, dans l'esprit du public, des méprises d'autant plus graves qu'elles se sont propagées, consciemment ou non, par la presse et la TV : en abusant des personnes trop crédules ou très mal informées, elles nuisent à la cause que défendent les fondations authentiques ». Toutefois, la loi du 4 juillet 1990 précitée, qui a prévu un régime propre aux fondations d'entreprise, n'a pas pour autant écarté la possibilité pour les entreprises de créer une fondation reconnue d'utilité publique ou une fondation sous égide, dépourvue de la personnalité morale et abritée par une autre fondation comme la Fondation de France.

La loi du 4 juillet 1990 créant les fondations d'entreprise a également créé les fondations abritées. Il s'agit de fondations dépourvues de personnalité juridique propre qui sont accueillies au sein de fondations reconnues d'utilité publique. Elles sont créées par l'affectation irrévocable de biens, droits ou ressources à une fondation reconnue d'utilité publique dont les statuts ont été approuvés à cette fin. C'est la fondation mère qui décide ou non d'accueillir la fondation abritée, dont elle assurera la gestion des biens. Parmi les pionniers figure la

[10] Loi n° 87-571 du 23 juill. 1987 sur le développement du mécénat.

Fondation Cartier pour l'Art contemporain qui détient une grande collection d'œuvres et d'objets de collection.

Enfin, la fondation reconnue d'utilité publique, forme historique de la fondation, reste la forme la plus prestigieuse. Toutefois, elle exige une dotation initiale très importante pour lui assurer des revenus suffisants et lui permettre de remplir durablement son objet, d'avoir une activité suffisamment importante et un rayonnement justifiant la reconnaissance d'utilité publique. La création d'une fondation n'est possible que si son indépendance et sa solidité financière sont assurées. Parmi ces fondations, on peut citer la Fondation Antoine de Galberg.

Au regard des nombreuses critiques faites au droit français, relatives à la rigidité, la lourdeur et la complexité de constitution des fondations, le législateur a créé le fonds de dotation qui a su attirer des collections privées.

B. Le choix récent des fonds de dotation

Les fonds de dotation[11] ont été créés en droit français par la loi du 4 août 2008 de modernisation de l'économie[12] pour favoriser le développement d'initiatives d'intérêt général, sur le modèle des *endowment funds* américains. Aux termes de cette loi, « le fonds de dotation est une personne morale de droit privé à but non lucratif qui reçoit et gère, en les capitalisant, des biens et droits de toute nature qui lui sont apportés à titre gratuit et irrévocable et utilise les revenus de la capitalisation en vue de la réalisation d'une œuvre ou d'une mission d'intérêt général ou les redistribue pour assister une personne morale à but non lucratif dans l'accomplissement de ses œuvres et de ses missions d'intérêt général ». Ainsi, cette structure combine les avantages de l'association loi de 1901 et de la fondation, sans leurs inconvénients. Doté de la personnalité juridique, le fonds de dotation est constitué d'une allocation irrévocable de biens pour la réalisation d'une mission ou d'une œuvre d'intérêt général. Il est créé par simple déclaration et dépôt des statuts à la préfecture. Il collecte des

[11] Y. Vincent, « Le fonds de dotation, ou comment concilier philanthropie et optimisation fiscale : un outil à (re)découvrir », *Droit des sociétés* n° 1, janv. 2014, étude 1.
[12] Art. 140 de la loi n° 2008-776 du 4 août 2008 de modernisation de l'économie.

fonds d'origine privée, qu'il peut soit constituer en dotation dont il utilise les fruits, soit consommer pour accomplir sa mission. Il peut mener lui-même cette mission, ou financer un autre organisme d'intérêt général pour son accomplissement. Le fonds de dotation bénéficie du régime fiscal du mécénat. La seule contrainte a été posée par la loi sur l'économie sociale et solidaire du 31 juillet 2014 et un décret du 22 janvier 2015, qui a posé le principe d'un montant minimal de la dotation fixé à 15.000 euros[13]. Le même décret a permis la mise en place d'un clausier qui « n'a aucune valeur normative mais a seulement pour objet d'éclairer les créateurs de fonds de dotation sur les bonnes pratiques en matière de rédaction des statuts : la liberté des créateurs de fonds dans la rédaction des statuts demeure »[14].

Les fonds de dotation connaissent un grand succès. Près de 2.500 fonds de dotation ont été créés à ce jour[15]. La proportion des fonds dans le secteur « action artistique et culturelle », secteur le plus important, est de 22,4%[16].

Dans ce contexte, les fonds de dotation apparaissent comme un cadre intéressant pour accueillir les collections privées. Parmi les collections importantes, on peut citer le fonds de dotation de Bernard Magrez à Bordeaux, celui de Laurent Dumas (Emerige) à Paris, ou celui d'Hélène et Édouard Leclerc à Landernau. Par ailleurs, le fonds de dotation est également un outil pour des fondations étrangères installées en France. Ainsi, certaines fondations de droit suisse gérant des collections ont créé en France des fonds de dotation qui permettent de récolter des fonds ou des œuvres auprès de mécènes et de leur permettre de profiter des déductions fiscales liées au mécénat d'entreprise ou de particuliers.

Ainsi, le droit français offre différents outils aux collectionneurs, personnes physiques ou personnes morales, pour assurer la pérennité de leurs collections, de sorte que le chiffre de 10% pour les collections organisées sous ces formes à but non lucratif peut étonner. En outre, il

---

[13] Décret n° 2015-49 du 22 janv. 2015 relatif aux fonds de dotation. V. aussi F. Perrotin, « Encadrement des fonds de dotations », LPA 26 janv. 2015, n° 18, p. 4.
[14] http://www.economie.gouv.fr/daj/fonds-dotation
[15] Au 31 déc. 2017, le site du Centre français des fondations et des fonds de dotation en recense précisément 2.494.
[16] http://www.economie.gouv.fr/files/files/directions_services/daj/fondsdedotation/pdf/categorie_fds_dotation.pdf [dernière visite 15 mai 2018]

est possible de combiner ces modèles et de faire certains montages efficaces. Enfin, la constitution d'une structure permet le financement par le mécénat, assurant ainsi la pérennité de la collection. Si la diversité des outils ne permet pas de comprendre ce chiffre, peut-être faut-il se demander si les règles gouvernant ces fondations sont adaptées aux spécificités des collections.

II. L'adaptation des règles aux spécificités des collections

Une explication au faible recours aux fondations et fonds de dotation par les collectionneurs, personnes physiques ou personnes morales, peut sans doute être trouvée dans l'inadaptation des règles les gouvernant aux besoins de ces collectionneurs. Un premier risque, commun à toutes les formes d'accueil de la collection, est le risque de dispersion de la collection. Sauf clause d'inaliénabilité, la collection pourra être vendue, en tout ou en partie par son propriétaire, qu'il s'agisse d'une personne physique, d'une société ou d'une fondation. Dans cette dernière structure, on pourra toutefois envisager d'intégrer la collection dans l'objet statutaire pour rendre plus délicate la dispersion. En revanche, deux autres difficultés sont plus spécifiques aux fondations et aux fonds de dotation. D'une part, le rattachement requis à l'intérêt général est parfois délicat. D'autre part, les règles de gouvernance ne permettent pas de pérenniser aisément le lien entre la collection et le collectionneur.

A. L'adaptation de l'objet à l'intérêt général

Quelle que soit la structure choisie, le but d'une fondation doit correspondre à la réalisation d'une œuvre d'intérêt général sans but lucratif[17]. L'intérêt général requis signifie que la fondation peut avoir un intérêt philanthropique, éducatif, scientifique, social, familial ou culturel, sans que cette liste soit exhaustive, et qu'elle ne doit pas concerner les intérêts particuliers ou personnels des fondateurs. Est ainsi une œuvre d'intérêt général ce qui présente notamment « un caractère [...] culturel ou concourant à la mise en valeur du patrimoine artistique, à la défense de l'environnement naturel ou à la diffusion de la culture, de la langue »[18]. Cette exigence de conformité à l'intérêt

[17] Art. 18 de la loi n° 87-751 du 23 juill. 1987 sur le développement du mécénat.
[18] Art. 200 et 238 bis du CGI.

général peut être délicate à mettre en œuvre dans le secteur privé. Ainsi, l'objet de la structure créée par une société pour abriter sa collection doit se conformer à l'intérêt général.

Dans le cadre de la fondation reconnue d'utilité publique, le contrôle se fait *a priori*. À cet égard, le Conseil d'État a pu juger que « la conservation et la diffusion au public d'un patrimoine artistique » constituent un objet conforme à l'intérêt général[19].
S'agissant des fonds de dotation, le clausier[20] précise que « l'objet du fonds doit être rédigé avec précision, afin que sa mission d'intérêt général, au sens des dispositions fiscales relatives au mécénat (articles 200 et 238 bis du code général des impôts), s'en déduise clairement. Recopier uniquement les termes de l'article 140 de la loi de modernisation de l'économie ne renseigne pas sur l'objet du fonds »[21]. Ainsi, si le fonds est opérateur, son « activité doit être non lucrative, sa gestion désintéressée, et le fonds ne doit pas fonctionner au profit d'un cercle restreint de personnes ; le fonds doit exercer directement des actions de nature philanthropique, éducative, scientifique, sociale, humanitaire, sportive, familiale, culturelle ou qui concourent à la mise en valeur du patrimoine artistique, à la défense de l'environnement naturel ou à la diffusion de la culture, de la langue et des connaissances scientifiques françaises »[22]. S'il est redistributeur, « sa gestion doit être désintéressée et il contribue financièrement à une activité d'intérêt général menée par un autre organisme, qui doit être lui-même éligible au régime fiscal du mécénat »[23].

Dès lors, cette exigence d'intérêt général exclut que la fondation soit constituée dans le seul intérêt du ou des fondateurs ou de leur famille[24]. Au-delà, il semble que la fondation ou le fonds affectataire d'une collection doive exposer celle-ci au public. À cet égard, un parallèle peut être fait avec certaines déductions fiscales prévues pour la constitution des collections. En effet, il a été récemment proposé, dans

---

[19] CE 27-02-2006, n° 264447, Arm ; Lebon, p. 91.
[20] *Cf. supra*, https://www.economie.gouv.fr/files/files/directions_services/daj/fondsdedotation/clausier/clausier-fds-dotation.pdf
[21] Référence.
[22] Art. 2 du clausier, p. 5.
[23] *Ibidem*.
[24] Sur ce point, v. notamment B. Clavagnier, « L'intérêt général dans tous ses états », JurisAssociations 2016, n° 546, p. 47.

le cadre d'un rapport parlementaire sur le marché de l'art[25], de clarifier la question de la présentation des collections au public. En effet, l'article 238 bis AB du Code général des impôts permet aux entreprises qui font l'acquisition d'œuvres originales d'artistes vivants de déduire le prix d'acquisition du résultat de l'entreprise. Cette déduction est soumise à une double condition : la limite de cinq pour mille du chiffre d'affaire et l'accessibilité au public. À cet égard, le rapport note la différence d'interprétation qui apparaît entre les travaux parlementaires de la loi n° 2003-709 du 1er août 2003 relative au mécénat, qui envisageait cette accessibilité de façon large[26], et la doctrine de l'administration fiscale qui exige une accessibilité à un public qui dépasse nécessairement les salariés et les clients de l'entreprise[27]. Le rapport propose ainsi de revenir à une lecture plus souple permettant de sécuriser les opérations d'acquisition des collections des entreprises, rejoignant ainsi un autre rapport sur la notion de cercle restreint dans le cadre de la qualification de l'intérêt général qui préconisait aussi une redéfinition de ce cercle[28]. Une telle redéfinition pourrait encourager l'affectation de collections d'entreprise à des fondations et des fonds de dotation.

B. L'adaptation de la gouvernance

L'adaptation de la gouvernance est une autre question importante. En effet, sans tomber dans le cliché de la « danseuse du président », il est évident qu'un lien affectif existe entre le collectionneur et sa collection. Dès lors, même si l'affectation de la dotation d'une fondation ou d'un fonds de dotation est irrévocable et pose un écran juridique entre le fondateur et la structure sans but lucratif, il est compréhensible que ce fondateur souhaite garder sinon le contrôle, au moins la surveillance de la collection qu'il apporte. Dès lors, comment concilier ce lien entre

---

[25] Rapport d'information n° 4234 présenté à l'assemblée nationale le 16 novembre 2016 par la commission des affaires culturelles et de l'éducation *en conclusion des travaux de la mission d'information relative au* marché de l'art, et présenté par Stéphane Travert.

[26] F. Perrotin, « Des propositions pour doper le marché de l'art », LPA 10 févr. 2017, n° 30, p. 5.

[27] BOI-BIC-CHG-70-10-20151202.

[28] Y. Blein, *Qualification d'intérêt général des organismes recevant des dons – Notion de cercle restreint*, Rapport mars 2016 (publié en juill. 2016).

collectionneur et collection et la nécessaire indépendance des dirigeants, exigée pour assurer le but d'intérêt général ?

S'agissant de la fondation reconnue d'utilité publique, forme historique de ces structures, les statuts types approuvés par le Conseil d'État le 13 mai 2012, révisés en août 2017, posent des lignes directrices quant à sa gouvernance[29]. D'abord, le conseil d'administration comporte au moins les trois premiers collèges énumérés dans la liste, à savoir un collège de fondateurs, un collège de membres de droit, un collège de personnalités qualifiées, ainsi que, le cas échéant un collège de salariés et/ou un collège d'"amis" de la fondation. En outre, il est précisé que « en application du principe d'indépendance des fondations vis-à-vis des fondateurs, l'effectif du collège des fondateurs doit être au plus égal à celui du collège des membres de droit et ne doit donc pas dépasser le tiers du total des sièges du conseil d'administration ». En outre, « le collège des membres de droit représente l'intérêt général : il doit donc disposer d'au moins un tiers du total des sièges ». Ainsi, pour la section de l'intérieur du Conseil d'État, l'indépendance d'une fondation par rapport à ses fondateurs n'est pas assurée lorsque la présidence ne résulte pas d'une élection par le conseil d'administration mais est dévolue de droit à l'un de ses fondateurs et lorsque le collège des fondateurs peut seul proposer les personnalités susceptibles d'être cooptées dans le collège des membres associés[30]. Toutefois, il a pu être admis que le président soit de droit, sa vie durant, le fondateur (Fondation Royaumont) puis son conjoint (pour la Fondation Maeght et la Fondation Vasarely)[31].

S'agissant des fondations d'entreprise, la composition du conseil est plus souple puisqu'il ne comprend pas de droit des représentants des pouvoirs publics. Le conseil doit être composé des fondateurs et de leurs représentants, des représentants du personnel des entreprises et des personnalités qualifiées dans les domaines d'intervention de la fondation. La disparition de la première catégorie permet de garder un plus grand contrôle que dans les FRUP, toutefois, il faut prendre garde au risque de requalification en filiale. En effet, à défaut d'indépendance entre la fondation et l'entreprise, une relation de contrôle pourrait être

[29] https://www.service-public.fr/associations/vosdroits/R31090

[30] Avis CE sect. intérieur, Rapport public 2008, EDCE n° 59, p. 75.

[31] Exemples cités dans le Mémento pratique Francis Lefebvre, Associations – Fondations – Congrégations – Fonds de dotation, 2014, n° 78015.

établie au sens de l'article L. 233-3 du Code de commerce pour les sociétés commerciales, ce qui pourrait non seulement constituer un motif de retrait de l'autorisation préfectorale, mais également emporter une requalification en filiale commerciale si la fondation investissait la sphère commerciale en plus de l'absence d'autonomie à l'égard de ses fondateurs.

Enfin, pour les fonds de dotation, il faut noter que le clausier aborde la gouvernance en rappelant l'esprit de la loi qui « laisse aux créateurs de fonds une grande liberté d'organisation du conseil d'administration et impose seulement qu'il soit composé d'au minimum trois membres ». En outre, il indique que « la présence d'un administrateur de l'organisme créateur du fonds de dotation au sein du conseil d'administration du fonds n'est pas de nature à remettre en cause le caractère désintéressé de la gestion du fonds. En effet, rien n'interdit qu'il y ait identité de dirigeant avec l'organisme adossé dans le statut juridique et fiscal d'un fonds de dotation, dès lors que celui-ci a pour objet de redistribuer ses revenus pour assister un organisme d'intérêt général »[32]. Toutefois, il faut noter que les fonds de dotation reprennent parfois l'équilibre de la composition du conseil des FRUP en prévoyant la représentation de trois collèges : le collège des fondateurs, le collège des mécènes et le collège des personnalités qualifiées.

Ainsi, l'adaptation de la gouvernance est une question de dosage afin de trouver un équilibre entre contrôle de la collection et indépendance de la structure d'accueil de la collection. Recherche de l'équilibre qui va en faveur du fonds de dotation.

En conclusion, les structures offertes aux entreprises pour abriter les collections du secteur privé ne permettent pas d'assurer la pérennité des collections. Toutefois, en fonction des choix opérés par les collectionneurs, la collection peut avoir une vie au-delà de celle de son propriétaire personne physique ou personne morale. Ainsi, le risque de dispersion n'est pas totalement endigué mais le droit peut apporter sa pierre à l'édifice.

---

[32] Clausier préc., p. 9.

L'enrichissement des collections publiques avec transfert de propriété : les dons et legs des collectionneurs

Apolline SANS
Juriste en droit du patrimoine culturel
Diplômée du Master Marché de l'art de l'École du Louvre

Introduction

Selon un « adage muséal » assez connu « un musée qui n'acquiert pas est un musée qui meurt ». C'est par cette phrase que j'aimerais introduire mon propos relatif à l'enrichissement des collections publiques grâce aux dons et legs de collections privées. Il est vrai que la force de nos collections publiques françaises réside dans leur perpétuel renouvellement et accroissement, ce depuis l'émergence des musées et jusqu'à nos jours.
Usant tantôt de la force, comme les saisies révolutionnaires, de la contrainte, par les arrêts en douanes, ou de prérogatives régaliennes, comme le droit de préemption, les méthodes d'acquisition des musées sont multiples. Cependant, il en est une dont l'importance, du fait peut-être de sa multiplicité, reste trop souvent mise de côté : les libéralités, dons et legs des collectionneurs privés.
La question du financement pour l'acquisition des œuvres d'art a toujours été un enjeu majeur pour les musées. La Réunion des Musées Nationaux[1], créée en 1896, a notamment eu pour rôle celui de caisse nationale des musées, permettant, entre autres, de rendre le mécanisme d'acquisition indépendant de la volonté des gouvernements. Elle a également permis d'abolir la règle de comptabilité publique qui obligeait les musées, en cas de reliquat des crédits d'acquisition, à reverser la somme à l'État, « empêchant toute constitution de fonds de réserves permettant l'achat d'œuvres exceptionnelles, et encourageant l'achat d'objets de second ordre, de peur de perdre le bénéfice de ces

[1] Pour plus d'informations sur l'histoire de la Réunion des Musées Nationaux, voir Agnès Callu, *La Réunion des musées nationaux (1870-1940) : genèse et fonctionnement*, Thèse de l'École des Chartes, 1994.

crédits »[2]. Cependant, même avec cette nouvelle entité juridique, les moyens financiers ne furent jamais assez abondants pour prétendre à l'acquisition de l'ensemble des œuvres dignes des musées nationaux. Les achats ne sont donc pas suffisants pour enrichir de manière conséquente les musées. Partant, il est intéressant de se pencher sur les mécanismes juridiques ayant permis d'enrichir les collections sans entamer, en principe, les crédits : les dons et legs, recevant la qualification juridique de libéralités.

Ces dernières sont consenties par des acteurs souvent mis de côté dans la sphère publique alors qu'ils jouent, encore aujourd'hui, un rôle primordial dans l'enrichissement des collections publiques : les « collectionneurs donateurs »[3].

L'on peut essayer de donner une définition simplifiée du « collectionneur ». Il ne s'agit pas uniquement de la personne qui acquiert des œuvres d'art, mais de la personne qui acquiert une pluralité d'œuvres afin de former un ensemble cohérent, et qui cherche à perfectionner sa collection en vendant certaines de ses œuvres pour en acquérir de plus belles. La collection d'œuvres d'art est donc le résultat de ce hobby et consiste en un ensemble cohérent rassemblé en fonction du goût du collectionneur. Les collections privées s'opposent aux collections publiques en ce qu'elles appartiennent à une personne privée qui possède donc, dans une certaine mesure, les prérogatives de la propriété privée, à savoir l'usus, le fructus et l'abusus. Par ailleurs, il n'y a pas d'obligation de présentation au public, contrairement aux collections publiques. Enfin, elles peuvent être aliénées et ne bénéficient pas, en principe, de l'imprescriptibilité attachée aux collections publiques[4].

Le collectionneur devient « collectionneur donateur » lorsqu'il décide de faire cadeau de tout ou partie de sa collection à l'État ou à une collectivité territoriale, souvent au profit d'un musée déterminé. Cette décision entraîne un transfert de propriété au bénéfice de la personne publique, intégrant ces œuvres dans les collections publiques leur

---

[2] Agnès Callu, *ibid.*

[3] Cité *in* Véronique Long, *Mécènes des deux mondes, les collectionneurs donateurs du Louvre et de l'Art Institute de Chicago, 1879-1940*, Presses universitaires de Rennes, 2007.

[4] Sauf pour les collections privées relevant de l'appellation « Musée de France », qui, sont imprescriptibles en vertu de l'article L451-3 du Code du patrimoine, et qui voient leur cession encadrée dans certaines circonstances en vertu de l'article L451-10 du Code du patrimoine.

faisant perdre par conséquent leur statut de collection privée.
Cette relation entre la propriété privée et le domaine public, bien que parfois occultée, demeure une réalité historique indéniable. Il convient dès lors de mettre en lumière ce lien en se penchant sur l'enrichissement des collections publiques d'œuvres d'art par les dons et legs des collectionneurs privés.
Cette étude se concentrera principalement sur les libéralités réalisées au profit des musées nationaux. Cependant, il est important de souligner que de nombreux musées territoriaux ont bénéficié de libéralités importantes qui ont même parfois été à l'origine de la constitution du musée local. Par ailleurs, si l'on analysera uniquement les libéralités faites en nature, il est également nécessaire de rappeler que nombre de libéralités en numéraire ont permis d'étoffer les budgets des acquisitions et partant d'enrichir de manière indirecte les collections publiques.
Il sera donc d'abord nécessaire de rappeler le contexte historique et juridique de la pratique des dons et legs (**I**), avant d'essayer d'analyser la signification de ces libéralités et leurs limites (**II**), puis d'étudier le rôle imparti aux musées dans l'acceptation des collections privées au sein de leurs collections (**III**).

I. Remise en contexte historique et juridique de la pratique des libéralités

La figure du « collectionneur donateur » est, en France, historiquement marquée par une forte proportion masculine, issue d'un milieu social très favorisé, des hommes souvent veufs ou célibataires[5].
L'histoire des « collectionneurs donateurs » doit être reliée à celle de l'histoire du droit des libéralités[6]. De manière très succincte, l'on peut rappeler que l'essor des dons et legs serait daté de la deuxième moitié

[5] Observations faites par Véronique Long, *op. cit.*, p. 167 ; ce portrait pourrait s'expliquer en partie par le système juridique français qui protège largement le patrimoine familial. Un père de famille collectionneur ne pourrait, par exemple, léguer l'ensemble des œuvres de sa collection sans risquer d'entamer la quotité disponible bénéficiant à ses ayants droit.

[6] Pour cette partie, nous avons pu lire la thèse de Mélina Girardin, *Les legs et donations d'artistes et de leurs héritiers aux collections publiques,* présentée dans le cadre de sa thèse, 2003, voir aussi Jean-Luc Marais, *Histoire du don en France 1800 – 1939,* Presses universitaire de Rennes, 1999.

du XIXe siècle. En effet, après que l'État a cherché à contrôler de manière étroite l'emploi des dons et legs, dans un contexte de rivalité avec l'Église, les politiques du Second Empire puis de la Troisième République favorisent largement le recours aux libéralités privées. Si dans un premier temps, notamment sous le Second Empire, ces biens sont majoritairement orientés vers les plus nécessiteux, la destination de ces ressources se diversifie peu à peu à partir de la seconde moitié du XIXe siècle. Les sociétés savantes, organismes privés, mais également les écoles, les universités, organismes publics, et pour ce qui nous concerne les musées, en bénéficient peu à peu. Ces libéralités pouvaient être faites sous forme numéraire ou en nature. En effet à cette époque, un intérêt grandissant pour le musée se dessine et celui-ci est peu à peu adopté comme un instrument éducatif, didactique qui n'est plus seulement réservé aux artistes mais ouvert également aux amateurs éclairés.

Ces gestes de générosité peuvent prendre deux formes dont il est nécessaire de rappeler les différences d'un point de vue juridique.

Les dons comme les legs ont pour finalité de transmettre la propriété d'un bien au profit d'une autre personne, physique ou morale, et ce à titre gratuit ; ils sont regroupés sous l'appellation de libéralités. Cependant, le don se distingue du legs du fait du moment de la survenance du transfert de propriété. En effet, le don est réalisé du vivant du propriétaire, donc du collectionneur, alors que le legs ne peut prendre effet qu'à la mort de ce dernier.

Il est important de noter que le don possède une particularité en ce qu'il peut prendre deux formes : le don manuel ou le don par acte authentique. Le don manuel consiste en la remise de la main à la main du bien visé, dans notre cas une œuvre d'art. Cette seule remise permet de former le don. Il s'agit donc d'un contrat imparfait puisque l'écrit n'est pas nécessaire *ad validitatem*[7]. La seconde forme du don est le don par acte authentique, aussi appelé don par acte notarié ou donation. Il est passé par devant notaire et un écrit accompagne obligatoirement

---

[7] Rappelons qu'une jurisprudence française, Cass. civ. 1re, 13 janv. 2016, n° 14-28.297, a rappelé que « *l'acceptation d'une donation dans les formes prescrites par la loi n'est exigée que pour les donations passées en la forme authentique* » et que partant, comme le souligne Xavier Pres, « *les dons manuels échappent donc à tout formalisme* », voir Xavier Pres, « Collections muséales, heurs et malheurs du formalisme des dons manuels », *Jurist Art etc.*, 2016, n° 35, p. 38.

cet acte permettant au nouveau propriétaire de disposer d'une preuve matérielle et tangible de ce geste gracieux.
Comme l'a souligné Véronique Long, il est rare qu'un collectionneur fasse don de la totalité de sa collection de son vivant[8]. En effet, même si une clause de réserve d'usufruit, permettant de garder la nue-propriété des œuvres, atténue cette séparation le collectionneur perd alors la faculté de se détacher d'un certain nombre de pièces et donc de perfectionner sa collection[9]. Souvent, le « collectionneur donateur » fait don de son vivant d'un nombre limité de pièces. Ce sont donc les legs qui permettent de faire entrer de manière importante les œuvres au sein des musées. Ce mode d'enrichissement des collections reste donc majoritairement tributaire des décès de grands collectionneurs. L'on pourra ainsi penser à la mort d'Isaac de Camondo en 1911 qui a permis de faire entrer son abondante collection au musée du Louvre dès 1913 ou aux nombreux dons et legs des membres de la famille Rothschild[10]. Cette pratique des dons et legs reste aujourd'hui largement d'actualité. À titre d'exemple, on peut citer les deux donations sous réserve d'usufruit d'octobre 2016 et de juillet 2019 des collectionneurs américains Marlene et Spencer Hays. Elles ont permis d'enrichir les collections publiques de plus de deux cent quatre-vingt œuvres qui seront affectées au musée d'Orsay à la mort des collectionneurs (Spencer Hays est décédé en mars 2017).
Si ces gestes de générosité de la part des collectionneurs privés sont indispensables à l'enrichissement des collections publiques, ils ont pu être vus comme ambigus, d'aucuns y voyant une certaine « générosité calculée »[11].

---

[8] Véronique Long, *Mécènes des deux mondes*, *op. cit.*, p. 203.
[9] Voir le très beau témoignage cité par Véronique Long dans son ouvrage *Mécènes des deux mondes*, *op. cit. « Une lettre du Baron Basile de Schlichting témoigne de ses réticences à ce sujet : «* L'idée de céder toute ma collection d'objets d'art au musée du Louvre par acte de donation à titre de nue-propriété me prive d'une des plus grandes jouissances de collectionneur, celle de la pleine liberté de faire des échanges à son gré, d'éliminer tel objet en faveur d'un autre, plus beau, toujours en vue d'un perfectionnement progressif », p. 203.
[10] Voir Pauline Prevost-Marcilhacy, *Les Rothschild, une dynastie de mécènes en France*, co-édition Louvre, BNF et Somogy, 2016. Ce travail a permis de répertorier environ cent-vingt mille œuvres entrées dans les collections publiques grâce aux libéralités des membres de cette famille.
[11] Terme employé par Pascale Samuel, *Les dons, donations et legs d'œuvres d'art aux musées*, mémoire de DESS présenté dans le cadre du Master Gestion des institutions culturelles, Université Paris-Dauphine, 1994, p. 25.

II. Dons et legs, entre geste de philanthropie et « générosité calculée »

La question du désintéressement du « collectionneur donateur » est souvent soulevée lorsque celui-ci réalise une libéralité, mais il est rare qu'il explique les motivations de sa générosité.
La réalisation d'un don ou d'un legs par un collectionneur au profit des collections publiques est souvent liée à recherche, consciente ou non, « [...] de gloire et d'immortalité [...] »[12]. En effet, il n'est pas rare qu'un musée propose d'afficher publiquement le nom des plus grands « collectionneurs donateurs ». Le musée du Louvre a par exemple proposé de graver littéralement ces noms dans le marbre et de les présenter sur une plaque accrochée dans la rotonde d'Apollon. Une sorte d'immortalité est ainsi promise aux donateurs. Par ailleurs, ces derniers n'hésitent pas à entourer leurs libéralités de conditions, qualifiées en droit de charges.
Ces charges ne doivent pas être négligées par les musées car si leur respect n'est pas assuré, le don ou le legs peut être révoqué à la suite d'une action en révocation de la part de l'ancien propriétaire ou de ses ayants droit. Le risque est donc de voir l'œuvre retourner en mains privées.
Il faut souligner que l'exigence des conditions est souvent proportionnelle à la qualité ou au nombre d'œuvres proposées à l'entrée dans les collections publiques. Ainsi, l'on peut passer de l'exigence de la présence du nom du donateur sur le cartel de l'œuvre à celle de l'exposition de l'ensemble des œuvres dans une ou plusieurs pièces dédiées, durant un temps déterminé, comme ce fut le cas pour le legs d'Isaac de Camondo au Musée du Louvre. En outre, si elles permettent souvent de garantir l'unité de la collection, ces charges posent des questions d'ordre juridique et éthique[13], notamment quant au principe de gratuité des libéralités. En effet, bien que le transfert de propriété soit fait à titre gratuit, il induit, dans ces cas précis, des dépenses à la charge du musée bénéficiaire[14].

---

[12] Véronique Long, *Mécènes des deux mondes*, *op. cit.*, p. 203.
[13] Cette réflexion rejoint celle menée par Madame Géraldine Goffaux Callebaut, « Les outils juridiques de l'éthique du mécénat », p. 161-170 *in Éthique et patrimoine culturel, Regard croisés*, Géraldine Goffaux Callebaut [sous la direction de], Ed. L'Harmattan, 2016.
[14] À noter que pour l'exemple du legs d'Isaac de Camondo, ce dernier avait, en plus de sa collection, légué une somme de 100 000 francs afin d'acquitter les « frais de

Ces charges peuvent être très handicapantes pour les musées encore aujourd'hui. L'exemple du legs du Duc d'Aumale à l'Institut de France, personne morale de droit public à statut particulier, est fameux. Le collectionneur avait en effet assorti son legs d'une interdiction de tout changement dans la présentation des œuvres, ainsi que de tout prêt et toute aliénation. Ces conditions, toujours appliquées aujourd'hui, sont des obstacles importants au développement et à l'attractivité du Musée Condé de Chantilly.

Cependant, la recherche de « l'immortalité » n'a pas été l'unique moteur des « collectionneurs donateurs ». Ainsi, le but patriotique du don ou du legs a pu être mis en avant[15]. Les œuvres d'art conservées dans les musées reflètent la culture française et sont vues comme « le trésor intellectuel du pays »[16]. Il convient donc d'alimenter et d'enrichir ces musées. Le don fait par Moreau-Nélaton en 1906 de la figure de La République peinte par Daumier[17] réalisée à l'occasion de la naissance de la Deuxième République en 1848 est un exemple de ce patriotisme.

D'autres « collectionneurs donateurs » constituent leur collection dans le seul but d'en faire don par la suite au musée : ce fut par exemple le cas d'Ernest Grandidier. Grâce à la donation de ce dernier en 1894, les collections publiques ont bénéficié d'un ensemble inédit et complet de porcelaines chinoises, constitué dans une optique pédagogique et d'illustration de l'histoire de la porcelaine en Chine[18].

Enfin, il convient de rappeler qu'un certain nombre de libéralités se fait de manière anonyme, ce qui permet de relativiser la « recherche de gloire et d'immortalité » des collectionneurs donateurs, souvent ancrée dans l'imaginaire collectif.

Si l'initiative des libéralités revient aux collectionneurs, ces outils juridiques restent des contrats et nécessitent par conséquent

---

déplacement » des œuvres, voir les archives, AN 20150044/70 (1).

[15] Pour plus de précision, voir Véronique Long, *Mécènes des deux mondes, op. cit.*, p. 179.

[16] Louis Courajod, « Eugène Piot et les objets d'art légués au Musée du Louvre », *Gazette des Beaux-Arts,* mai 1890, p. 395-396, cité in Véronique Long, *Mécènes des deux mondes, op. cit*, p. 179.

[17] Honoré Daumier, *La République*, 1848, huile sur toile, Musée d'Orsay, Paris, RF 1644.

[18] Pour plus d'informations, voir Véronique Long, « Les collectionneurs d'œuvres d'art et la donation au musée à la fin du XIXe siècle : l'exemple du Musée du Louvre » *in Romantisme*, 2001, n° 112, La collection, p. 45-54, p. 51.

l'acceptation des deux parties, y compris celle du musée. Si cet accord peut paraître de prime abord évident, l'on a pu constater que ces derniers se réservaient le droit de choisir quelles œuvres issues de collections privées pourraient intégrer les collections publiques.

III. La réception des collections privées par les musées : une entrée sélective

L'entrée des collections privées dans les collections publiques a été et ne peut être qu'encouragée par les musées qui y voient un moyen d'enrichir leurs collections tout en conservant leurs budgets dédiés aux acquisitions. Cependant, ces libéralités, et les charges qui y sont afférées, peuvent parfois entraîner des effets pervers et défigurer les musées au risque de les transformer en « petits musées particuliers »[19]. Par ailleurs, l'enrichissement progressif des musées qui acquièrent des œuvres de plus en plus prestigieuses permet de légitimer une certaine exigence qualitative des œuvres qui leur sont proposées. D'une attitude ouverte où la plupart des donations étaient acceptées, sans réelle évaluation qualitative, des procédures strictes d'acquisition et d'évaluation des œuvres se sont mises en place, notamment à la suite de la réforme de la loi relative aux musées de France du 4 janvier 2002. Ainsi, l'acceptation des libéralités par les musées est évaluée selon deux modalités en fonction que le musée possède ou non la personnalité juridique.

Pour les musées en bénéficiant, soit la plupart des grands musées comme le Musée du Louvre ou le Musée d'Orsay, le processus suit trois étapes.

Les libéralités sont d'abord soumises à une réunion de « conseil-acquisition ». Un collège de conservateurs et le président de l'établissement public y assistent et délibèrent sur la poursuite ou non de l'examen de la libéralité en conseil scientifique de l'établissement.

Ce dernier conseil est composé de conservateurs mais également de personnes qualifiées, extérieures au musée, qui peuvent être des collectionneurs. La question de la pertinence du projet d'acquisition est à nouveau soumise à l'avis des participants.

La dernière étape consiste en la défense du projet devant la Commission des acquisitions du musée. Cette commission est composée, pour le cas

---

[19] Auguste Marguillier, « Musées et collections », *Mercure de France*, 1er juin 1914, p. 639, cité *in* Véronique Long, *Mécènes des deux mondes*, *op. cit.*, p. 211.

du Musée d'Orsay, de onze membres, nommés par leurs pairs ou par arrêté du ministère de la Culture. L'adoption d'un projet de libéralités est alors soumise au vote à bulletin secret et adopté à la majorité simple. Il est à noter que pour les libéralités assorties de charges, la procédure d'acquisition est assortie d'une étape supplémentaire puisqu'un arrêté du ministre de la Culture est requis en vertu de l'article R423-1 du Code du patrimoine.

En revanche, pour les musées ne bénéficiant pas de la personnalité juridique, les acquisitions ne peuvent se faire que par le biais de la Réunion des Musées Nationaux qui pilote cinq commissions d'acquisition thématiques. Enfin, lorsque le musée est un service à compétence nationale et que la valeur du bien dépasse un certain seuil, alors un arrêté du ministre de la Culture est nécessaire pour acter l'acquisition.

Cependant, ce processus a vocation à évoluer prochainement, le ministère de la Culture ayant annoncé le 24 mars 2017[20] une réforme de la procédure d'acquisition destinée à renforcer la vigilance à l'égard des faux.

Si le droit impose un chemin particulier pour pouvoir intégrer les collections privées dans le domaine public, il est intéressant de souligner que les critères d'intégration d'une œuvre au sein des collections publiques restent très flous. Si l'on peut s'appuyer sur ceux énoncés par l'article L1 du Code du patrimoine[21], l'on peut aussi supposer que ces éléments restent des notions cadres.

Il n'existerait donc pas de critères précis d'intégration des œuvres dans les collections publiques. Chaque acquisition se fait au cas par cas.

Néanmoins, l'on peut supposer que la présentation d'une libéralité comprenant une œuvre permettant de compléter les lacunes des collections d'un musée sera fortement favorisée.

Cependant il est d'autres œuvres que l'on pourrait qualifier d'avant-gardistes, et dont l'intégration aux collections n'est pas toujours aisée. Ainsi, dans son ouvrage *Histoire de musées-Souvenirs d'un conservateur*, Michel Laclotte rappelle que « certaines formes d'art

---

[20] Communiqué de presse du ministère de la Culture, accessible en ligne : [http://www.culturecommunication.gouv.fr/Presse/Archives-Presse/Archives-Communiques-de-presse-2012-2017/Annee-2017/Reforme-de-la-chaine-d-acquisition-dans-les-musees-nationaux].

[21] Art. L1 du Code du patrimoine : *« Le patrimoine s'entend au sens du présent code, de l'ensemble des biens [...] présentant un intérêt historique, artistique, archéologique, esthétique, scientifique ou technique »*.

n'étaient pas encore reconnues comme essentielles à la fin des années 1970. Par exemple dans le domaine du siège, quand je montrais des chaises de Thonet, beaucoup de membres du Comité ou du Conseil les considéraient comme de vulgaires chaises de bistrots. Ce n'était pas encore entré dans la grande histoire de l'art, pas plus que la photographie d'ailleurs »[22].
La frilosité des musées français pour l'entrée de certaines œuvres a pu laisser des séquelles durables dont on trouve encore aujourd'hui des traces dans l'histoire des collections publiques. Au cours du XXe siècle, cela a notamment été le cas de la célèbre affaire du legs Caillebotte[23].

Gustave Caillebotte (1848-1894) était un artiste peintre, collectionneur et ami des impressionnistes dont il acquit certaines toiles pour les soutenir et les encourager. Décédé prématurément en 1894, il légua à l'État français l'ensemble de sa collection en application de ses dispositions testamentaires de 1876, confirmées en 1883. Auguste Renoir fut désigné exécuteur testamentaire et était à ce titre responsable du respect des charges grevant ce legs. En effet, Caillebotte tenait à ce que les tableaux de la collection n'aillent ni dans un grenier ni dans un musée de province, mais bien au Musée du Luxembourg, alors musée des artistes vivants, et plus tard au Louvre. Or la collection léguée comportait soixante-six tableaux et le règlement du Musée du Luxembourg limitait à trois le nombre d'œuvres exposées par artiste. L'ensemble de la collection ne pouvait donc pas être exposé. Les protagonistes ont alors cherché à moduler cette charge. Dans un premier temps, Renoir a proposé au musée de faire un premier choix dans les œuvres et de conserver sous forme de dépôt dans les mains de la famille celles restantes. Mais cette proposition fut écartée. Par la suite, les conservateurs proposèrent que l'ensemble du legs soit accepté mais qu'une partie seulement soit exposée au Musée du Luxembourg, le reste devant rejoindre en dépôt les Musées de Fontainebleau et de Compiègne qui étant des annexes des musées nationaux ne pouvaient être considérés comme des musées de province. Ce compromis fut d'abord accepté par les héritiers mais le frère de Caillebotte, Martial, se

---

22 Michel Laclotte, *Histoire de musées – Souvenirs d'un conservateur*, Ed. Scala, 2003, p. 218.
23 Voir Pierre Vaisse, *Deux façons d'écrire l'histoire. Le legs Caillebotte,* Ed. Orphys, 2014, et les archives conservées aux Archives nationales, cote AN 20144790/80.

rétracta et refusa finalement de signer cet accord, l'estimant trop loin de la lettre du testament.
Ce n'est qu'en 1895 qu'une solution fut trouvée. Une décharge partielle de legs fut opérée autorisant l'État à faire un choix parmi les œuvres qui lui ont échu, le reste redevenant la propriété des ayants droit. Ce sont ainsi environ quarante tableaux qui furent choisis par l'État au lieu des soixante-six composants la collection initiale. Parmi les œuvres qui rejoignirent les collections publiques on peut compter des chefs-d'œuvre comme la Balançoire[24] de Renoir ou encore le Bal du moulin de la Galette[25].
Dès 1908, Martial Caillebotte proposa à nouveau à l'État certaines œuvres issues de la collection de son frère dont il était resté propriétaire. Mais il dû essuyer un refus et fit dès lors jurer à sa femme et ses enfants de ne plus jamais s'adresser aux musées nationaux. Cette position entraîna en 1928 le refus de l'épouse veuve de Martial Caillebotte de faire don au Musée du Louvre de vingt-cinq tableaux restés en sa possession et préalablement refusés par l'État.
Cette histoire montre bien l'évolution de l'histoire de l'art et de l'histoire du goût au sein des musées et permet d'illustrer les difficultés rencontrées quant à l'entrée de certaines œuvres au sein des collections nationales françaises.

Conclusion

Ce court exposé aura permis, je l'espère, de démontrer la place historique, primordiale et précurseur des collectionneurs donateurs dans l'enrichissement des collections publiques. Ils constituent un maillon essentiel dans la chaîne de patrimonialisation des biens culturels en identifiant, collectionnant et valorisant les œuvres dignes d'intérêt, avant de les faire entrer, parfois non sans difficultés, dans les collections publiques et de les offrir, de manière plus ou moins ostensible, à l'ensemble de la Nation.

---

[24] Pierre-Auguste Renoir, *La balançoire*, 1876, huile sur toile, Musée d'Orsay, Paris, RF 2738.
[25] Pierre-Auguste Renoir, *Bal du moulin de la Galette*, 1876, huile sur toile, Musée d'Orsay, Paris, RF 2739.

Éléments de bibliographie

Actes du 6e colloque interdisciplinaire Icône-Image, Les musées et le marché de l'art, Ed. Obsidiane-les Trois P, 2010
Callu Agnès, *La réunion des musées nationaux 1870-1940, genèse et fonctionnement*, Thèse de l'École des Chartes, 1994
Cornu Gérard, *Vocabulaire juridique*, Ed. Quadrige, 2007
Frier Pierre-Laurent, *Droit du patrimoine culturel*, Ed. Presses universitaires de France, 1997
Georgel Chantal [sous la direction de], *La jeunesse des musées*, coédition RMN et Musée d'Orsay, 1994
Girardin Mélina, *Les legs et donations d'artistes et de leurs héritiers aux collections publiques de 1818 à 1969*, travail présenté dans le cadre de sa thèse soutenue en 2005
Goffaux Callebaut Géraldine [sous la direction de], *Éthique et patrimoine culturel, Regards croisés*, Ed. L'Harmattan, 2016
Long Véronique, *Mécènes des deux mondes, les collectionneurs donateurs du Louvre et de l'Art Institute de Chicago, 1879-1940*, Ed. Presses universitaires de Rennes, 2007
Long Véronique, « Les collectionneurs d'œuvres d'art et la donation au musée à la fin du XIXe siècle : l'exemple du Musée du Louvre », Romantisme, 2001, n° 112, La collection, p. 45-54
Laclotte Michel*, Histoires de musées, souvenirs d'un conservateur*, Ed. Scala, 2003
Marais Jean-Luc, *Histoire du don en France 1800-1939*, Presses universitaire de Rennes, 1999
Pomian Krzysztof, *Collectionneurs, amateurs et curieux, Paris Venise : XVIe – XVIIIe siècle*, Ed. Gallimard, 1987
Près Xavier, « Collections muséales, heurs et malheurs du formalisme des dons manuels », Jurist Art etc., 2016, n° 35, p. 38
Samuel Pascale, *Les dons, donations et legs d'œuvres d'art aux musées*, Mémoire présenté dans le cadre du DESS Gestion des institutions culturelles, Université Paris-Dauphine, 1994
Vaisse Pierre, *Deux façons d'écrire l'histoire : le legs Caillebotte*, Ed. Orphys, 2014

Webographie :

Site internet du musée d'Orsay, processus d'acquisition : [http://www.musee-orsay.fr/fr/collections/acquisitions/processus-

dacquisition.html], consulté le 19 février 2017
Communiqué de presse du ministère de la Culture : http://www.culturecommunication.gouv.fr/Presse/Archives-Presse/Archives-Communiques-de-presse-2012-2017/Annee-2017/Reforme-de-la-chaine-d-acquisition-dans-les-musees-nationaux

Les archives privées

Stéphane DUROY
Professeur de droit public
Université Paris-Saclay
Laboratoire IEDP

Lorsqu'on parle de collections, publiques ou privées, j'ai bien conscience que l'on ne pense pas spontanément aux archives. C'est sans doute que contrairement aux œuvres d'art, elles semblent beaucoup moins propices à la délectation. En forçant le trait, on pourrait dire qu'il ne s'agit que de tas de papiers poussiéreux, qui n'ont guère qu'un intérêt scientifique, auquel ne peuvent se montrer sensibles que quelques savants, historiens, chartistes, juristes, mais qui ne sont pas aussi évidemment désirables que la Bugatti Type 358 figurant sur l'affiche de notre colloque.

C'est pourtant des archives et spécialement des archives privées qu'il m'incombe de vous parler, en essayant de vous convaincre, comme Jérôme Fromageau a commencé à le faire hier, que les archives peuvent aussi faire vibrer.

Si donc les archives peuvent faire vibrer, si une passion des archives est possible, cette dernière ne s'est portée qu'assez tardivement sur les archives privées. En effet, l'intérêt des historiens et des archivistes pour les archives privées, ne s'est manifesté qu'à compter du XIXe siècle. C'est à la fin du XIXe siècle, plus précisément en 1891, que Charles Victor Langlois et Henri Stein, publient un ouvrage de référence : « Les archives de l'histoire de France », dans lequel ils consacrent de substantiels développements aux archives privées, sous l'intitulé « familles et châteaux »[1]. Mais, il faudra encore attendre1949, pour que cet intérêt s'institutionnalise sous la forme d'un service des archives privées, au sein des archives nationales.
C'est plus récemment, en 1988, qu'a été créé l'Institut Mémoires de l'édition contemporaine (IMEC), installé depuis 2004 dans l'ancienne

---

[1] Ch.-V. Langlois et H. Stein, *Les Archives de l'histoire de France*, Paris, Alphonse Picard et fils 1891-93.

abbaye d'Ardenne, aux portes de la ville de Caen (Calvados). Cet institut, au statut juridique d'association, même si la puissance publique est très présente dans la vie de cette association, se présente comme réunissant le plus important catalogue d'archives privées de France[2].

Du côté des juristes, dès le début du XIXe siècle, la jurisprudence s'attache à distinguer les archives qui sont la propriété de l'État ou d'autres personnes publiques[3] et qui seront considérées plus tardivement, à la fin du XIXe siècle, comme des archives publiques appartenant au domaine public[4], et les archives privées qui sont des propriétés privées[5].

De cette jurisprudence, il ressort qu'il existe deux grandes catégories d'archives privées. Les vraies et les fausses. Les vraies sont des archives qui ne répondent pas aux caractéristiques des archives publiques et sont donc des propriétés privées. Les fausses sont des archives qui ont la qualité d'archives publiques, mais qui sont entrées en possession de particuliers, autrement dit en mains privées, dont nous verrons bientôt qu'elles peuvent faire l'objet d'actions en revendication imprescriptibles.

Le législateur s'est aussi emparé des archives. L'article L. 211-1 du Code du patrimoine définit les archives de façon générale en ces termes :

« Les archives sont l'ensemble des documents, quels que soient leur date, leur lieu de conservation, leur forme et leur support, produits ou reçus par toute personne physique ou morale et par tout service ou organisme public ou privé dans l'exercice de leur activité ».

Il définit ensuite, par son article L. 211-4, les archives publiques de la façon suivante :

---

[2] L'Institut abrite des fonds d'auteurs, de revues et de presse, des fonds d'éditeurs ainsi que des fonds d'institutions et d'associations.

[3] Cour royale de Paris, 8 mai 1829, Barras c/ Préfet de la Seine, Recueil général des lois et des arrêts, Sirey n° 22, p. 995 et s. ; Recueil critique de jurisprudence et de législation, 1829, p. 186.

[4] Sur l'affirmation de l'appartenance au domaine public des archives publiques : Trib. civ. de Gap, 30 oct. 1895, Héritiers Amatc/ Abbé Guillaume, DP 1897. II. 54 ; CA Nancy, 16 mai 1896, Dufresne c/ L'État, DP 1896. II. 411 ; Trib. civ. de Lyon, 25 janv. 1899, Département du Rhône, de la Loire, de l'Isère etc. c/ les héritiers de Verna, DP 1899. II. 230.

[5] Cour de cassation, 31 mars 1858, Barba c/ de Saint-Simon et Hachette, D. 1858, p. 145 ; CA Paris, 11 déc. 1865, Préfet de l'Yonne c/ Succession de Sérilly, DP 1865. II.220.

« Les archives publiques sont :

a) Les documents qui procèdent de l'activité de l'État, des collectivités territoriales, des établissements et entreprises publics ;
b) Les documents qui procèdent de l'activité des organismes de droit privé chargés de la gestion des services publics ou d'une mission de service public.
c) Les minutes et répertoires des officiers publics ou ministériels ».

Les archives privées, quant à elles, ne font l'objet que d'une définition en creux par l'article L. 211-5 qui dispose :
« Les archives privées sont l'ensemble des documents définis à l'article L. 211-1 qui n'entrent pas dans le champ d'application de l'article L. 211-4 ».
Autrement dit, les archives qui ne sont pas des archives publiques sont des archives privées.
Ainsi sommairement définies, et tardivement institutionnalisées, les archives privées ont cependant de longue date fait l'objet de protections (**I**), qui favorisent à plus ou moins long terme une entrée dans les collections publiques (**II**).

I. Les protections des archives privées

On peut distinguer trois grandes catégories de protections, celles assurées par les propriétaires eux-mêmes, les familles (**A**), celles assurées par la puissance publique (**B**), celles assurées par les familles et la puissance dans le cadre d'un contrat de dépôt (**C**).

A. Les protections assurées par les propriétaires successifs

Ce sont en effet les familles qui assurent en premier lieu la protection matérielle des archives qui sont en principe leur propriété. Elles ne le font peut-être pas toujours à la perfection, mais suffisamment bien pour qu'un certain nombre de fonds d'archives anciens soient parvenus jusqu'à nous et finissent par entrer dans des fonds d'archives publics.

Pour illustrer cette protection matérielle familiale, j'évoquerai en premier lieu le cas du fonds d'archives Diderot-Vandeul. Ce fonds d'archives, du philosophe des lumières Denis Diderot, fut dans un premier temps conservé par sa fille Mme de Vandeul, puis fut transmis

à ses ayants droits, le dernier en date ayant été le baron Le Vavasseur et au final la succession Le Vavasseur.
Ce fonds, connu de quelques spécialistes dès le XIXe siècle, a surtout été inventorié par l'historien de la littérature Herbert Dieckmann à la fin des années 40. Dans un article publié en 1985, peu de temps avant sa mort, intitulé « L'épopée du Fonds Vandeul » il relatait notamment, le déménagement du fonds en 1940[6]. Conservé à Paris dans l'appartement du baron Le Vavasseur, il fut transporté, à l'approche de l'armée allemande, au château des Ifs près de Fécamp (Tourville les Ifs). Installé dans le salon du château, il fut ensuite isolé dans un grenier pour être maintenu à l'abri des Allemands qui occupaient le château. Il y demeura, pour rester cette fois à l'abri des Américains, qui occupèrent aussi le château en 1944.
C'est dans un autre château normand[7], proche de Bayeux, que fut conservé le fonds d'archives constitué par Turgot (1727-1781), intendant du Limousin puis contrôleur général des finances, l'un des plus hauts personnages de l'État. Bien que son histoire soit moins bien documentée que celle du fonds Diderot, on imagine aisément que ce fonds a fait l'objet de quelque attention familiale, dans un château situé au cœur de l'espace historique de la bataille de Normandie, à quelques kilomètres seulement des plages du débarquement.

La protection par les familles peut aussi prendre des formes plus juridiques. C'est ainsi que le fils de l'écrivain Émile Zola, le docteur Jacques Émile Zola, avait dans son testament introduit une disposition ainsi rédigée :
« Je demande que les souvenirs qui me viennent de mon père et de ma mère ne soient jamais vendus ».
Nonobstant cette disposition très claire, une clause d'inaliénabilité, la fille du docteur Zola, en possession matérielle de ces souvenirs, comprenant notamment le manuscrit original du fameux article de l'Aurore « J'accuse », avait décidé, en 1987, de les vendre par l'intermédiaire de la société Sotheby's à Monaco.
Saisi par un autre membre de la famille Zola (François Émile Zola), le président du tribunal de grande instance de Paris, intervenant en qualité de juge des référés, a décidé qu'il serait sursis à la vente.

---

[6] H. Dieckmann, *L'épopée du Fonds Vandeul*, *in* Revue d'histoire littéraire de la France, PUF 1985/6 (n° 85), p. 156.
[7] Le château de Manneville situé sur la commune de Lantheuil (Calvados).

La Cour d'appel de Paris a confirmé cette mesure de sursis, jugeant après avoir rappelé les termes de la clause que : « En cet état et en présence de son père encore vivant, Brigitte Émile Zola épouse Place, ne saurait suivre sur son projet qui tend directement à la dispersion définitive et irrémédiable des composants d'une collection, dès lors que ce projet a suscité l'opposition d'un descendant direct d'Émile Zola et que cette même opposition n'a pas été jugée à ce jour injustifiée ou abusive »[8].
Aux protections par les familles, se sont ajoutées plus récemment les protections par la puissance publique.

B. Les protections assurées par la puissance publique

Elles sont au nombre de trois : protection au titre des monuments historiques, protection au titre des archives historiques, protection au titre des trésors nationaux.

La protection au titre des monuments historiques est la première protection qui a pu être mise en œuvre pour protéger un fonds d'archives privées. Elle a rarement été utilisée, contrairement au classement d'autres types d'objets mobiliers. Pour l'illustrer, on peut cependant évoquer, de nouveau, le fonds d'archives Diderot-Vandeul. Il a en effet été classé par un décret du 5 décembre 1951 signé du président du Conseil René Pleven[9].
Faisant application de la loi du 31 décembre 1913, le décret dispose que « sont classés comme documents dont la conservation présente pour l'histoire nationale un intérêt public, les manuscrits des ouvrages de Denis Diderot, les copies de ces manuscrits, les documents originaux concernant la personne, l'œuvre, la famille et le pays d'origine de cet écrivain, possédés en indivis par etc… ».
Dans l'affaire du manuscrit de Zola, « J'accuse », c'est encore la procédure de classement, plus précisément une décision plaçant les documents litigieux sous le régime de l'instance de classement, qui a été mise en œuvre, et ce, alors même que l'administration disposait

[8] CA Paris, 7 déc. 1987, Sté Sotheby's Monaco et autres c/ François Émile Zola et autres, Semaine juridique 1988, II. 21148, note J.-F Barbièri.
[9] Décret du 5 déc. 1951 portant classement de manuscrits, *JO* 14 déc. 1951, p. 12290.

d'une procédure de protection spécifique des archives depuis la loi de 1979 sur les archives[10].

En 2003, c'est encore à la procédure de classement au titre des monuments historiques que l'autorité administrative a eu recours, pour protéger un manuscrit autographe de Marcel Proust intitulé : « À propos du style de Flaubert ». L'arrêté de classement (08-04-2003) a été pris après que le bien en question ait en premier lieu fait l'objet d'un refus de certificat d'exportation (16 mars 2000). L'arrêté de classement a donc ici, pris le relais d'un refus de certificat d'exportation, comme cela s'était produit dans la fameuse affaire du tableau « Le Cercle de la rue Royale », resté longtemps la propriété de M. Hottinguer avant que d'entrer finalement dans les collections du Musée d'Orsay, non sans avoir fait l'objet d'un contentieux qui devait précisément trancher la question de la possible succession entre décision de refus d'exportation et décision de classement[11]. Le manuscrit de Proust est encore à ce jour la propriété de la librairie Jean-Claude Vrain.

La protection des archives historiques est quant à elle possible depuis la loi de 1979, relative aux archives. L'article L. 212-15 du code du patrimoine, issu de cette loi, dispose que : « Les archives privées qui présentent pour des raisons historiques un intérêt public peuvent être classées comme archives historiques, sur proposition de l'administration des archives, par décision de l'autorité administrative ». Aux termes de l'article L. 212-17 du même code : « À défaut du consentement du propriétaire, le classement d'archives privées peut être prononcé d'office par décret pris sur avis conforme du Conseil d'État ».

Ces classements demeurent relativement rares. Depuis 1979, la liste des archives historiques ne comprend qu'une dizaine d'arrêtés. Ils concernent :

- Les archives de la société Pathé-Cinéma classées le 15 décembre 1989.
- Les archives du site industriel du Creusot classées le 21 mars 1989.
- Les archives de la société L'Imagerie d'Épinal classées le 4 avril 1989 (dessins originaux de 1796 à 1988).
- Les archives du château de Maintenon classées le 29 mars 2002.

[10] Elle n'a sans doute pas été utilisée car les souvenirs en question ne comprenaient pas que des manuscrits.

[11] CAA Paris, 27 juin 2000, Ministre de la culture c/ Hottinguer, AJDA 2000, p. 947, concl. S. Brottons ; CE, 21 juin 2001, Ministre de la culture c/ Hottinguer, n° 223936.

- Les archives historiques de la société Hachette classées le 29 mars 2002.
- La bibliothèque ancienne de Camille Flammarion classée le 29 mars 2002.
- Les archives et la bibliothèque du château de Serrant classées le 11 décembre 2002.
- Les archives de la famille de Bourmont (château du même nom en Maine et Loire) classées le 25 février 2013.
Les archives (chartrier) du château d'Anjouy (Cantal) classées le 19 décembre 2013.
Les archives de la grande Loge nationale française, classées le 19 décembre 2013.
Une troisième protection peut résulter de l'appartenance des archives privées à la catégorie des trésors nationaux.

L'article L. 111-1 du Code du patrimoine dispose que : « Sont des trésors nationaux : 5° Les autres biens présentant un intérêt majeur pour le patrimoine national au point de vue de l'histoire, de l'art ou de l'archéologie ».
Cette qualité est plus précisément reconnue à l'occasion d'une demande de certificat d'exportation, qui sera refusé si la qualité de trésor national est reconnue par le ministre, après avis de la commission consultative des trésors nationaux.
Le bien qui présente les qualités d'un trésor national à la suite d'un refus de certificat d'exportation, peut faire l'objet, selon les termes de l'article L. 121-1 du code du patrimoine, d'une procédure d'offre d'achat du bien par la puissance publique, dans les trente mois qui suivent la décision qualifiant le bien de trésor national.

Depuis 2007, on comptabilise une douzaine de décisions de refus relatives à des fonds d'archives privées[12]. Plus concrètement, il s'agit :
- Des archives composées de manuscrits autographes et de feuillets dactylographiés de Vassily Kandinsky (3 mai 2007).
- Des archives personnelles de Guy Debord (29 janvier 2009).

---

[12] Suite à un avis de la CADA en date du 19 janv. 2017, une liste précise des trésors nationaux ayant fait l'objet d'un refus de certificat a été diffusée, couvrant la période 1993-2017. Outre les exemples précités on comptabilise 19 décisions de refus de certificat d'exportation concernant des archives privées entre 1993 et 2007. On comptabilise donc 31 décisions de refus concernant des archives sur les 232 décisions de refus prises depuis 1993.

- Des archives Turgot (29 mars 2011).
- Des manuscrits et dactylogrammes de Michel Foucault (28 mars 2012).
- Du manuscrit musical autographe de César Franck : Variations symphoniques pour piano et orchestre 1885 (15 juin2012).
- De la copie manuscrite intégrale des Mémoires d'outre-tombe (29 décembre 2013).
- Du manuscrit en partie autographe de Berlioz pour l'opéra les Troyens (9 novembre 2014).
- Des archives personnelles d'Édouard Glissant (romancier et poète héritier de Césaire) (28 novembre 2014).
- Du registre de comptes des travaux du château royal d'Amboise (1er juin 2015).
- D'un album de plans et vues de Trianon réalisé sous la direction de Richard Mique avec une reliure aux armes de Marie-Antoinette (23 octobre 2015).
- Du manuscrit autographe de Stéphane Mallarmé : « Jamais un coup de dés n'abolira le hasard » (6 novembre 2015).
- D'un album de photos composé par Léon Maufras. 113 tirages par Gustave Legray, véritable galerie de portraits du second Empire (14 novembre 2016).

C. La protection résultant d'un contrat de dépôt

Assez curieusement, le contrat de dépôt d'archives privées dans un dépôt d'archives publiques n'est pas spécialement évoqué par les dispositions du Code du patrimoine, relatives aux archives privées.
Il apparaît subrepticement à l'article L. 213-6 disposant que : « Les services publics d'archives qui reçoivent des archives privées à titre de dons, de legs, de cession ou de dépôt sont tenus de respecter les stipulations du donateur, de l'auteur du legs, du cédant ou du déposant quant à la conservation et la communication de ces archives ».
Le contrat de dépôt d'archives privées obéit en conséquence aux dispositions du code civil, notamment les dispositions des articles 1915 et 1927.
Le premier dispose que : « Le dépôt, en général, est un acte par lequel on reçoit la chose d'autrui, à la charge de la garder et de la restituer en nature ».

Le second dispose lui que : « Le dépositaire doit apporter, dans la garde de la chose déposée, les mêmes soins qu'il apporte dans la garde des choses qui lui appartiennent ».
Tout aussi curieusement, le site internet des Archives de France, insiste sur les inconvénients du dépôt. Il souligne que le propriétaire privé conserve ses titres de propriété, en conséquence, sauf dispositions particulières, le décès du propriétaire a pour conséquence le transfert de propriété aux héritiers. Il signale par ailleurs que la révocation du dépôt est toujours possible.
Le dépôt est cependant encouragé, comme en attestent les différents sites des archives départementales qui l'évoquent tous longuement, avec reproduction d'un contrat type de dépôt.
Il est fréquemment utilisé en pratique, nonobstant les réserves évoquées par l'administration des archives et constitue souvent la première étape d'un processus d'entrée dans les collections.

De tels contrats peuvent aussi être conclus avec des institutions privées. C'est le cas s'agissant de l'IMEC évoqué dans l'introduction. Si certains fonds sont donnés à l'Institut, il semble que pour beaucoup, ils font l'objet, au moins dans un premier temps, d'un contrat de dépôt.
Ils peuvent encore être conclus avec des notaires, comme l'illustre la remarquable affaire du manuscrit des *Mémoires d'Outre-tombe*, déposé chez un notaire parisien. En 1836, François-René de Chateaubriand, par contrat, cède à ses éditeurs Delloye et Sala, les droits sur ses *Mémoires* déposés dans le coffre du notaire. Chateaubriand meurt en 1848. En 1850, l'éditeur vient reprendre quelques éléments, déclarant dans un procès-verbal : « Je lui laisse les autres ». Pendant 160 ans, les notaires successifs ont conservé les manuscrits, jusqu'à ce qu'en 2013, le dernier en date décide de les vendre. Le processus de vente a été interrompu par un refus de certificat d'exportation délivré le 26 novembre 2013. Mais, de surcroît, le parquet de Paris estimant que le notaire n'avait aucun droit sur les manuscrits en cause, a engagé contre lui des poursuites pour abus de confiance.
Il a été condamné par une décision du tribunal correctionnel de Paris en date du 10 décembre 2015. Le tribunal a notamment souligné que « il ne peut y avoir acquisition par prescription pour le gardien d'un objet ». Cette condamnation a été confirmée par la Cour d'appel de Paris le 13 décembre 2016[13].

---

[13] Sur cette affaire voir : T. de Ravel d'Esclapon, *Les « petits papiers » de*

Les protections que nous venons d'évoquer n'ont pas pour effet de faire entrer les archives privées en cause dans les collections publiques. C'est à cette entrée que nous allons maintenant nous intéresser.

II. L'entrée dans les collections publiques

Empruntant les formules utilisées par le code général de la propriété des personnes publiques (CGPPP), je distinguerai successivement les modes d'acquisition à l'amiable d'archives privées (**A**) puis les modes d'acquisition selon des procédés de contrainte (**B**), pour évoquer enfin la technique particulière de la revendication (**C**).

A. Les modes d'acquisition à l'amiable

Il s'agit en premier lieu de l'achat. Pour reprendre quelques-uns des exemples précités, les archives de Diderot classées au titre des monuments historiques, ont été achetées à la famille et sont entrées dans les collections de la BNF au début de l'année 1952.
Les archives Zola, dont le fameux « J'accuse » ont fait également l'objet d'un achat à la famille en 1991.
La plupart des archives privées considérées comme des trésors nationaux, ont fait aussi l'objet d'achats. C'est notamment le cas des archives Turgot qui ont été acquises pour la coquette somme de 8,5 millions d'euros grâce au mécénat de la banque de France[14]. C'est aussi le cas du registre des comptes des travaux du château d'Amboise ou des archives de Michel Foucault. La fréquence des achats s'explique par les dispositions de l'article L. 121-1 du Code du patrimoine disposant que : « Dans le délai de trente mois, prévu à l'article L. 111-6, l'autorité administrative peut dans l'intérêt des collections publiques, présenter une offre d'achat ».
Les autres modes d'acquisition amiables sont les dons et legs. La liste

---

Chateaubriand : à qui appartient son manuscrit ?, Dalloz actualité : https://www.dalloz-actualite.fr.

[14] Signalons aussi l'acquisition en 1998 du manuscrit des Mémoires de Turenne ; en 2000 du manuscrit autographe de Poèmes de René Char, enluminé par Joan Miró ; en 2003 du manuscrit du « Journal du voleur » de Jean Genet ; en 2013 des archives de Michel Foucault ; en 2015 d'un album des plans et vues de Trianon aux armes de Marie-Antoinette ; en 2016 de Variations symphoniques pour piano et orchestre de César Franck ; en 2016 du manuscrit en partie autographe des Troyens d'Hector Berlioz ; en 2016 du registre de comptes des travaux du château d'Amboise.

des trésors nationaux permet aussi d'en identifier quelques-uns. Ainsi, le manuscrit autographe de « Vol de nuit » de Saint Exupéry a été donné par sa propriétaire, en 1998, à la BNF. Les documents photographiques provenant du fonds Charles Nègre ont été donnés sous réserve d'usufruit au Musée d'Orsay.

Les dons et legs sont de manière générale source de contentieux. En effet, ils sont fréquemment contestés par les héritiers directs ou plus indirects. Pour illustrer cette dernière catégorie d'héritiers, mérite d'être signalée l'affaire du fonds d'archives du philosophe et écrivain Émile Cioran.

Les manuscrits de Cioran ont fait l'objet d'une donation en 1995 au profit de la Bibliothèque Jacques Doucet. Or, une brocanteuse chargée de débarrasser l'appartement et la cave de la compagne d'Émile Cioran (Simone Boué), y a découvert un autre ensemble de manuscrits, décrit par un notaire chargé de l'inventaire comme un lot de débarras ne méritant pas description. Parmi ces manuscrits figurait celui « De l'inconvénient d'être né », qu'elle a cherché à mettre en vente.

À la demande de la bibliothèque, la Cour d'appel de Paris a bloqué en 2005 la vente des manuscrits. Mais finalement, la Cour d'appel de Paris, par un arrêt du 11 mars 2011 a jugé que la brocanteuse était bien propriétaire des manuscrits litigieux. Elle a débouté la chancellerie des Universités, confirmant le jugement du tribunal de grande instance de Paris du 3 décembre 2008.

Suite à cette décision, une vente est intervenue en avril 2011 à l'hôtel Drouot. Un certain nombre de pièces ont été acquises par une société appartenant à un homme d'affaires d'origine roumaine (George Brailoiu) qui a souhaité en faire don à l'État roumain.

La dation en paiement est encore une possibilité. La liste des trésors nationaux publiée en mai 2017 permet encore de l'illustrer. C'est une dation en paiement qui a permis l'acquisition en 1998 de différentes archives, notamment photographiques, de Picasso.

B. Les modes d'acquisition selon des procédés de contrainte

Le code général de la propriété des personnes publiques (CGPPP) vise pour commencer la nationalisation et l'expropriation. Ces modes d'acquisition d'archives privées n'ont guère, aujourd'hui, d'effectivité concernant nos archives privées. Ces procédés ont certes joué un rôle au moment de la Révolution. La sécularisation des biens du clergé, puis

la confiscation des biens des émigrés, ont en effet fortement contribué à faire entrer des archives privées dans les collections publiques[15].
Il y a eu certes, plus récemment, des nationalisations d'entreprises en 1946, puis en 1981-82, qui ont pu avoir pour effet également de transformer des archives d'entreprises privées en archives publiques (Renault, etc.). Mais, depuis les privatisations de 1986 et celles qui ont suivi, le temps n'est plus aux nationalisations. Ces mouvements de nationalisations puis de privatisations posent cependant des questions importantes concernant le statut des archives de ces entreprises, que je ne fais que signaler.
Aussi, si l'on ne s'attarde pas davantage sur les nationalisations et expropriations, le principal mode d'acquisition selon des procédés de contrainte est le droit de préemption.
Le Code du patrimoine dans son Livre II Archives contient une sous-section 3 consacrée au droit de préemption des archives privées (art L. 212-30 à L. 212-37).
Aux termes de l'article L. 212-32 il apparaît que : « S'il l'estime nécessaire à la protection du patrimoine d'archives, l'État exerce, sur tout document d'archives privées mis en vente publique, un droit de préemption par l'effet duquel il se trouve subrogé à l'adjudicataire ».
Il s'agit d'une technique régulièrement utilisée au profit de la BNF ou des Archives de France.
Ainsi, le rapport 2015 sur l'activité des services d'archives fait état d'aides financières apportées à 15 services d'archives territoriaux pour l'acquisition de documents anciens (le plus souvent des préemptions). Est notamment signalée la préemption par les archives municipales de Dunkerque d'un ensemble de correspondances de Dominique Lemaire (1739-1818) négociant dunkerquois devenu colon à Saint Domingue, retraçant l'histoire de son installation puis la révolution haïtienne.
Le rapport d'activité de l'année 2011 fait lui état de 38 préemptions, dont les fameuses archives Robespierre, préemptées chez Sotheby's à un peu plus de 1 million d'euros.
La liste des trésors nationaux met aussi en évidence l'importance de l'exercice du droit de préemption. Ainsi en 1998 c'est par exercice du droit de préemption qu'est acquis pour la BNF le manuscrit autographe de « Une Saison en enfer » de Rimbaud. En 2002, c'est encore par exercice du droit de préemption que sont acquis pour la BNF une

[15] Pour des archives ecclésiastiques : Trib. civ. de Gap, 30 oct. 1895, Héritiers Amat c/ Abbé Guillaume, DP 1897. II. 54, relatif au cartulaire de la chartreuse de Durbon.

correspondance et le premier document photographique connu de Nicéphore Niepce.

C. Le cas particulier des actions en revendication d'archives publiques en mains privées

L'action en revendication n'est pas à proprement parler un mode d'acquisition. En effet, cette action est utilisée par une personne publique qui s'estimant propriétaire d'un bien, en l'espèce des archives publiques, appartenant au domaine public, demande au juge d'enjoindre à un propriétaire privé, entre les mains duquel elles se trouvent, de les restituer à la personne publique qui n'a jamais cessé d'en être propriétaire. En résumé, elle permet à une personne publique de rentrer en possession d'archives publiques qui se trouvaient, pour des raisons factuelles diverses, en mains privées.

Ces actions en revendication, qui sont tout comme les biens relevant du domaine public imprescriptibles, tendent à se multiplier depuis quelques années.

L'exemple le plus remarquable est celui des archives du général du premier Empire, François Charles Louis de Chasseloup-Laubat. Mort en 1833 il avait constitué tout au long de sa vie militaire, administrative (il fut Conseiller d'État) et politique (il fut Pair de France) un fonds d'archives.

En 2003, un de ses descendants a voulu vendre ce fonds dans une salle des ventes. C'est alors que le ministère de la défense a cherché à obtenir l'empêchement de la vente. Son argument tenait en quelques mots. Le fonds d'archives du général Chasseloup-Laubat est constitué pour l'essentiel d'archives publiques qui appartenant au domaine public de l'État doivent lui être restituées.

Depuis 2003, toutes les juridictions administratives et judiciaires ont été saisies de ce litige. En 2011 le Conseil d'État avait estimé que l'affaire posait une question sérieuse de compétence et que le Tribunal des conflits devait être saisi[16]. Le Tribunal des conflits a, en 2012, jugé que : « les archives publiques appartiennent au domaine public et sont régies par les principes d'inaliénabilité et d'imprescriptibilité…», mais que : « l'action en revendication de telles archives, introduite par une personne de droit public à l'encontre d'une personne de droit privé en

[16] CE, 9 nov. 2011, Ministre de la défense c/ Murat de Chasseloup-Laubat, req. n° 331500, Rec, T, p. 922.

possession de laquelle se trouvent ces documents, relève de la compétence des juridictions judiciaires, sous réserve d'une éventuelle question préjudicielle posée au juge administratif en cas de difficulté sérieuse portant sur la détermination du caractère public desdites archives »[17].

Le Tribunal de grande instance de la Rochelle, saisi de l'action en revendication, a jugé en 2013 que les archives Chasseloup-Laubat étaient des archives privées[18]. La Cour d'appel de Poitiers a confirmé ce jugement en 2014. Mais en 2015, la Cour de cassation a cassé cet arrêt[19] et renvoyé l'affaire devant la Cour d'appel de Paris.

Cette dernière a tout d'abord écarté une question prioritaire de constitutionnalité (QPC) visant l'article L. 211-4 du code du patrimoine[20]. Puis, sur le fond, elle a jugé sur le fondement des articles L. 211-4 du Code du patrimoine et de l'article L. 2112-1 du Code général de la propriété des personnes publiques (CGPPP), que les archives Chasseloup-Laubat sont des archives publiques et que la demande en revendication présentée par le ministère de la défense doit être accueillie[21].

Le Tribunal de grande instance de Paris s'est prononcé dans le même sens, à propos d'archives constituées par le maréchal du premier Empire Bessières (1768-1813)[22].

Deux autres affaires ont également fait l'objet de contentieux remarqués.

L'une concerne un ensemble de télégrammes (313) produits par le général de Gaulle entre 1940 et 1942. Le Tribunal de grande instance de Paris a jugé en 2013 que ces télégrammes constituaient des archives publiques[23]. La Cour d'appel de Paris, dans le cadre de l'appel formé contre ce jugement, a décidé de saisir le Tribunal administratif de Paris d'une question préjudicielle, estimant qu'il existait en l'espèce une

---

[17] TC, 9 juill. 2012, Ministre de la défense c/ Murat de Chasseloup-Laubat, Rec, p. 514.

[18] TGI La Rochelle, 26 mars 2013, Ministère de la défense c/ Murat de Chasseloup-Laubat, n° 12/00363.

[19] Cass civ 1, 21 oct. 2015, req. n° 14-19807.

[20] CA Paris, 18 oct. 2016, M. Murat de Chasseloup-Laubat, n° 16/13254.

[21] CA Paris, 28 mars 2017, M. Murat de Chasseloup- Laubat, n° 15/23576.

[22] TGI Paris, 12 mai 2016, Ministère de la défense c/ M. X, n° 14/16060.

[23] TGI Paris, 20 nov. 2013, État c/ Asso du musée des lettres et manuscrits et Sté Aristophil, n° 12/06156 ; AJDA 2014, p. 226, note O. Agnus.

difficulté sérieuse portant sur la détermination du caractère public des archives en cause. Par un jugement du 12 mai 2017, le Tribunal administratif de Paris a jugé que les télégrammes constituaient des archives publiques[24].

L'autre affaire, concerne des documents produits par le Maréchal Pétain, lorsqu'il était chef de l'État français, parmi lesquels un tapuscrit de l'appel du général de Gaulle, dont certains paragraphes ont été cochés ou surlignés par Philippe Pétain. Leur qualité d'archives publiques a été retenue devant le Tribunal de grande instance de Paris en 2014[25], confirmée par la Cour d'appel de Paris en 2015[26] et confirmée encore par la Cour de cassation en 2017[27].

Pour l'heure, on observe donc très clairement que la tendance de la jurisprudence est de faire droit aux actions en revendication de l'État, en affirmant la qualité d'archives publiques des documents litigieux, et ce alors même que les raisonnements suivis par le juge ne semblent pas satisfaisants, en particulier au regard de l'application dans le temps du droit régissant les archives publiques[28]. Plus précisément, alors que les juges devraient pour apprécier la qualité d'archives publiques d'un document, se placer à sa date de production, pour vérifier s'il pouvait être considéré à cette date comme une archive publique, ils se contentent d'appliquer l'article L.211-4 définissant les archives publiques, issu de la loi de 1979 relative aux archives, au risque de faire d'une archive privée au temps de sa production, une archive publique relevant du domaine public, pouvant donc être revendiquée sans indemnisation pour le possesseur.

On mesure tout l'intérêt patrimonial d'une telle procédure qui permet aux personnes publiques, surtout à l'État, d'enrichir ses collections sans bourse délier. Elle constitue assurément un progrès par rapport à des techniques plus despotiques, je pense au dépôt dans les archives du ministère des affaires étrangères du manuscrit complet des mémoires du duc de Saint Simon[29], ordonné par Louis XV, ou encore, beaucoup plus récemment, c'était en 1968-69, à la saisie et à l'enlèvement « manu

---

[24] TA Paris, 12 mai 2017, Cour d'appel de Paris, n° 1602472/6-1.

[25] TGI Paris, 3 avr. 2014, État ministère de la culture c/ SARL La librairie Jean-Claude Vrain, n° 12/14221.

[26] CA Paris, 24 nov. 2015, n° 14/09606.

[27] Cass. civ. 1°, 22 févr. 2017, Société librairie Jean-Claude Vrain, n° 16-12.922.

[28] Sur cette question de fond : S. Duroy, *Domaine public et archives publiques : réouverture d'un « carton » resté longtemps en sommeil*, RDP 2016, p. 891.

[29] Cass., 31 mars 1858, Barba c/ de Saint-Simon et Hachette, D. 1858 p. 145.

militari », des documents se trouvant au domicile de l'amiral Muselier[30], tumultueux compagnon de route du général de Gaulle pendant la seconde guerre mondiale, mais elle n'en demeure pas moins problématique pour le droit « inviolable et sacré » qu'est le droit de propriété, selon les termes de la déclaration des droits de l'homme de 1789.

Mais, quel que soit le bien-fondé juridique de ces actions en revendication d'archives, elles illustrent, comme les protections et les différents modes d'acquisitions sus-évoqués, une volonté politique d'enrichissement des collections d'archives et de construction d'une mémoire nationale, qui a connu avec la période révolutionnaire une impulsion remarquable et qui aujourd'hui encore, en dépit des débats récurrents sur la sélection des archives et le financement des mètres linéaires d'archives, n'est dépourvue ni de cohérence ni d'utilité publique.

[30] CE, 10 oct. 1969, Consorts Muselier, Rec. P. 432 ; RA 1970, p. 29, concl. Braibant ; RDP 1970, p. 774, note M. Waline.

Acquérir, documenter, intéresser, publier : les missions du conservateur à la Fondation Gandur pour l'Art

Jean Claude GANDUR
Président
Isabelle TASSIGNON
Conservatrice des collections Archéologie et Ethnologie

Constituées il y a près de 40 ans les collections de Jean Claude Gandur ont été envisagées dès le début dans la perspective de former un jour un patrimoine culturel à partager. Leur principale raison d'être est donc leur accessibilité au plus grand nombre. Ces collections relèvent de quatre domaines : l'archéologie, les arts décoratifs, les beaux-arts et plus récemment l'ethnologie, quatre ensembles qui continuent de s'accroître régulièrement. Si la collection archéologique avait été exposée anonymement dès 2001[1], ce n'est qu'en 2010 que ces collections ont été dévoilées au public, avec la création de la Fondation Gandur pour l'Art (FGA). Cette fondation de droit suisse est ainsi dépositaire de collections qui ont vocation à être publiques.

Faire un travail de diligence sur la provenance des objets, s'acquitter des taxes lors de l'entrée sur le territoire, préserver et entretenir la collection, prêter les objets constituent les obligations spécifiques du collectionneur qui, à l'aube du XXIe siècle, garantissent l'éthique des collections[2]. Ces obligations sont inscrites dans les statuts de la FGA. Deux autres conditions fondamentales s'y ajoutent : la nécessaire publication scientifique des collections et leur inaliénabilité. Une fois intégrés à ses collections, seuls les objets de qualité inférieure peuvent être revendus pour racheter un objet de meilleure qualité, à condition qu'il soit de fonction équivalente. Ce principe est extrêmement strict : par exemple, un ex-voto au dieu Harpocrate ne pourra être remplacé que par une autre offrande à la même divinité, mais mieux conservée ou de meilleure qualité.

---

[1] *Reflets du divin. Antiquités pharaoniques et classiques d'une collection privée. Musée d'art et d'histoire, Genève, 30 août 2001-3 février 2002*, Genève, 2001.

[2] Manlio Frigo, « The impact of the Unidroit Convention on international case law and practice: an appraisal », *Unif. L. Rev.*, 20 (2015), p. 626-636.

Les collections ethnologiques et archéologiques représentent la moitié de l'ensemble des collections. La plus anciennement constituée (dès 1978, pour les tout premiers objets), la collection archéologique est aussi la plus riche, avec des artefacts provenant de l'ensemble du bassin méditerranéen. Reflet de la passion du collectionneur pour l'Égypte, la collection d'artefacts égyptiens y est largement prédominante, puisqu'elle correspond à plus de la moitié de la collection archéologique. Le reste est constitué d'objets grecs, romains et proche-orientaux.

I. Accroître les collections

A. Acquisition et bonne pratique archéologique

« Devenir une vitrine pour l'éthique », selon l'expression d'Antoinette Maget, est, en ce début de XXIe siècle, le défi majeur qui préside à la constitution des collections publiques et privées[3]. Étant donné la nature-même des collections, un travail de diligence préalable à l'acquisition d'un objet et à sa publication scientifique s'impose de manière particulièrement aiguë à la FGA. Membre de l'ICOM depuis 2013 et de l'Association des Musées Suisses depuis 2019, la FGA développe ses collections archéologiques et ethnologiques dans ce souci d'éthique et s'est dotée d'une équipe de conservateurs professionnels, archéologues et historiens de l'art ; par ailleurs, elle a mené systématiquement et de concert avec le Musée d'Art et d'Histoire de Genève une recherche sur la provenance et l'authenticité des objets. Rappelons que, outre les questions d'inauthenticité, les objets circulant sur le marché peuvent être au cœur de trois types de fraudes : le vol (objets volés soit à un État, soit à un propriétaire privé) ; l'exportation illicite avant l'entrée en vigueur des lois applicables à leurs pays respectifs, ou l'exportation illicite après l'entrée en vigueur de ces lois[4]. En ces temps troublés, où le trafic illicite de biens culturels prospère partout, il est de notre devoir de redoubler de précautions lorsqu'il s'agit d'acquérir un bien archéologique ou ethnologique. Ainsi, la collection proche-orientale n'est-elle aujourd'hui plus augmentée vu l'origine douteuse de

[3] Antoinette Maget, *Collectionnisme public et conscience patrimoniale. Les collections d'antiquités égyptiennes en Europe*, Paris, 2009, p. 380 *pass.*
[4] Sur ces questions, voir Antoinette Maget, *Collectionnisme public et conscience patrimoniale,* p. 515-516.

nombreux objets circulant sur le marché. Ne pas acquérir d'objets provenant de ces régions en conflit est peut-être le moyen le plus sûr de court-circuiter le trafic et par là, le pillage des sites archéologiques. La même remarque vaut pour certains biens culturels africains[5]. Rien ne justifie et ne justifiera jamais le pillage.

Les conservateurs des collections archéologiques et ethnologiques accomplissent au quotidien un travail d'enquête approfondi sur les objets qui pourraient être acquis, en se renseignant au préalable sur la réputation des vendeurs. Il faut tout particulièrement se prémunir d'objets, qui volés ou pillés, auraient pu être blanchis par un passage « purificatoire » en exposition[6]. On doit donc mener une critique des informations qui nous sont fournies par les galeristes et maisons de vente, et s'assurer que l'objet proposé n'a pas été volé. Les listes rouges des biens culturels répertorient le patrimoine signalé comme volé (bases de données d'Interpol, de l'Unesco et de l'ICOM, l'Art Loss Register). De ce point de vue, il est à souhaiter qu'une base de données unique, simple et réalisée par des archéologues, soit un jour mise à disposition des personnes chargées de réaliser ce travail de diligence. Encore faut-il que l'objet ait été signalé comme volé par les États ou les collectionneurs, ce qui n'est pas forcément le cas…

Il est ensuite demandé au marchand de fournir des informations circonstanciées sur la manière dont il a acquis l'objet ainsi que des documents prouvant qu'ils sont en ordre d'importation (certificat de bien culturel et document 11.97/11.95 pour l'importation en Suisse). C'est là probablement la phase la plus délicate de l'enquête car les anciens propriétaires d'œuvres d'art tiennent généralement à garder l'anonymat[7].

Si un certain nombre de galeristes veillent à s'adapter aux nouveaux standards d'éthique, il n'en va malheureusement pas de même pour tous[8]. Nous appliquons à toute proposition d'achat les principes de la critique historique : le détenteur précédent de l'objet est-il connu comme collectionneur ? Que collectionnait-il ? Y a-t-il eu des catalogues/des inventaires de sa collection ? L'objet est-il par hasard

---

[5] Éric Huysecom, « Des spoliations coloniales et post-coloniales au trafic illicite contemporain », dans *Le code de déontologie de l'ICOM pour les musées, 1986-2016* (à paraître).

[6] La question a été développée ailleurs : Jean Claude Gandur, « *Due Diligence* : les derniers maillons de la chaîne », *Unif. L. Rev.*, 20 (2015), p. 651-655, et part. p. 652.

[7] Jean Claude Gandur, « *Due Diligence* », p. 652.

[8] Antoinette Maget, *Collectionnisme public et conscience patrimoniale,* p. 387-388.

mentionné dans une très ancienne collection ? De ce point de vue, d'anciens ouvrages tels que *L'Antiquité expliquée*[9], ou les répertoires de S. Reinach[10], – pour ne citer qu'eux en archéologie classique – peuvent fournir des indications (ainsi pour un pilier janiforme de l'ancienne collection Giovanni Capranesi, constituée dans la seconde moitié du XIXe siècle). Quand on ne trouve aucun indice d'appartenance à une ancienne collection bien connue, la question à se poser est celle de la cohérence et de la plausibilité de la collection dont il est censé provenir. À cet égard, le web constitue une appréciable source d'informations, depuis les catalogues de vente jusqu'aux collections muséales en ligne, en passant par les sites de généalogie ou les divers textes que l'on peut trouver sur les blogs : toutes ces informations doivent être croisées et sont bien sûr toujours à considérer selon les principes élémentaires de la critique historique. Les résultats obtenus lors de ces enquêtes préliminaires limitent ainsi considérablement le nombre d'objets susceptibles d'entrer dans les collections.

B. Acquisition et bonne pratique scientifique

Assurer la cohérence scientifique de la collection

La collection de la FGA est une collection au plein sens du terme, c'est-à-dire un ensemble d'objets réunis autour d'un écheveau de fils conducteurs dont la matière-même est ici l'homme et ses dieux[11]. Si le critère esthétique est primordial dans le choix d'un objet qui entre dans les collections de la FGA, ce n'est évidemment pas le seul. C'est surtout une collection scientifiquement cohérente et ce souci de cohérence guide nos choix, quitte à nous faire renoncer à tel objet rare et beau mais qui ne trouverait pas sa place dans nos collections. Nos collections archéologiques et ethnologiques font sens, indépendamment l'une de l'autre, et l'une avec l'autre. La collection archéologique s'articule autour de quelques grands thèmes, tous intimement liés : l'Égypte, et particulièrement Alexandrie, ses pharaons, ses princes et ses dieux, les

---

[9] Dom Bernard de Montfaucon, *L'Antiquité expliquée et représentée en figures*, Paris, 1719.

[10] Salomon Reinach, *Répertoire de la statuaire grecque et romaine*, Paris, 1906-1930 ; *id.*, *Répertoire des reliefs grecs et romains*, Paris, 1909-1912.

[11] Sur la définition de la collection, voir Elina Moustaira, *Art collections, private and public : a comparative legal study,* Heidelberg-New York-Dordrecht-London, 2015, p. 1-3.

divinités du bassin méditerranéen, – notamment leurs représentations sur bronze –, les pratiques cultuelles, officielles ou personnelles, lesquelles touchent parfois à la magie, et surtout les syncrétismes religieux, et plus largement culturels, en cours dans le bassin méditerranéen antique. Cet intérêt pour la relation de l'homme au divin est par ailleurs le dénominateur commun entre les différentes collections archéologiques et ethnologiques – collections ethnologiques qui comprennent principalement des objets d'Amérique précolombienne et d'Océanie. Nous cherchons ainsi, par le biais des cultes et des rituels, à constituer une collection aussi représentative que possible des grandes cultures qui rayonnèrent dans le bassin méditerranéen ancien, dans l'Amérique précolombienne et en Océanie.

Par ailleurs, nous privilégions aussi la notoriété, voire la cohérence de la collection à laquelle l'objet a appartenu. Plusieurs objets anciennement acquis ont appartenu à des collectionneurs célèbres : Tigrane Pasha, Émile C. Amélineau, Augustus Pitt-Rivers, Pierre Loti ou encore Émile Zola…[12] D'autres noms sont peut-être moins connus du grand public, mais sont ceux d'érudits ou de collectionneurs avertis du XIXe siècle, comme Félix-Bienaimé Feuardent, Eugène Mutiaux, Abraham Adda, Gustave Mustaki… Nous veillons aussi, dans toute la mesure du possible, à ne pas dissocier des lots qui faisaient sens au moment où le premier collectionneur a constitué sa collection, quand le contexte d'acquisition est intéressant : ainsi avons-nous acquis récemment, en deux fois, une partie de l'ancienne collection de Gaspard Théodore Mollien, diplomate français en Colombie au milieu du XIXe siècle. Ces ensembles forment, du point de vue historique, un témoignage intéressant en soi sur le collectionnisme ancien qu'il nous semble important de préserver.
Si un objet parvient à franchir les différentes étapes de la critique et est intégré à nos collections, les conservateurs rédigent une étude scientifique approfondie, qui servira une base à une publication ultérieure.

[12] Voir à ce propos Christiane Ziegler, « Trésors artistiques, univers des dieux : les arts du métal dans la collection égyptienne de la Fondation Gandur pour l'Art », dans *Les Bronzes égyptiens*, Berne, 2014, p. 28-29.

II. Documenter et préserver

Les deux conditions requises à l'accroissement des collections sont leur préservation et leur documentation. Chaque artefact qui entre dans la collection fait ainsi l'objet d'une fiche d'inventaire détaillée munie de tous les documents d'archives disponibles (anciens catalogues de vente mentionnant l'objet, littérature scientifique et littérature « grise », certificat de bien culturel, photos d'archives, rapports de restauration, et tout ce qui a trait au dossier d'achat) dans la base de données *Museum Plus*, logiciel spécifiquement dédié aux collections muséales. Cette base recense toutes les œuvres dont est dépositaire la FGA, toutes collections confondues ; elle est régulièrement enrichie de nouveaux documents d'archives (nouvelles photos, récents rapports de restauration ou notices révisant le contenu des premières notices scientifiques). Véritable mémoire archivistique des collections, la base de données *Museum Plus* est un outil en constant accroissement et en perpétuelle évolution.
Le travail de documentation passe aussi par des campagnes photographiques systématiques (chaque objet disposant d'une photographie de publication et de photos d'identité) qui, à terme, couvriront l'ensemble de nos collections. La numérisation 3D de quelques-unes des œuvres, qui a débuté en 2017, permettra de les présenter sur notre site web. Par ailleurs, certains objets (vases antiques ou objets comportant des décors peu lisibles à la photographie) nécessitent pour leur publication, des dessins techniques. Dans certains cas, des radiographies permettant de mettre en évidence d'anciennes restaurations : tout ceci rejoint alors le dossier de documentation publiable de l'objet.
Une fois acquis, les objets rejoignent un espace d'exposition où ils sont conservés dans les meilleures conditions (température et hygrométrie constantes et adaptées aux divers matériaux, éclairage adapté), selon les standards définis par l'ICOM ; ces conditions d'exposition sont d'ailleurs aussi requises des musées auxquels la FGA prête des objets. La restauration des objets qui entrent dans nos collections et leur entretien régulier (stabilisation de la corrosion des bronzes, nettoyage des pierres, consolidations ou dérestaurations éventuelles…) sont deux autres obligations auxquelles la Fondation consacre une importante part de son budget annuel. Souvent, ces objets qui ont appartenu à d'anciennes collections n'ont été ni nettoyés, ni publiés. Requérant l'intervention de spécialistes, ces travaux de nettoyage réservent alors

parfois d'agréables surprises qui apportent régulièrement des informations nouvelles sur nos objets : ainsi, le nettoyage d'un sphinx en calcaire a-t-il fait apparaître une inscription dédicatoire en grec jusque-là inconnue.

III. Construire l'intérêt public

Alors que l'idée même de collection privée rime encore trop souvent, dans l'esprit du public, avec celle d'une collection d'accès difficile, réservée à quelques *happy few* ou à une élite universitaire, l'objectif que nous poursuivons est de rendre notre collection visible et compréhensible à un public aussi large que possible. Ces démarches s'inscrivent dans un projet global de construction de l'intérêt public[13], exactement comme le ferait un musée. L'accessibilité de nos collections repose sur quelques lignes de force humanistes à savoir que l'art est un vecteur de dialogue entre les cultures et qu'il a un rôle à jouer dans la société actuelle ; que le partage de ces biens culturels et des connaissances qu'ils véhiculent permet de mieux se comprendre ; que l'art doit être mis à la disposition du plus grand nombre, et particulièrement des couches fragilisées de nos sociétés. En d'autres termes, ces collections n'ont d'intérêt que si elles sont vues, partagées et expliquées au plus grand nombre, selon des moyens adaptés. Ceci rejoint en quelque sorte la déclaration que faisait récemment Guillaume Cerutti, ancien directeur général du Centre Pompidou, selon qui « plus que jamais, l'avenir des collections publiques passe par le développement des collections privées »[14].

A. Exposer

Pour ce faire, la FGA mène une politique d'ouverture aux autres institutions muséales, en prêtant ses œuvres pour des expositions (ainsi en 2015, 320 objets archéologiques ont été prêtés pour diverses expositions, dont une exposition qui a fait le tour du Japon[15]) ou à long

---

[13] J. A. Sánchez Cordero Dávila, « The Private Art Collections », *Unif. L. Rev.*, 20 (2015), p. 617-625, et part. p. 618.

[14] Propos recueillis par Martine Robert, « Aux donateurs les musées reconnaissants », *L'Œil*, n° 697 (janv. 2017), p. 104-105, et part. p. 105.

[15] R. S. Bianchi, *Ancient Egypt Art and Magic, Treasures from the Fondation Gandur pour l'Art*, Hokkaido, Asahikawa Museum of Art, 17 avr.-21 juill. 2015; Fukui, Fukui

terme à des musées, dans le cadre de partenariats[16]. Outre la visibilité que ces prêts confèrent aux objets de la collection, ils sont aussi l'occasion de confronter nos œuvres au regard de nos collègues travaillant dans les musées. En 2017, la FGA s'est impliquée aux côtés de l'équipe de la villa romaine de Pully afin de réaliser une exposition archéologique spécialement dédiée aux enfants, consacrée aux relations homme-animal dans l'Antiquité[17]. Ensemble, nous avons mis en œuvre les moyens de rendre cette exposition accessible aux enfants souffrant de diverses formes d'exclusion. Depuis 2018, nous participons aux *Journées européennes du Patrimoine* en ouvrant notre collection archéologique au public et en organisant des visites guidées.

B. Communiquer

La communication sur ce que sont ces objets, d'où ils viennent, est, à côté du devoir de diligence, le second axe de nos activités. Cette communication se fait à des niveaux divers et selon un degré de détail qui varie en fonction du type de média et du public visé. Trois types de communication visent trois publics différents : une communication de niveau élémentaire (qui doit toucher un public jeune), une communication de niveau muséal (visant un public intéressé), et enfin une communication de niveau académique (étudiants, chercheurs ou public érudit). Au niveau élémentaire, la communication doit aujourd'hui passer par les réseaux sociaux : c'est actuellement *Instagram*, où tous les jours sont postés deux nouveaux objets ou tableaux issus de nos collections. Dans ce cas, seule une identification rapide des objets est fournie ; si nécessaire, nous assurons un suivi des questions qui sont posées sur les œuvres. La présence de ces œuvres sur Instagram a pour objectif de susciter l'intérêt du visiteur et de l'inciter à découvrir nos trésors sur le site de la FGA. Le site internet de la FGA est en effet actuellement le moyen privilégié de communiquer sur nos collections et d'en montrer toute la diversité.
En effet, parmi les projets que porte actuellement la FGA, il y a la mise en ligne de *Museum Plus*, la base de données dans laquelle sont

---

Fine Arts Museum, 3 juill.-30 août 2015 ; Tokyo, Shoto Museum of Art, 6 oct.-23 nov. 2015; Gunma, Museum of Art, Tatebayashi, 5 janv.-21 mars 2016.

[16] Ainsi, pour la collection Beaux-Arts, le partenariat établi avec le Musée Reina Sofia de Madrid.

[17] *Archéonimaux*, villa romaine de Pully, du 25 sept. 2017 au 23 déc. 2018.

cataloguées toutes les œuvres de nos collections (c'est *l'e-Museum Plus*) et qui permet à l'e-visiteur d'accéder à toutes les données scientifiques relatives à nos objets. Ici encore, tant pour ce qui touche à la recherche sur la provenance de l'objet archéologique ou ethnologique qu'à son étude scientifique, nous privilégions une communication en toute transparence. Toutes les informations scientifiques de base (identification, origine géographique présumée, matériaux, date, provenance et bibliographie éventuelle) y sont accessibles. S'il est, à terme, envisagé que tous les objets de la FGA s'y trouvent, c'est actuellement les trois quarts de nos collections qui sont en ligne. De plus, convaincue qu'il faut apprendre à regarder autrement les objets en mettant les nouvelles technologies à leur service, la FGA prévoit de développer sur son site web une interface où seront déposés les objets numérisés en 3D : l'e-visiteur aura ainsi l'occasion de voir les tout petits objets (amulettes, bijoux…) de manière magnifiée et de les manipuler virtuellement tout en disposant de toutes les informations scientifiques qu'ils recèlent – exactement comme ils ne pourraient jamais le faire dans un vrai musée.
Enfin, le rapport annuel, qui présente les comptes et les activités de la Fondation au cours de l'année écoulée, s'adresse à tous puisqu'il paraît annuellement sous forme de livre, mais est aussi accessible en ligne. Pour notre dernier rapport annuel, nous avons inauguré une série d'essais des conservateurs présentant, sous une forme relevant de la bonne vulgarisation, un objet des collections dont ils s'occupent.

IV. Publier

Si nous voulons mettre en œuvre de nouveaux médias pour faire connaître nos collections, nous voulons aussi en faire comprendre le sens : car qu'est-ce qu'un objet archéologique ou ethnologique sans une étude scientifique de qualité ? Faire apparaître l'objet au grand jour, le faire connaître, en donner l'accès aux spécialistes directement ou par voie de publication, tels sont les objectifs que la FGA poursuit en publiant le matériel dont elle est dépositaire. La publication scientifique de l'objet apparaît comme le seul moyen de le faire revivre, en en donnant l'accès à la communauté scientifique. La vie même de la collection passe par sa publication.
Au niveau « académique », nous privilégions ainsi deux modes d'expression pour nos publications : une publication en ligne, sur le site web, et des publications traditionnelles. « L'œuvre du mois » est

accessible en ligne sur le site de la FGA. À l'instar de ce qui se pratique sur les sites web de nombreux musées, nous avons récemment instauré la mise en ligne d'une notice scientifique relative à un objet particulièrement intéressant, signée d'un conservateur (avec archivage des anciennes notices). Outre le fait que cela donne une visibilité aux travaux scientifiques des conservateurs ou des mandataires chargés d'étude, c'est, pour la Fondation, le moyen de présenter des dossiers complets relatifs aux œuvres, – et particulièrement tout ce qui concerne le devoir de diligence. Le troisième avantage est que cette publication permettra à terme, grâce à un système d'archivage des notices, de montrer l'existence de la vie scientifique, mais aussi le réseau de chercheurs dans lequel s'inscrit la Fondation.

La publication de catalogues raisonnés participe aussi de cette volonté de donner un nouveau statut aux œuvres, qui de pur plaisir de collectionneur deviennent accessibles aux chercheurs et au public. Il y a tout d'abord les catalogues d'exposition, édités seuls ou en partenariat[18]. Par ailleurs, la FGA a commencé une publication systématique de ses collections. Sans parler de ce qui relève des beaux-arts, nous avons déjà publié un premier volume de 108 bronzes égyptiens et nous prévoyons à terme de publier toutes nos collections. À cela, nous pourrions en ajouter une troisième, que nous comptons mettre sur pied prochainement : les conférences « grand public » sur des objets de la Fondation. Il est donc pour nous primordial que les objets soient publiés et accessibles à la communauté scientifique. De ce point de vue, pour soutenir sa politique de recherche et de publication, la FGA s'est dotée d'une équipe de cinq conservateurs qui non seulement sont chargés d'étudier le matériel qui entre dans les collections, mais qui insèrent la FGA dans un réseau académique et muséal ; à ces scientifiques s'ajoutent des mandataires, spécialistes d'une discipline, qui étudient certains types d'objets spécifiques ainsi que deux documentalistes, un régisseur et un coordinateur des prêts. À cet égard, en Suisse, et peut-être même en Europe, la FGA est

---

[18] Pour ne citer que les principaux : *Les bronzes égyptiens. Fondation Gandur pour l'Art*, Genève, 2014 ; Robert S. Bianchi, *Ancient Egypt Art and Magic, Treasures from the Fondation Gandur pour l'Art*, Museum of Fine Arts, Saint Petersburg, Florida, 2011 ; pour les ouvrages publiés en partenariat : *Reflets du divin. Antiquités pharaoniques et classiques d'une collection privée. Musée d'art et d'histoire, Genève, 30 août 2001-3 février 2002*, Genève, 2001 ; *Corps et esprits. Regards croisés sur la Méditerranée antique*, Genève-Milan, 2014 ; *Migrations divines*, Paris, 2015.

probablement un des rares cas de fondation de ce type, vouée à l'archéologie et aux beaux-arts, à employer autant de professionnels : à nouveau, cette structure l'apparente à un musée.

Conclusion

Si nous sommes particulièrement attentifs à rendre nos collections vivantes aujourd'hui, nous souhaitons également qu'elles soient pérennes. Nous voulons donc qu'à l'avenir, et même après la disparition du fondateur et de l'équipe actuellement en place, ces collections continuent de s'accroître dans le même souci d'éthique, de cohérence et d'ouverture que celui qui nous anime actuellement. Il est de notre responsabilité de conserver cette collection vivante et accessible à tous.

La fiscalité française favorise-t-elle l'accès aux collections privées ?

Armelle VERJAT
Docteur en droit
Chercheur-associé Institut Droit Éthique Patrimoine
Université Paris-Saclay

Le droit fiscal français n'appréhende pas la collection comme une universalité de fait[1] ; il identifie des objets, des éléments individuels susceptibles d'intégrer la collection mais pouvant exister en dehors d'un tel ensemble. Reprenant *in extenso* la directive européenne du 28 novembre 2006[2], l'article 98 A de l'annexe 3 au Code général des impôts liste les biens susceptibles d'être qualifiés d'objets de collection. Aux côtés des timbres, on y trouve notamment les objets de collections naturalistes ou ethnographiques, dès lors qu'ils ne sont pas neufs[3]. Plus généralement, selon l'administration fiscale, « le point de savoir si un bien constitue un objet de collection est une question de fait qui doit être appréciée, cas par cas », et « découle de l'application d'un ou plusieurs des critères suivants : l'ancienneté ; la rareté ; l'importance de son prix, lequel doit être sensiblement supérieur à la valeur d'un bien similaire destiné à un usage courant ; l'arrêt de la fabrication du bien ; la provenance ou la destination[4] ; l'intérêt historique qu'il présente ; le

---

[1] Sur cette notion, v. not. E. Meiller, « L'universalité de fait », *RTD civ.* 2012. 651.

[2] Dir. 2006/112/CE du Conseil, *JOUE* L 347/1 du 11 déc. 2006. Selon le droit douanier de l'Union européenne, « la notion de collection n'est pas autrement caractérisée que par ses éléments constitutifs », *Dictionnaire comparé du droit du patrimoine culturel*, CNRS Éditions.

[3] Selon l'article 98 A de l'annexe 3 au Code général des impôts, sont considérés comme objets de collections les « timbres-poste, timbres fiscaux, marques postales, enveloppes premier jour, entiers postaux et analogues, oblitérés ou bien non oblitérés mais n'ayant pas cours et n'étant pas destinés à avoir cours » ainsi que les « collections et spécimens pour collections de zoologie, de botanique, de minéralogie, d'anatomie, ou présentant un intérêt historique, archéologique, paléontologique, ethnographique ou numismatique ». Il existe en outre une définition spécifique des véhicules de collection (et motocyclettes), Circ. douanière n° FCPD1421298C du 8 sept. 2014, *Bulletin officiel des douanes* n° 7032 ; W. Hannecart-Weyth « Voitures de collection – L'autre eldorado fiscal », *JAC* n° 25/2015, p. 45.

[4] L'utilisation faite du bien doit être différente de sa destination initiale, BOI-TVA-

fait qu'il ait appartenu à un personnage célèbre »[5], qu'il fasse l'objet de « transactions spéciales en dehors du commerce habituel des objets similaires utilisables » ou qu'il illustre une période de l'évolution des réalisations humaines[6].

Si, à n'en pas douter, ces critères permettent de retenir au titre des objets de collection ceux issus des collections les plus atypiques, il n'en reste pas moins que, d'un point de vue fiscal, l'objet de collection est circonscrit et se distingue de l'objet d'art et de l'objet d'antiquité. Ces deux derniers ont toutefois vocation à être inclus dans notre propos, car ils peuvent faire partie d'une collection au sens retenu dans le cadre de ce colloque[7] et suivent, en tout état de cause, un régime fiscal proche de celui des objets de collection. Ainsi, sont notamment des œuvres d'art et d'antiquité[8], les tableaux, gravures, statues, tapisseries, céramiques ou photographies, auxquels s'ajoutent les œuvres d'art audiovisuel, les livres et manuscrits, ou encore « les éléments faisant partie intégrante de monuments artistiques, historiques ou religieux et provenant du démembrement de ceux-ci, ayant plus de cent ans d'âge »[9].

L'ensemble de ces biens est susceptible d'intégrer autant une collection publique qu'une collection privée, c'est-à-dire détenue par une personne relevant du droit privé, personne physique ou morale, œuvrant dans un but lucratif ou non. Cette détention privée exclut-elle tout accès du public à la collection ? Faut-il considérer que privé rime avec caché ?

SECT-90-10, 11 avr. 2014, § 360.

[5] BOI-RPPM-PVBMC-20-10, 31 déc. 2018, § 70.

[6] BOI-TVA-SECT-90-10, 11 avr. 2014, § 360. Ces critères sont issus notamment de CJCE, 10 oct. 1985, aff. 252/84. La définition fiscale de l'œuvre d'art ou de collection n'est toutefois pas unique, comme le montre les développements qui suivent sur l'évaluation des objets d'art et de collection et les meubles meublants.

[7] Est ici retenue la définition de droit français du *Dictionnaire comparé du droit du patrimoine culturel* (CNRS Éditions), selon laquelle la collection est un « ensemble de biens mobiliers et immobiliers dont la réunion présente un intérêt historique, artistique ou scientifique distinct de la valeur des éléments qui le composent », plus large que celle de l'article R. 111-3 du code du patrimoine qui ne semble inclure que les ensembles mobiliers. *Cf. supra,* l'intervention de M. Roellinger.

[8] Ces notions ne sont pas développées ici car la délimitation entre les notions d'objet de collection, d'art ou d'antiquité n'a pas d'incidence sur les mesures fiscales, qui s'appliquent généralement dans les trois cas. Pour plus de précisions, v. not. art. 98 A de l'annexe 3 au CGI ; BOI-TVA-SECT-90-10, 11 avr. 2014, § 130 ; É. Mirieu de Labarre, « Le statut fiscal de l'objet d'art », *Droit fiscal* n° 20/206, p. 20 et J. Fingerhut, « L'art, le droit douanier et le droit fiscal », *Droit fiscal* n°41/2017, p. 493.

[9] BOI-RPPM-PVBMC-20-10, 31 déc. 2018, § 40.

Et surtout quel rôle le droit fiscal joue-t-il dans l'exposition des objets ? Comme indiqué précédemment, la notion de collection en tant que telle n'est pas reconnue par le droit fiscal, qui ne favorise pas davantage la cohérence d'ensemble que le bien lui-même, élément de cet ensemble. Aussi, plutôt que l'accès du public aux collections, il sera surtout question de l'accès aux objets (de collection, d'art ou d'antiquité), c'est-à-dire essentiellement de leur exposition au public[10]. Néanmoins, la collection ne sera pas oubliée car sera également évoqué le rôle de la fiscalité française dans le maintien ou au contraire la dispersion des ensembles d'objets, constitutifs d'une collection, notamment à l'épreuve de l'accès à ces ensembles. Il apparaît que plusieurs dispositifs fiscaux spécifiques peuvent inciter le collectionneur à montrer les œuvres qu'il détient, sans pour autant toujours tenir compte de la cohérence d'ensemble. Mais, dans le même temps, certaines dispositions fiscales peuvent être vues comme un frein indirect à l'exposition de ces mêmes œuvres.

Les incitations fiscales à l'accès aux collections en mains privées

L'étude des mesures fiscales visant les objets de collection, d'art ou d'antiquité montre que, si elles sont susceptibles d'encourager l'accès aux œuvres détenues par des personnes physiques ou morales de droit privé, leur objectif premier est généralement tout autre. Ainsi, certaines contribuent à l'enrichissement des collections publiques, et d'autres au maintien d'ensembles patrimoniaux ou à la constitution de collections privées.

Enrichissement des collections publiques : l'exposition garantie ?

Deux mesures fiscales encouragent les collectionneurs privés (ou leurs héritiers ou donataires) à remettre à l'État tout ou partie de leurs biens à caractère historique ou artistique, contribuant ainsi à l'enrichissement des collections publiques[11]. Ces deux dispositifs nécessitent un transfert de la propriété du bien à l'État, ce qui ne permet plus de le qualifier de

[10] Il est bien entendu admis que l'accès peut être limité, à un public de scientifiques par exemple, pour des raisons de conservation des œuvres, notamment pour les archives ou livres.

[11] Pour une application de ces deux dispositions aux archives, v. not. C. Tourtier Bonazzi Chantal, « La loi de défense du patrimoine national et les Archives », *La Gazette des archives*, n° 105, 1979. p. 112.

privé. Toutefois, sous certaines conditions, une réserve de jouissance peut être accordée au collectionneur privé ; tout en ne lui appartenant plus, le bien est alors placé sous sa responsabilité. Cette réserve de jouissance n'est pas exclusive de toute exposition de l'œuvre, bien au contraire. En l'accordant, l'État exige le plus souvent en contrepartie que le bien soit accessible au public ; elle semble dès lors garantir l'accès au bien, qui n'est qu'hypothétique dans le cas où l'État en est le dépositaire.

1. Tout d'abord, le Code général des impôts accorde une exonération des droits de mutation à titre gratuit à l'acquéreur, le donataire, l'héritier ou le légataire d'une œuvre d'art, de livres, d'objets de collections ou de documents de haute valeur artistique ou historique dont il fait don à l'État[12]. Même si la valeur patrimoniale des biens ainsi reçus peut évidemment l'y inciter, aucune disposition légale ou règlementaire n'impose à l'État de les exposer au public. À défaut de charges dictées par le donateur, l'État est libre de disposer des biens comme il l'entend et n'est tenu ni de les rendre accessibles au public, ni d'en conserver la cohérence en tant que collection. Selon la doctrine administrative, « le donateur a la faculté de demander que le bien faisant l'objet de sa libéralité soit affecté par l'État à un musée départemental ou communal »[13], sans faire expressément référence à son éventuelle exposition[14]. Toutefois, s'agissant d'une libéralité, ledit donateur peut en principe imposer tout type de conditions ou charges au bénéficiaire[15],

---

[12] C. patr., art. L. 122-3 ; CGI, art. 1131. Ce n'est pas le collectionneur lui-même qui transfère tout ou partie de sa collection à l'État mais la personne à qui il a souhaité la transmettre, à condition bien entendu que ledit collectionneur n'ait pas assorti le don ou le legs d'une interdiction d'aliéner la ou les œuvres. Les aspects techniques et procéduraux de cette mesure ne sont pas détaillés ici, v. à ce sujet BOI-ENR-DMTG-10-20-30-80, 1er avr. 2015 ; O. Dantil, « Collections publiques – Acquitter ses impôts en "monnaie d'art" », *JAC* n°27/2015, p. 44.

[13] BOI-ENR-DMTG-10-20-30-80, 1er avr. 2015, § 50. Il en va différemment en cas de dation en paiement, v. ci-après et CAA Paris, 11 juin 2015, n° 13PA02966, *AJCT* 2015. 593, obs. J.-D. Dreyfus.

[14] L'affectation de l'œuvre à un musée peut néanmoins avoir un impact sur son accès ; il est en effet possible d'admettre que la remise d'une œuvre à un musée local (plutôt qu'à un musée national dont la collection est déjà riche) renforce la probabilité de son exposition.

[15] L'administration fiscale rappelle que « l'offre de donation faite à l'État peut être assortie de certaines conditions ou réserves », BOI-ENR-DMTG-10-20-30-80, 1er avr. 2015, § 50.

parmi lesquelles l'obligation de favoriser l'accès aux œuvres remises. Sa générosité peut donc être dictée par la volonté de voir les œuvres données exposées au public ou encore de conserver l'unité d'une collection en interdisant sa dispersion[16].
Lorsque le donateur souhaite conserver la jouissance des biens donnés, comme l'y autorise la loi[17], l'accessibilité des œuvres dépend de sa seule volonté. Il peut garder l'usage exclusif des biens donnés, sans que l'État ne puisse lui imposer leur présentation au public[18]. Il peut au contraire exposer les œuvres et même s'y engager dans l'offre de donation[19]. Par principe temporaire[20] et dictée par la seule satisfaction du donateur, cette réserve de jouissance peut devenir illimitée à la demande du donateur, lorsque « les biens donnés sont attachés à un immeuble, en raison de motifs historiques ou artistiques »[21]. Elle bénéficie alors, après le donateur, « successivement aux personnes auxquelles l'immeuble sera transmis »[22], sous réserve d'un maintien *in situ* des œuvres et de leur exposition au public. S'il semble commandé par la préservation de la cohérence d'un ensemble immeuble-meubles, ce maintien *in situ* assorti de l'obligation d'accès aux œuvres est en fait la contrepartie de la réserve illimitée de jouissance. En effet, à défaut d'une telle réserve ou si elle reste temporaire, ni ce maintien *in situ*, ni même l'accès au public ne s'imposent, peu importe la nécessité de conserver la cohérence

---

[16] Bien entendu, l'État peut refuser d'agréer la libéralité si les charges lui semblent démesurées ou inadaptées ou fixer des conditions à leur mise en œuvre (BOI-ENR-DMTG-10-20-30-80, 1er avr. 2015) ; il peut en outre obtenir leur révision en cas de difficulté d'application (CGPPP, art. L. 2222-12 s.).

[17] CGI, art. 1131.

[18] Sans ôter toute effectivité à l'article 1131 du code général des impôts, l'État conserve néanmoins la possibilité d'édicter des conditions lors de l'agrément de la donation ou de refuser celui-ci si la réserve de jouissance lui semble, par exemple, présenter des dangers pour la conservation des biens.

[19] Notons toutefois que le Modèle d'offre de donation n'envisage la visite du public que lorsque le donateur est une personne morale, BOI-LETTRE-000099, 26 août 2013. Rien n'empêche une personne privée de s'y engager. Si cet engagement est repris au titre des conditions d'agrément, le donateur ne devrait plus pouvoir s'y soustraire, sauf à renoncer à la réserve de jouissance.

[20] CGI, art. 1131. En principe, pour une personne physique, la réserve de jouissance s'éteint avec la mort du donateur, ou le cas échéant de son conjoint ; pour une personne morale, elle prend fin à sa dissolution, ou à défaut, dans un délai maximal de 25 ans.

[21] CGI, art. 1131.

[22] *Id.* Personnes qui ne sont pas nécessairement des héritiers mais de potentiels acquéreurs à titre payant.

immeuble-meubles. En outre, en cas d'option pour une réserve de jouissance illimitée, le non-respect des engagements de maintien *in situ* et d'accès du public fait disparaître l'apparente nécessité de préserver la cohérence de l'ensemble patrimonial : il suppose la remise des biens à l'État et acte donc la séparation de l'immeuble et du meuble.

2. Constitutive de l'un des principaux modes d'enrichissement des collections publiques[23], la dation en paiement permet, quant à elle, de s'acquitter des droits de mutation à titre gratuit ou de l'impôt sur la fortune immobilière (IFI)[24] par la remise « d'œuvres d'art, de livres, d'objets de collection, de documents, de haute valeur artistique ou historique »[25]. Aucune disposition légale ou règlementaire ne garantit l'exposition au public des biens transférés dans les collections publiques par ce biais, cette éventualité étant laissée à l'appréciation de l'État ou de la personne dépositaire[26]. Toutefois, la « haute valeur

---

[23] « Pour les musées nationaux des beaux-arts, le montant des dations a dépassé à huit reprises le montant des crédits d'acquisition qui leur sont attribués » et, pour les années 1988-2008, « la moyenne du montant des dations venues enrichir ces musées représente 70% du montant » de ces crédits, J.-P. Changeux, S. Stcherbatcheff, « La dation en paiement : 40 ans de succès », *La Revue du Trésor* n° 5, mai 2008, p. 340. La diversité du patrimoine recueilli dans les collections publiques par ce biais est également soulignée, p. 343. Les œuvres acquises par dation peuvent venir directement des ateliers des artistes (succession Picasso ou Chagall) et non des seuls collectionneurs. Les œuvres des artistes vivants peuvent être admises (v. rép. min. à B. Bourg-Broc, n° 92506, *JOAN* du 20 juin 2006), ce qui n'est pas sans faire penser au dispositif fiscal mexicain permettant aux artistes de payer leurs impôts par la remise d'œuvres aux collections publiques, F. Laffaille, « *Pago en especie* : payer l'impôt en œuvres d'art », *JAC* n°2015/21, p. 40.

[24] Anciennement ISF, impôt de solidarité sur la fortune. Les autres impôts ne sont pas visés ; v. en particulier le refus d'extension de la dation en paiement des impôts locaux, Rép. min. à J.-L. Masson, n° 05329, *JO Sénat* du 2 juill. 2009.

[25] C. patr., art. L.122-1 ; CGI, art. 1716 bis ; v. égal. CGI, ann. 2, art. 384-A et 384-0 A bis. Les aspects techniques et procéduraux de cette mesure ne sont pas détaillés ici, v. à ce sujet BOI-SJ-AGR-50-20, 6 nov. 2018 ; F. Bouglé, « Art et transmission patrimoniale » [2], *Revue juridique de l'Ouest*, 1999-2, p. 131 ; O. Dantil, « Collections publiques – Acquitter ses impôts en "monnaie d'art" », *JAC* n°27/2015, p. 44 ; P. Noual, *L'être et l'avoir de la collection. Essai sur l'avenir juridique des corpus artistiques*, thèse, université Toulouse 1 Capitole, 2016, p. 523 s.

[26] Si les biens offerts en dation n'intègrent pas nécessairement un musée national, le demandeur ne peut imposer le dépôt dans un musée déterminé, l'État devant disposer librement des œuvres proposées en dation, CAA Paris, 11 juin 2015, n° 13PA02966, *AJCT* 2015. 593, obs. J.-D. Dreyfus.

artistique ou historique »[27] reconnue à l'objet mobilier ainsi acquis laisse supposer qu'il sera montré, de manière temporaire, si ce n'est continue. Ainsi, « celui qui offre des œuvres en dation a l'assurance que celles-ci font partie d'un patrimoine collectif ouvert à tous »[28].
En revanche, la dation peut indirectement favoriser le démembrement des collections, et ce à plusieurs titres. Tout d'abord, lors de l'instruction de la demande, la Commission interministérielle compétente peut ne retenir « que certains biens présentés dans l'offre ou proposer au demandeur la substitution ou l'adjonction d'autres biens à son offre »[29]. Elle est ainsi susceptible de « recomposer » une collection ou de compléter des collections publiques existantes. Même si le collectionneur privé conserve la possibilité de refuser la proposition de la Commission afin de préserver la cohérence de sa collection[30], les considérations patrimoniales ayant guidé les choix de la Commission peuvent entrer en contradiction avec le respect de l'intégrité de la collection privée dont émanent les biens. Ensuite, lorsque la valeur libératoire d'un bien est supérieure aux droits exigibles, ne sont accordés ni soultes[31], ni avoirs ou crédits sur des droits futurs. Dès lors, le contribuable n'est pas incité à donner un ensemble de biens si seuls certains d'entre eux suffisent à régler l'impôt dû. Fiscalement, cela peut même l'encourager à morceler sa collection, de façon à conserver les objets non immédiatement nécessaires au règlement de l'impôt mais utiles pour une potentielle dette fiscale ultérieure. Enfin, même si l'offre de dation vise une collection entière, et est acceptée dans sa globalité, rien n'interdit à l'État de déposer les œuvres constituant cette collection dans différents musées, dispersant sur le territoire ce qui pourrait constituer un ensemble[32].

---

[27] V. not. F. Bouglé, « Art et transmission patrimoniale » [2], *Revue juridique de l'Ouest*, 1999-2, p. 144.

[28] J.-P. Changeux, « Le patrimoine en danger : l'espoir des dations », *Revue de l'Art* n° 88, 1990, p. 9. L'avis de la Commission interministérielle sur un projet de dation vise à déterminer l'importance patrimoniale de l'œuvre : « mérite-t-elle d'être présentée dans nos Musées Nationaux ? », *id.*, p. 7.

[29] CGI, annexe 2, art. 384-0 A bis.

[30] Sous réserve toutefois d'avoir la capacité financière de refuser l'avantage fiscal de la dation.

[31] BOI-SJ-AGR-50-20, 23 sept. 2013, § 100 et 290. V. le cas signalé du versement d'une soulte par la société des amis du Louvre pour l'acquisition d'une œuvre dont la valeur libératoire était supérieure à celle de la dette fiscale, cité par F. Bouglé, « Art et transmission patrimoniale » [2], *Revue juridique de l'Ouest*, 1999-2, p. 157, note 71.

[32] Ce n'est toutefois pas la solution qui a été retenue lors de la succession de Picasso,

La dation étant un mode de paiement de l'impôt (et non une libéralité, comme précédemment)[33], l'administration fiscale retient par principe que « le demandeur n'est pas admis à stipuler à son profit une réserve de jouissance portant sur les biens offerts »[34]. Dès lors, une offre de dation peut être valablement refusée si son acceptation risque de porter « atteinte à l'intérêt de l'État, qui ne pourrait disposer librement des œuvres »[35], en imposant par exemple leur affectation à un musée désigné. Toutefois, dans au moins quatre cas, des objets remis en dation ont été replacés ou maintenus dans un monument privé[36]. Cette possibilité, non formalisée dans les textes et rarement mise en œuvre, est loin de ne constituer qu'une faveur accordée à certains collectionneurs, elle présente un triple avantage pour la conservation et la mise en valeur du patrimoine. En premier lieu, la réserve de jouissance[37] est conditionnée par un accès du public aux biens remis en dation, ce qui n'est pas juridiquement garanti par la dation elle-même[38]. Ainsi, plus que le transfert du bien dans les collections publiques, c'est la réserve de jouissance accordée au collectionneur privé qui garantit

---

qui a donné lieu à la création du musée éponyme à Paris.

[33] Le fait que la dation en paiement soit prévue dans la partie « Acquisitions à titre onéreux » du code général de la propriété des personnes publiques (art. L. 1111-5) montre l'enjeu budgétaire de la mesure, contrairement aux dons et legs.

[34] BOI-SJ-AGR-50-20, 23 sept. 2013, § 100.

[35] CAA Paris, 11 juin 2015, n° 13PA02966, *AJCT* 2015. 593, obs. J.-D. Dreyfus. En l'espèce, l'offre de dation de la Ville de Bayonne était assortie « d'une condition d'affectation des œuvres [au musée Bonnat], ainsi qu'en atteste notamment la lettre adressée le 23 mai 2011 par le maire de Bayonne au bureau des agréments et rescrits de la direction générale des finances publiques, aux termes de laquelle il indiquait que "l'hypothèse d'une dation avec un seul dépôt provisoire des œuvres à Bayonne doit être écartée, car cela priverait le Musée Bonnat-Helleu des œuvres les plus belles et les plus rares, diminuant ainsi sensiblement l'intérêt du legs pour le public" et précise qu'"une exposition des œuvres dans un autre musée serait en outre contraire aux dispositions du testament" [ayant désigné le Musée Bonnat comme légataire universel] ».

[36] Il en est ainsi des douze tentures de l'histoire d'Alexandre remises en dation en 1988 tout en étant maintenues au château d'Haroué. L'une d'elles a disparu dans l'incendie de l'atelier de restauration Bodin en 1997, tout comme les quatre tapisseries de l'Histoire de Diane données en dation en 1979 et conservées au château d'Anet jusqu'à leur destruction. Deux panneaux de portes ont également été réinstallés au château de la Bâtie d'Urfé suite à une dation. Dans le dernier cas, le dépôt est postérieur à la dation puisque le portrait du duc de Noailles, remis en dation à l'État en 1993, n'est en dépôt au château de Maintenon que depuis 1999.

[37] Il est parfois question de « dation avec maintien *in situ* ».

[38] P. Laffitte, Rapp. n° 399 du 20 juin 2011, Sénat.

l'accès aux œuvres, celui-ci en étant la condition *sine qua none* non écrite[39]. En outre, « cette disposition, si elle était mieux connue, éviterait peut-être que certains châteaux ne se vident de leur mobilier... »[40]. Tout en allégeant la charge fiscale du contribuable, elle permet en effet de maintenir voire de réintégrer des meubles dans leur cadre historique, favorisant la cohérence de l'ensemble patrimonial immeuble-meubles, et ce dans l'esprit de la servitude de maintien dans les lieux, adoptée dans le cadre de la loi relative à la liberté de création, à l'architecture et au patrimoine[41]. Enfin, la réserve de jouissance peut contribuer à sauvegarder l'intégrité d'ensembles mobiliers, telles que des bibliothèques[42] ou des collections, dont la valeur patrimoniale résulte non de chaque objet pris individuellement mais de son rassemblement cohérent. Combinée à des dations successives (chaque année en paiement de l'ISF-IFI par exemple), elle permet la conservation de l'ensemble le temps du transfert progressif à l'État des biens le constituant[43]. Au terme de ce transfert, la collection ou la bibliothèque peut alors soit être maintenue *in situ* compte tenu de ses liens historiques ou artistiques avec l'immeuble, soit être déplacée dans un autre lieu sous la responsabilité de l'État ou d'un dépositaire désigné par lui. Outre qu'elle laisse la possibilité au collectionneur de continuer à enrichir la collection[44], la première solution présente l'avantage de garantir l'accès à la collection comme évoqué précédemment.

---

[39] « La possibilité existe de maintenir des œuvres importantes dans leur cadre historique, à condition, bien entendu, qu'elles soient accessibles au public et bien protégées », J.-P. Changeux, « Le patrimoine en danger : l'espoir des dations », *Revue de l'Art* n°88, 1990, p. 9.

[40] J.-P. Changeux, « Le patrimoine en danger : l'espoir des dations », *Revue de l'Art* n° 88, 1990, p. 9. Néanmoins, le risque de dispersion du mobilier semble être autant le résultat du montant des droits de mutation (conduisant à « vendre le meuble pour garder l'immeuble » selon J.-P. Changeux (p. 5) ; v. égal. F. Bouglé, « Art et transmission patrimoniale » [2], *Revue juridique de l'Ouest*, 1999-2, p. 138) que des règles civiles du partage.

[41] C. patr., art. L. 622-1-2.

[42] Sur ce point, v. not. M. Roux, *Les dations aux bibliothèques*, Mémoire d'étude Enssib, M. Poulain dir., 2013.

[43] Selon P. Laffitte (Rapp. n° 399 du 20 juin 2011, Sénat), « la dation a [déjà] permis [...] de sauvegarder l'intégrité d'ensembles mobiliers [...] par remise "échelonnée" de ces ensembles à l'État ».

[44] « Rien n'empêche les particuliers de faire l'acquisition d'une œuvre dans le but avoué de dation », F. Bouglé, « Art et transmission patrimoniale » [2], *Revue juridique de l'Ouest*, 1999-2, p. 162. Toutefois, l'offre de dation n'est pas recevable lorsque les biens sont détenus depuis moins de cinq ans par l'intéressé, à moins qu'ils ne soient

Avec la dation comme avec la donation, la réserve de jouissance illimitée favorise l'accès au public de biens appartenant à des collections publiques mais maintenus dans des mains privées. Elle contribue aussi à la préservation de la cohérence d'ensembles, ce qui conduit à s'interroger sur l'articulation de ces dispositifs fiscaux avec les nouveaux articles L. 622-1-1 et L. 622-1-2 du code du patrimoine. En effet, le classement d'un ensemble ou d'une collection d'objets mobiliers au titre des monuments historiques ne limite-t-il pas les possibilités de remise en dation ou de donation d'une seule partie de ces objets ? De même la servitude de maintien dans les lieux, susceptible de grever des objets mobiliers attachés à un immeuble classé par des liens historiques ou artistiques remarquables, permet-elle une dation ou une donation ? Pour l'heure, cette éventualité nécessite des autorisations particulières ou une réserve de jouissance illimitée. Peut-être cette dernière devrait-elle dès lors devenir la norme dans ces cas particuliers, ce qui pourrait nécessiter toutefois des ajustements légaux ou règlementaires.

Création et maintien des collections privées : l'exposition favorisée

Plusieurs avantages fiscaux visant les meubles à caractère historique ou artistique sont conditionnés par l'exposition desdits meubles. Ici encore le maintien de la collection en tant qu'entité n'est pas favorisé, les règles fiscales incitant seulement à rendre accessibles au public les œuvres, prises individuellement, ou éventuellement constituant un ensemble avec un immeuble, cet accès n'étant pas prévu par le code du patrimoine ou d'autres textes juridiques.

3. Les dispositifs fiscaux en faveur des immeubles privés classés ou inscrits au titre des monuments historiques retiennent généralement une approche civiliste de la notion d'immeuble, si bien que les meubles attachés à perpétuelle demeure, au sens de l'article 525 du code civil (immeubles par destination), peuvent bénéficier d'avantages fiscaux similaires à l'immeuble auquel ils sont liés[45]. Ainsi, les dons de mécénat en faveur des monuments historiques privés (ouvrant droit à une

---

entrés en sa possession par mutation à titre gratuit (CGI, art. 1716 bis).

[45] Les aspects techniques et procéduraux des mesures présentées ci-après ne sont pas détaillés.

réduction d'impôt sur le revenu ou les sociétés[46]) peuvent permettre de financer des dépenses de conservation ou de restauration d'objets classés ou inscrits exposés au public dans un immeuble historique auquel ils sont attachés à perpétuelle demeure[47]. Peuvent également être déduites dans le cadre du régime de l'impôt sur le revenu les primes d'assurance de ces mêmes objets situés sur le parcours de visite[48]. Dans les deux cas, l'avantage est soumis à une ouverture au public de l'immeuble au minimum 40 jours par an. Pour le mécénat, le propriétaire doit s'engager à maintenir cette ouverture pendant 10 ans à compter de la fin des travaux. L'exonération des droits de mutation à titre gratuit, quant à elle, vise non seulement les immeubles par nature et par destination, mais aussi « les biens meubles qui en constituent le complément historique ou artistique »[49], qu'ils soient ou non protégés au titre des monuments historiques. Ici aussi l'ouverture au public est requise, au moins 60 jours par an[50], et ce pour une durée indéterminée, sauf accident de la vie[51]. Dans ces trois dispositifs, l'avantage fiscal n'a d'existence qu'en présence d'un immeuble protégé au titre des monuments historiques, immeuble auquel les meubles sont attachés, soit physiquement (scellement), soit en raison de leur lien historique ou artistique, et qui doit être accessible au public dans les mêmes conditions que lesdits meubles. Au-delà de l'accès aux œuvres, ces mesures fiscales ont indéniablement vocation à préserver les liens existants entre la collection privée et l'immeuble dans lequel elle est conservée, ce qui n'est pas sans rappeler la servitude de maintien *in situ* instaurée par la loi relative à la liberté de création, à l'architecture et au patrimoine[52].

Ceci est particulièrement significatif pour le régime d'exonération des droits de mutation, dont la mise en œuvre nécessite la signature d'une convention entre le(s) repreneur(s) et l'État. En effet, si l'avantage fiscal n'est pas conditionné par la présence de meubles dans le monument[53], il n'en reste pas moins que, selon le ministère en charge

---

[46] CGI, art. 200, 2 bis et 238 bis, 1, f ; C. patr., art. L. 143-2-1 et L. 143-15.
[47] BOI-IR-RICI-250-10-20-30, 12 sept. 2012, § 230.
[48] BOI-RFPI-BASE-20-60, 25 janv. 2017, § 60.
[49] CGI, art. 795 A.
[50] Décr. n° 2003-1238 du 17 déc. 2003 (mod. décr. n° 88-389 du 21 avr. 1988), *JO* du 24, convention-type, art. 3.
[51] *Id.*, art. 4.
[52] C. patr., art. L. 622-1-2, créé par L. n° 2016-925 du 7 juill. 2016, *JO* du 8, art. 75.
[53] Rép. min. à M. Caldaguès, n° 20660, *JO Sénat* du 11 juin 1992.

de la culture, « le but recherché par le texte, et qui doit être poursuivi dans toute la mesure du possible, est de maintenir sur place un ensemble mobilier qui soit cohérent avec l'immeuble qui l'abrite »[54]. L'inventaire du mobilier concerné est « dressé contradictoirement par les héritiers, donataires ou légataires, les représentants de la direction régionale des affaires culturelles et de la direction des finances publiques du lieu de situation de l'immeuble »[55], ce qui signifie que les bénéficiaires de l'exonération comme les services de l'État peuvent (re)composer la collection existante, le critère principal étant le lien des meubles avec l'immeuble (et éventuellement le coût fiscal de l'opération, qui légitime l'intervention des services fiscaux), et non l'unité de la collection elle-même puisque les meubles ne constituant pas le « complément historique ou artistique » de l'immeuble doivent être écartés[56]. Les éléments de décor (meubles ou immeubles par destination) ainsi identifiés sont les seuls à être exonérés ; ils sont listés en annexe de la convention, ainsi que leurs conditions d'entretien et de présentation[57]. Ils doivent en effet être maintenus sur le parcours de visite, ce qui garantit leur accès au public[58], sauf en cas de rupture de la convention, qui impose aux signataires de payer les droits de mutation à titre gratuit. Cette rupture peut résulter de la fermeture du monument (et donc de la non-accessibilité à la collection), du non-entretien du mobilier ou encore de la mutation à titre onéreux de tout ou partie des biens exonérés[59]. Ainsi, théoriquement la vente d'un ou plusieurs meuble(s) entraîne la perte de l'exonération des droits de mutation pour l'ensemble immeuble-meubles, le coût fiscal pouvant dépasser le montant même de la vente. Cette éventualité peut être analysée de deux façons. Elle peut être vue comme défavorable au maintien et à l'accès aux collections en considérant qu'elle incite les repreneurs du monument à limiter, voire à exclure tout meuble de la convention[60]. Au

---

[54] Circ. n° 2006/005 du 21 juill. 2006, *BOMCC* n° 156, août 2006, p. 21.

[55] BOI-ENR-DMTG-10-20-30-60, 12 sept. 2012, § 60.

[56] Il est toutefois possible que la collection ne soit composée que d'éléments constituant le complément historique ou artistique de l'immeuble, et ne soit donc pas menacée.

[57] Décr. n° 2003-1238 du 17 déc. 2003 préc., convention-type, annexe 1. Cette liste ne peut être communiquée au public qu'avec l'autorisation écrite des héritiers, donataires ou légataires, BOI-ENR-DMTG-10-20-30-60, 12 sept. 2012, § 60.

[58] Décr. n° 2003-1238 du 17 déc. 2003 préc., art. 2 et 6.

[59] *Id.*, art. 11.

[60] Cette exclusion n'interdit évidemment pas aux collectionneurs de maintenir le mobilier sur le parcours de visite mais ils ne pourront bénéficier de l'exonération des

contraire, dans l'hypothèse où la promesse de l'exonération (plutôt que le risque potentiel de sa remise en cause) dicte le comportement des repreneurs du monument, la mesure paraît favorable à la pérennité de la collection comme ensemble, et de surcroît sa préservation au sein de l'immeuble avec lequel elle constitue une cohérence.

4. Outre le patrimoine historique, des mesures fiscales visent l'art contemporain en encourageant l'exposition des œuvres, directement ou indirectement. Ainsi, ouvrent droit à une réduction d'impôt dans le cadre du régime du mécénat les dons versés aux organismes publics ou privés, dont la gestion est désintéressée, et qui ont pour activité principale notamment l'organisation d'exposition d'art contemporain[61], c'est-à-dire d'œuvres sur tout support d'artistes-auteurs vivants ou décédés depuis moins de 70 ans[62]. Comme les précédentes, cette disposition fiscale ne garantit pas l'exposition d'une collection en tant qu'ensemble ; l'organisme bénéficiaire des fonds est laissé libre dans la composition de l'exposition qu'il organise, exposition qui peut comprendre autant des collections entières que des œuvres issues de plusieurs collections, privées ou publiques. Il s'agit donc d'une mesure favorisant l'accès aux œuvres d'art contemporain en tant qu'individualité et non en tant que collection, et ce indépendamment du statut public ou privé de celle-ci.
Il en est de même de l'autre dispositif fiscal incitant, mais cette fois-ci de manière indirecte, à l'accès aux œuvres privées d'art contemporain. L'article 238 bis AB du code général des impôts accorde aux entreprises une déduction spéciale (extra-comptable) de la somme correspondant au prix d'acquisition d'une œuvre inscrite dans un compte d'actif immobilisé, sous réserve qu'elle soit exposée pendant cinq ans[63]. La vocation première de cette mesure est d'encourager la création contemporaine[64] et de soutenir le marché de l'art contemporain

droits de mutation à titre gratuit pour ceux-ci.

[61] CGI, art. 200, 1, f et art. 238 bis, 1, e.

[62] Sont visés les dessins, peintures, sculptures, photographies, vidéographies, ainsi que les installations et performances, BOI-IR-RICI-250-10-20-10, 10 mai 2017, § 250 et 260.

[63] L'entreprise doit informer le public du lieu d'exposition et des possibilités d'accès au bien, ce par des indications attractives sur le lieu même de l'exposition et par tous moyens promotionnels adaptés à l'importance de l'œuvre.

[64] Seules les œuvres originales d'artistes vivants sont éligibles.

français[65], mais l'exposition de l'œuvre est une « contrepartie essentielle et obligatoire de l'avantage fiscal »[66]. Selon la doctrine administrative, cette condition est considérée comme remplie lorsque l'œuvre est exposée dans un musée – où elle est mise en dépôt, et dont le caractère public ou privé est indifférent – ou par une région, un département, une commune ou un de leurs établissements publics ou encore par un établissement public à caractère scientifique, culturel ou professionnel. Les modalités d'accès à l'œuvre ne sont pas précisées dans ces cas, il en va différemment lorsque l'exposition est sous la responsabilité de l'entreprise bénéficiaire de la déduction fiscale. Les conditions posées par l'administration fiscale dans cette dernière hypothèse ont conduit le législateur à modifier l'article 238 bis AB du code général des impôts, afin de permettre une application plus large de la mesure. En effet, en 2003, constatant que les entreprises avaient « peu recouru à cette possibilité, destinée, à l'origine à encourager la constitution de collections d'entreprise »[67], en raison notamment de l'« effet dissuasif » des contraintes d'exposition, les parlementaires ont opté pour une rédaction plus souple du texte. Les œuvres qui étaient « destinées à être exposées au public » doivent désormais être exposées « dans un lieu accessible au public », ce qui permet théoriquement de présenter les œuvres « sans qu'une salle d'exposition spécifique soit dédiée »[68]. En 2005, le texte a été une nouvelle fois modifié afin d'inclure au titre du public, les salariés de l'entreprise, tout en excluant toutefois une « délectation solitaire dans leurs bureaux »[69], en considérant que les entreprises « n'ont pas vocation à se transformer en galeries d'art »[70]. Malgré ces deux modifications à l'occasion desquelles la volonté du législateur a été réaffirmée, l'administration fiscale maintient une doctrine jugée encore restrictive puisqu'elle retient que « l'œuvre ne doit donc pas être placée dans un local réservé à une personne ou à un groupe restreint de personnes. Tel serait le cas [...] si le lieu d'exposition était réservé aux seuls clients de l'entreprise » ou si l'œuvre « n'est exposée que ponctuellement [à l'occasion d'une

---

[65] V. en ce sens l'amendement n° 39 rect. bis au projet de loi de finances rectificative pour 2005, Sénat, 20 déc. 2005.
[66] BOI-BIC-CHG-70-10, 7 août 2019, § 90.
[67] P. Nachbar, Avis n° 279, 7 mai 2003, Sénat.
[68] L. Hénart, Rapport n° 993 du 1er juill. 2003, Ass. nat. ; v. dans le même sens Y. Gaillard, *Rapport n° 278*, 7 mai 2003, Sénat.
[69] Y. Gaillard, CR Sénat, 20 déc. 2005.
[70] *Id.*

manifestation] au profit d'un public plus large, et non pendant toute la période de cinq ans »[71]. Un rapport parlementaire de 2016 suggère à l'administration fiscale de revenir sur cette interprétation, ceci « afin de favoriser l'appropriation et la mise en œuvre du mécénat des artistes vivants par le plus large spectre d'entreprises, y compris les petites et moyennes entreprises, et afin de remédier à l'insécurité juridique de cette nouvelle définition de la notion d'accessibilité au public qui inquiète un certain nombre d'entrepreneurs »[72].

5. Deux ultimes mesures fiscales peuvent conduire à favoriser l'accès au public de certaines œuvres, comprises dans une collection ou non. Elles visent respectivement les trésors nationaux et les objets classés au titre des monuments historiques. Compte tenu de leur intérêt public ou majeur[73], il est peu probable qu'une collection soit composée exclusivement de ce type de biens[74]. Dès lors, dans les deux cas, si l'accès aux œuvres est encouragé, il n'est pas question du maintien d'un ensemble cohérent d'objets[75].
Une réduction d'impôt est accordée pour les travaux de restauration d'objets mobiliers classés[76], sous réserve de leur exposition au public pendant cinq ans[77]. Pour remplir cette obligation, le collectionneur a la possibilité soit de montrer l'objet dans un immeuble ouvert au public

---

[71] BOI-BIC-CHG-70-10, 7 août 2019, § 90.

[72] S. Travert, *Rapport d'information déposé en application de l'article 145 du Règlement par la Commission des affaires culturelles et de l'éducation en conclusion des travaux de la mission d'information relative au marché de l'art*, Ass. Nat. n°4234, 16 nov. 2016. *Cf. supra,* l'intervention de Géraldine Goffaux-Callebaut.

[73] Sur la notion de trésor national, v. art. L. 111-1 du code du patrimoine ; sur la notion de monument historique classé, v. art. L. 622-1 du code du patrimoine.

[74] La collection du château de Flaugergues (Montpellier), rassemblant 62 objets mobilier monuments historiques, comprend à la fois des objets classés (les 21 janv. 1992 et 12 déc. 2006) et inscrits (le 23 nov. 2007).

[75] La nouvelle servitude de maintien dans les lieux, adoptée dans le cadre de la loi relative à la liberté de création, à l'architecture et au patrimoine (C. patr., art. L. 622-1-2) peut remplir ce type d'objectif mais, en l'état actuel des textes, elle ne présente aucune conséquence fiscale spécifique incitant à l'accès du public.

[76] CGI, art. 199 duovicies. Elle correspond à 18 % du montant des travaux retenus dans la limite de 20 000 euros, elle est donc plafonnée à 3 600 euros.

[77] Sauf cas particuliers, cette condition interdit la cession de l'objet (vente, cession d'un droit indivis, transmission à titre gratuit, échange ou apport en société, inscription à l'actif d'une entreprise individuelle, démembrement), BOI-IR-RICI-190, 12 sept. 2012, § 350.

au moins 40 jours par an[78], soit de le confier à un tiers « en vue de son exposition au public »[79]. Ainsi, même si la mesure a prioritairement vocation à encourager la restauration du mobilier classé dans le respect de la réglementation en vigueur[80] et à effectuer les travaux nécessaires à sa conservation[81], l'accès au public est juridiquement garanti, que l'œuvre soit en mains publiques ou privées. Sous réserve des éventuelles limitations nécessairement encadrées et contrôlées par les services de l'État[82], cet accès s'impose tant au collectionneur, s'il prend cette responsabilité, qu'aux organismes tiers potentiellement éligibles[83], ce qui est notable car ce n'est pas le cas pour les dispositions fiscales étudiées jusqu'à présent ni pour celle en faveur des trésors nationaux.

En effet, plutôt que l'accès au bien, la réduction d'impôt de 40 % accordée aux entreprises pour l'acquisition d'un trésor national (dont elle reste propriétaire) entraîne une obligation de « mise en dépôt gratuite »[84] pendant dix ans. L'organisme bénéficiaire de ce dépôt n'est pas tenu d'exposer le trésor national, sauf si l'entreprise propriétaire prescrit un accès au moins temporaire au public dans la convention de dépôt qui la lie à cet organisme. Cette absence de garantie légale se retrouve dans l'hypothèse de la réduction d'impôt de 90 % des

---

[78] CGI, annexe IV, art. 17 ter.

[79] BOI-IR-RICI-190, 12 sept. 2012, § 210.

[80] Les travaux doivent être autorisés et exécutés conformément au code du patrimoine.

[81] « Les dépenses de travaux qui, s'ils ne portent pas directement sur l'objet lui-même, sont effectués dans son environnement pour en assurer la conservation (par exemple : travaux pour la ventilation de la pièce dans laquelle l'objet est exposé, pose de films de protection ultra-violets sur les vitrages de cette pièce…) ouvrent droit à la réduction d'impôt, sous réserve que les travaux concernés aient été expressément prescrits par les services chargés des monuments historiques dans la décision d'autorisation des travaux portant sur l'objet lui-même », BOI-IR-RICI-190, 12 sept. 2012, § 90.

[82] BOI-IR-RICI-190, 12 sept. 2012, § 240.

[83] À savoir un musée de France ou une collectivité territoriale, une bibliothèque, un service d'archives ou une « personne publique ou privée occupant le domaine public maritime, fluvial, ferroviaire ou aéronautique, sous réserve qu'une convention tripartite ait été conclue à cet effet entre le propriétaire de l'objet, la personne publique ou privée à laquelle il est confié et les services de l'État chargés des monuments historiques », BOI-IR-RICI-190, 12 sept. 2012, § 220.

[84] CGI, art. 238 bis-0 AB. L'entreprise reste propriétaire du trésor national. Cette mesure est réservée aux personnes morales, la proposition de l'étendre aux particuliers n'ayant pas donné lieu à des mesures concrètes à ce jour, S. Travert, *Rapport* préc. (Proposition n° 8).

versements effectués pour l'acquisition d'un trésor national par l'État[85]. Néanmoins, dans les deux cas, même si les textes ne l'exigent pas, il est fort probable que le trésor national ainsi acquis soit exposé au public compte tenu de son statut particulier. C'est vraisemblablement un devoir patrimonial mais également politique, car cette exposition peut permettre de valoriser l'action des entreprises ayant permis l'acquisition de l'œuvre, et d'encourager d'autres à suivre cet exemple. Ceci apparaît d'autant plus important dans le cas où le trésor national est acquis par l'entreprise pour son propre compte (et non pour celui de l'État), puisque, l'obligation de dépôt venant s'ajouter à celle de consentir le classement du bien comme monument historique ou comme archive historique, et à l'interdiction de céder le bien pendant 10 ans, aucune application de la mesure n'était identifiée en 2011[86].
Ainsi, plusieurs dispositifs fiscaux prévoient au titre des contreparties de l'avantage accordé, l'obligation de rendre accessible les biens au public. Toutefois, l'exposition des œuvres ne constitue généralement pas l'objectif premier de la mesure et est en principe limitée dans le temps, temps variable, considéré par le législateur comme nécessaire à la compensation de la dépense fiscale engagée par l'État. Si le collectionneur peut être guidé dans sa volonté d'exposer l'œuvre au public par l'avantage fiscal qu'il pourrait en retirer, il peut aussi l'être par son seul souhait de partager sa passion pour les œuvres qu'il a rassemblées. Encore faut-il, dans cette dernière hypothèse, que la fiscalité ne freine pas ses ambitions.

Les freins fiscaux à l'accès aux collections privées

La fiscalité est-elle de nature à inciter le collectionneur privé à cacher les œuvres qu'il détient ? Si, aucune mesure fiscale n'a vocation à limiter l'exposition des œuvres, l'absence de dispositions spécifiques peut influer sur l'accès aux collections privées, en tout ou partie, d'autant qu'au-delà de la rationalité du droit fiscal, se dessine la « peur du fisc ».

---

[85] C. patr., art. L. 122-6 ; CGI, art. 238 bis-0 A ; BOI-IS-RICI-20-20, 12 sept. 2012. Cette mesure est également réservée aux seules personnes morales, aucune suite n'ayant été donnée à la proposition de l'étendre aux particuliers, S. Travert, *Rapport* préc. (Proposition n° 8).
[86] T. Laval, « Les dépenses fiscales du programme Patrimoines », *in* F. Benhamou et D. Thesmar, *Valoriser le patrimoine culturel de la France*, 2011, p. 128.

Les musées privés soumis à la pression fiscale ?

Selon le code du patrimoine, un musée est une « collection permanente composée de biens dont la conservation et la présentation revêtent un intérêt public et organisée en vue de la connaissance, de l'éducation et du plaisir du public »[87]. L'une des principales missions du musée étant la présentation de tout ou partie de la collection au public, l'accès partiel ou total à une collection paraît garanti par la création d'un musée. Dès lors, le caractère incitatif ou au contraire dissuasif du régime fiscal de ce type de structure peut avoir des répercussions sur la visibilité des collections privées, ainsi que sur le maintien de la cohérence de l'ensemble et la pérennité d'une collection. En effet, au-delà des potentielles difficultés de financement, les musées privés ne sont pas soumis à une fiscalité spécifique et les règles de droit commun peuvent s'avérer inadaptées voire pénalisantes. À de nombreuses reprises, plusieurs parlementaires ont identifié une « discrimination » et « une distorsion de concurrence » entre les musées publics et les musées privés[88], du fait notamment de la différence de traitement fiscal des premiers par rapport aux seconds[89]. Ce constat a conduit à la présentation d'un amendement dans le cadre des débats relatifs au projet de la loi relative à la liberté de création, à l'architecture et au patrimoine, en vue de la création d'une appellation « Musée privé de France », auquel auraient été attachés les mêmes avantages fiscaux que ceux accordés aux bénéficiaires de l'appellation « Musée de France »[90]. En effet, pour justifier l'absence de mise en œuvre d'un régime fiscal spécifique en faveur des musées privés, le ministre en charge de la

---

[87] C. patr., art. L. 410-1.

[88] Rép. min. à F. Vannson, n° 98706, *JOAN* du 16 mai 2017 ; rép. min. à F. Marlin, *JOAN* du 16 mai 2017, n°100972 ; rép. min. à M.-L. Fort, *JOAN* du 20 sept. 2016, n°90177 ; rép. min. à P. Gosselin, *JOAN* du 6 sept. 2016, n°98707 ; rép. min. à F. Marlin, *JOAN* du 26 juill. 2016, n°64060 ; rép. min. à F. Marlin, *JOAN* du 29 juill. 2014, n°58567 ; rép. min. à M. Saddier, *JOAN* du 29 juill. 2014, n°50713 ; rép. min. à P. Gosselin, *JOAN* du 29 juill. 2014, n°49404 ; rép. min. à C. Kert, *JOAN* du 29 juill. 2014, n°48760 ; rép. min. à J.-C. Taugourdeau, *JOAN* du 29 juill. 2014, n°47952 ; rép. min. à N. Ameline, *JOAN* du 29 juill. 2014, n°47953 ; rép. min. G. Huert, *JOAN* du 29 juill. 2014, n°47954 ; rép. min. à A. Moyne-Bressand, *JOAN* du 29 juill. 2014, n° 47580 ; rép. min. à B. Gilles, *JO Sénat* du 6 mars 2014, n°10772.

[89] V. not. F. Goliard, « Les musées privés : une fiscalité inadaptée », *JAC* n°42/2017, p. 41 s. ; v. égal. Union française des Amateurs d'armes, « Fiscalité des musées privés en France », 5 déc. 2014, www.armes-ufa.fr.

[90] Sénat, compte rendu intégral des débats, 12 févr. 2016.

culture a mis en avant à plusieurs reprises les contraintes résultant de l'appellation « Musée de France »[91]. Or, celle-ci ne vise pas l'ensemble des musées publics (puisque l'appellation est accordée sur demande, sous réserve du respect de conditions garantissant notamment la conservation et la présentation des collections[92]), et ne leur est pas réservée (certains musées privés sont éligibles). De plus, ce n'est pas cette appellation mais le statut public du musée qui lui permet de bénéficier de mesures fiscales spécifiques. La confusion vient du fait que les personnes privées à but non lucratif peuvent également, sous certaines conditions, jouir d'une fiscalité particulière et que l'appellation « Musée de France », est accordée aux seuls « musées appartenant à l'État, à une autre personne morale de droit public ou à une personne morale de droit privé à but non lucratif »[93]. Dès lors, les différences de traitement fiscal frappent essentiellement les musées à but lucratif, y compris s'ils sont gérés directement par les collectionneurs, mais sont-elles réellement de nature à décourager le collectionneur dans son projet de création d'un musée ?

1. Tout d'abord, les revenus générés par les droits d'entrée et les prestations annexes (boutique, restaurant, etc.), constituent la source principale de financement des musées privés. Or, les musées publics ne sont pas soumis à la taxe sur la valeur ajoutée (TVA) sur les droits d'entrée, conformément à l'article 256 B du code général des impôts[94]. Il en est de même des musées privés dits sans but lucratif (créés par une association ou une fondation notamment), gérés de manière désintéressée[95] lorsqu'ils bénéficient de subventions publiques[96] ou

---

[91] V. rép. min. préc.

[92] C. patr., art. L. 442-3.

[93] C. patr., art. L. 441-1. Selon le Conseil International des musées (ICOM), « un musée est une institution permanente sans but lucratif au service de la société et de son développement, ouverte au public, qui acquiert, conserve, étudie, expose et transmet le patrimoine matériel et immatériel de l'humanité et de son environnement à des fins d'études, d'éducation et de délectation », statuts de l'ICOM, adoptés le 24 août 2007.

[94] BOI-TVA-CHAMP-10-20-10-10, 4 févr. 2015, § 130.

[95] L'administration fiscale retient que « en raison de l'absence d'une véritable concurrence entre les divers musées et monuments historiques, la condition relative aux prix [...] à laquelle est, en principe, subordonné le bénéfice de l'exonération, peut être considérée comme sans objet. Elle sera présumée remplie dès lors que les établissements concernés bénéficient de subventions », BOI-TVA-CHAMP-30-10-30-10, 15 mai 2019, § 240.

[96] BOI-TVA-CHAMP-30-10-30-10, 15 mai 2019, § 240.

lorsque l'exposition des œuvres peut être considérée comme un service à caractère culturel rendu à leurs membres[97]. Pour les autres musées privés, la TVA est applicable dans les conditions fixées à l'article 279 du code général des impôts : le taux réduit de 10 % vise les droits d'accès au musée et les recettes des activités directement liées à la visite telles que les projections audiovisuelles (cinéma, vidéo ou diaporama) et les conférences[98], à l'exclusion des attractions non rattachées aux thèmes des objets exposés ou des lieux visités et des articles (cartes postales, diapositives, jouets, vêtements, souvenirs, etc.) – y compris s'il s'agit de reproductions des objets exposés – ou encore des ventes à consommer sur place (restaurants, buvettes, etc.)[99], toutes ces recettes étant soumises au taux de TVA qui leur est propre. Sur ce type de revenus, les musées publics ne sont pas traités différemment puisqu'ils sont assujettis à la TVA « pour leurs activités lucratives qui ne constituent pas le prolongement nécessaire de leurs activités à caractère culturel »[100]. Ils peuvent être considérés comme désavantagés par rapport aux propriétaires de monuments historiques classés ou inscrits exploitant un musée dans leur immeuble, puisqu'ils sont exonérés de TVA non seulement sur les droits d'entrée mais également sur les « ventes de cartes postales, photographies, brochures évoquant le château, etc., réalisés par les propriétaires de châteaux »[101].
Afin de mettre sur un pied d'égalité l'ensemble des musées, des parlementaires ont proposé d'harmoniser le taux de TVA applicable aux droits d'entrée[102]. Constatant qu'actuellement les musées privés sont implantés essentiellement en province, où le montant moyen des droits

[97] *Id.*, § 40 s.
[98] BOI-TVA-LIQ-30-20-50, 6 juin 2018, § 70.
[99] *Id.*, § 80.
[100] En ce sens, v. not. rép. min. à F. Vannson, n°98706, *JOAN* du 16 mai 2017 ou rép. min. à B. Gilles, n°10772, *JO Sénat* du 6 août 2015 ; rép. min. à F. Marlin, n°5002, *JOAN* du 14 août 2018. Il en est de même pour la CFE et la CVAE, v. not. BOI-IF-CFE-10-30-10-10, 27 mars 2019, § 260.
[101] BOI-TVA-CHAMP-30-10-60-20, 2 mars 2016, § 1. Sur l'application de cette doctrine administrative à l'ensemble des monuments historiques et non aux seuls châteaux, v. not. thèse A. Verjat, *Préservation et mise en valeur des monuments historiques privés : la fiscalité de l'impôt sur le revenu*, L'Harmattan, coll. *Droit du patrimoine culturel et naturel*, 2011.
[102] Ass. Nat., Proposition de loi relative aux musées privés, n° 2961, 8 juill. 2015. Dans le même esprit, la création d'un taux réduit à 15 % d'impôt sur les sociétés a été préconisé pour les musées ouverts, le taux de droit commun étant actuellement de 33 1/3 %.

d'entrée est plus faible qu'en Ile de France[103], et ne représentent que 15 % des entrées totales (59 millions annuelles) entraînant une recette fiscale limitée de 5 750 000 euros, ils soulignent que l'assujettissement de l'ensemble des musées à un taux super réduit de 2,1 % rapporterait « sans douleur » à l'État plus de 12 000 000 euros. Le caractère indolore de la mesure, fondé notamment sur les règles de gratuité pratiquée dans les musées publics[104], est discutable puisque l'augmentation du montant des droits d'entrée peut avoir une répercussion sur la fréquentation[105]. De même, l'apparente répercussion budgétaire qu'aurait cette mesure pour l'État doit être tempérée par le droit à déduction de la TVA d'amont, droit qui limite probablement la potentielle distorsion entre musées publics et privés.

2. Ensuite, la présentation des œuvres nécessite un local adapté. L'État et les collectivités territoriales bénéficient d'une exonération de taxe foncière pour les locaux affectés à un service public ou d'utilité générale et non productifs de revenus[106]. Selon la doctrine de l'administration fiscale, « il y a productivité de revenus quand la collectivité exerce dans l'immeuble une activité lucrative : agricole, industrielle ou commerciale »[107] ; au contraire, sont assimilées à des propriétés improductives de revenus celles où s'exerce une activité revêtant entre autres un caractère essentiellement culturel, éducatif ou touristique[108]. Si bien que les personnes publiques ne sont pas soumises à cette taxe pour les immeubles aménagés en musée dont elles sont propriétaires, y compris si le musée donne lieu à la perception de droits d'entrée. Du côté des structures de droit privé, aucune distinction n'est opérée selon que l'activité est exercée à but lucratif ou non ; l'ensemble des musées privés propriétaires de ses locaux est donc au contraire imposé à la taxe foncière[109]. Cette inégalité de traitement a été soulignée

---

[103] Montant moyen de 10 euros en Ile de France et 6,5 euros en province.

[104] Pour les musées de France, le montant des droits d'entrée doit être fixé de « manière à favoriser l'accès de ces musées au public le plus large », C. patr., art. L. 442-6.

[105] Toutefois, avec un billet à 16 euros, le musée Grévin a accueilli plus de 690 000 visiteurs en 2015, soit plus que le Panthéon mais moins que la Fondation Louis Vuitton avec un million de visiteurs pour un billet à 9 euros.

[106] CGI, art. 1382.

[107] BOI-IF-TFB-10-50-10-30, 10 janv. 2019, § 30.

[108] *Id.*, § 40.

[109] Les associations propriétaires de certains édifices affectés à l'exercice du culte (et dans lesquels peuvent être présentées des collections d'art religieux) sont toutefois exonérées (CGI, art. 1382).

et a conduit à un projet d'exonération de la taxe en faveur des musées privés recevant moins de 250 000 visiteurs par an[110]. Le même type de différence peut être identifié pour la cotisation foncière des entreprises (CFE), les collectivités territoriales étant par principe exonérées[111] contrairement aux personnes privées exerçant des activités considérées comme lucratives, qu'elles soient ou non propriétaires des locaux. Diverses propositions ont également été faites pour accorder une exonération partielle ou totale de cet impôt aux musées recevant moins de 250 000 visiteurs[112] ou moins de 450 000 visiteurs[113].

Au-delà de la dichotomie entre musées publics et musées privés, ces deux taxes annuelles sont-elles de nature à décourager le collectionneur à montrer sa collection ? Autrement dit, leur coût constitue-t-il un frein à la création d'un musée ? A priori non en ce qui concerne la taxe foncière, dans la mesure où la collection, qu'elle soit ou non montrée au public, nécessite un lieu de conservation, potentiellement soumis à la taxe foncière[114]. Néanmoins, il peut être admis que la surface nécessaire, et par conséquent le montant de la taxe foncière, augmente lorsque les œuvres sont exposées au public[115], et non conservées à un usage privatif[116]. Dans le cas où l'immeuble accueillant la collection est un monument historique géré civilement, son propriétaire peut en outre déduire de ses revenus le montant de la taxe foncière à 100 % en cas d'ouverture au public (au lieu de 50 % dans le cas contraire). Même si l'exposition des meubles constituant la collection n'est pas garantie,

---

[110] Ass. Nat., Proposition de loi relative aux musées privés, n° 2961, 8 juill. 2015, art. 3. V. égal. rép. min. à D. Gremillet, n° 0912S, *JO Sénat* du 22 août 2019.

[111] CGI, art. 1449, 1°; BOI-IF-CFE-10-30-10-10, 27 mars 2019, § 250.

[112] Ass. Nat., Proposition de loi relative aux musées privés, n° 2961, 8 juill. 2015, art. 4.

[113] Sénat, Proposition de loi relative aux musées privés, n° 429, 8 avr. 2014, art. 1er.

[114] De plus, la question de la taxe foncière ne vise que les cas où le lieu de conservation appartient au musée ou au collectionneur. S'il n'en est que locataire, il n'est pas redevable de cette taxe.

[115] La muséographie, les règles de sécurité et d'accessibilité (le musée relève de la réglementation des établissements recevant du public), comme les aménagements liés à l'accueil du public (sanitaires, vestiaires, billetteries, etc.), nécessitent des locaux suffisamment spacieux. Cette exigence n'implique toutefois pas nécessairement l'agrandissement du lieu de conservation de la collection (cas d'une collection installée dans un monument historique, par exemple).

[116] Le domicile du collectionneur est le principal lieu d'exposition et de stockage des collections privées. V. en ce sens N. Moureau, D. Sagot-Duvauroux, Marion Vidal, « Collectionneurs d'art contemporain : des acteurs méconnus de la vie artistique », *Culture Études* 2015/1.

puisque la mesure vise l'immeuble et non les meubles qu'il abrite, il n'en reste pas moins que cette disposition peut favoriser l'accès des lieux au public et limiter l'hypothétique frein fiscal à la création d'un musée privé, du fait de la taxe foncière. L'imposition au titre de la CFE découle, quant à elle, d'une activité professionnelle[117], telle que l'exploitation d'un musée à but lucratif[118]. En conservant sa collection à un usage privatif[119], le collectionneur échappe à cette taxe mais il est redevable de la taxe d'habitation.

3. Enfin, l'attractivité d'un musée passe par l'évolution de ses collections. Aussi, la fiscalité applicable à l'acquisition et à la vente des œuvres peut avoir des répercussions sur l'enrichissement et l'accès aux collections. Ici encore, une distinction est opérée entre les musées selon leur statut, distinction qui est indépendante de l'activité de musée. En particulier, les collectivités publiques et les organismes sans but lucratif d'intérêt général concourant à la mise en valeur du patrimoine artistique[120] peuvent, sous certaines conditions, recevoir des dons et legs exonérés de droit de mutation à titre gratuit ou encore faire appel au mécénat. Il en va différemment des structures lucratives, qui restent exclues malgré les propositions d'étendre le dispositif du mécénat au profit des musées privés situés en France et existants depuis plus de 2 ans pour les sommes « qui sont affectées à l'investissement dans les collections présentées au public »[121], en complément du dispositif applicable pour l'organisation des expositions d'art contemporain[122].
Les cessions d'objets d'art, de collection et d'antiquité sont soumises à une taxe forfaitaire correspondant à 6 % du prix[123], tout comme les exportations vers un État tiers à l'Union européenne. Cette taxe est à la charge du vendeur mais elle a nécessairement une incidence sur le coût de mise en vente de l'œuvre au musée, et doit être supportée par lui

[117] CGI, art. 1447.
[118] Les organismes sans but lucratif peuvent être exonérés de CFE, v. not. BOI-IF-CFE-10-20-20-20, 5 avr. 2017, § 20 s.
[119] BOI-IF-TH-10-20-10, 27 févr. 2019, § 190.
[120] Sont notamment éligibles « les versements effectués à travers les souscriptions ouvertes pour financer l'achat d'objets ou d'œuvres d'art destinés à rejoindre les collections d'un musée de France accessibles au public », BOI-IR-RICI-250-10-20-10, 10 mai 2017, § 130. Le statut de Musée de France n'est pas un critère déterminant, contrairement à celui d'intérêt général, BOI-IR-RICI-250-10-10, 10 mai 2017, § 90 s.
[121] Ass. Nat., Proposition de loi relative aux musées privés, n° 2961, 8 juill. 2015, art. 8.
[122] V. plus haut.
[123] CGI, art. 150 VI et 150 VK.

lorsqu'il souhaite céder un objet d'art, de collection ou d'antiquité considéré comme « mineurs » pour l'acquisition d'œuvres plus importantes ou en cas de remaniement de la collection. Plusieurs exonérations sont toutefois prévues afin de limiter les conséquences négatives de cette taxe d'un point de vue patrimonial. Ainsi, ne sont pas imposables les exportations temporaires, notamment lorsque « les contribuables acceptent de prêter [...] l'objet d'art, de collection ou d'antiquité dont ils sont propriétaires dans le cadre d'une exposition »[124]. Il en est de même des cessions au profit des musées de France ou des musées d'une collectivité territoriale, des bibliothèques publiques et des services d'archives[125]. Pour les autres musées, l'imposition dépend du statut du vendeur : les professionnels soumis à l'impôt sur le revenu ou sur les sociétés ne sont pas soumis à la taxe si le bien vendu est inscrit à l'actif de l'entreprise, contrairement aux particuliers ou aux personnes morales non assujetties à l'impôt sur le revenu ou sur les sociétés, ce qui est généralement le cas des organismes sans but lucratif. Ce champ d'application de la taxe conduit à une situation paradoxale puisque ce n'est ni la valeur artistique ou patrimoniale de l'œuvre, ni sa vocation à être ou non exposée au public qui compte mais sa provenance. Quant aux musées qui souhaitent vendre une ou plusieurs pièces de leur collection, le champ d'application de la taxe pénalise davantage les organismes sans but lucratif, et ce y compris s'il s'agit d'un musée de France, que les structures lucratives[126]. Dès lors, la proposition d'extension de l'exonération de la taxe aux « cessions réalisées au profit d'un musée privé existant depuis plus de 2 ans pour les montants destinés à être réinvestis dans leurs collections ayant vocation à être présentées au public »[127], devrait probablement être aménagée pour tenir compte des cas de *deaccessioning*, à moins que le dispositif fiscal n'ait justement

[124] BOI-RPPM-PVBMC-20-10, 31 déc. 2018, § 480.
[125] CGI, art. 150 VJ : BOI-RPPM-PVBMC-20-10, 31 déc. 2018, § 260 s.
[126] Le musée peut également opter pour la plus-value s'il est en mesure d'établir de manière probante la date et le prix d'acquisition de l'objet. Toutefois, le coût fiscal n'est pas nécessairement moindre, sauf si le bien est détenu depuis plus de vingt-deux ans, délai à partir duquel la plus-value est définitivement exonérée, CGI, art. 150 VL ; BOI-RPPM-PVBMC-20-20, 1er avr. 2014.
[127] Ass. Nat., Proposition de loi relative aux musées privés, n° 2961, 8 juill. 2015, art. 7.

vocation à limiter ces pratiques, moins répandues en France qu'aux États-Unis[128].

La « peur du fisc »

Même si les collectionneurs n'optent pas pour la création d'un musée pour des raisons personnelles ou fiscales, ils peuvent être amenés à déposer tout ou partie des œuvres de leur collection dans un musée en vue de leur exposition, en particulier temporaire[129]. Toutefois, un rapport parlementaire relatif au marché de l'art a identifié une « peur du fisc » susceptible de freiner ce type de prêts : « ayant "peur du gendarme", les propriétaires de collections répugneraient à les montrer »[130]. Ce frein est-il psychologique ? Les collectionneurs privés ont-ils de bonnes raisons de craindre l'administration fiscale ? Oui, si l'on en croit l'anecdote rapportée : « plusieurs collectionneurs qui avaient prêté des œuvres au Musée d'art moderne de la Ville de Paris, pour l'exposition "Passions privées" qui s'y est tenue en 1995-1996, se sont vus notifier un contrôle fiscal après ladite exposition – ce qui n'a pas été de nature à les inciter à montrer une nouvelle fois leurs collections au public »[131]. À défaut de précisions sur le type d'impôt concerné, deux pistes sont ici explorées.

4. Tout d'abord, citons le cas paradoxal de l'ancien impôt de solidarité sur la fortune (ISF). Paradoxal car le mobilier historique ou artistique était légalement exonéré d'ISF[132], ce qui aurait dû rassurer les collectionneurs. Toutefois, cette exonération était régulièrement questionnée voire remise en cause lors des débats parlementaires relatifs aux lois de finances[133]. Plusieurs amendements ont ainsi été déposés dans le but de réintégrer ces œuvres dans la base taxable de

---

[128] V. not. C. de Noblet, « Déclassement des œuvres, outil de gestion des collections muséales », *JAC* n° 28/2015, p. 27.

[129] Selon l'étude de N. Moureau, D. Sagot-Duvauroux et M. Vidal (« Collectionneurs d'art contemporain : des acteurs méconnus de la vie artistique » préc.), plus de la moitié des collectionneurs prêtent des œuvres à des musées.

[130] S. Travert, *Rapport* préc. Cette même peur, associée à celle des vols, conduit certains collectionneurs privés à ne prêter leurs œuvres que sous couvert d'anonymat, comme le montrent les catalogues de ce type d'exposition.

[131] *Id.*

[132] « Les objets d'antiquité, d'art ou de collection ne sont pas compris dans les bases d'imposition à l'impôt de solidarité sur la fortune », CGI, art. 885 I.

[133] V. not. J.-R. Pellas, « Les anamorphoses de l'impôt de solidarité sur la fortune et les œuvres d'art », *RFFP* n° 123/2013, p. 197.

l'ISF[134]. Même s'ils n'ont jamais été définitivement adoptés, ils ont pu créer une situation d'incertitude, identifiée comme nuisant au marché de l'art français : « les annonces régulières d'une éventuelle imposition [...] entraînent presque systématiquement et immédiatement une hausse des demandes de certificats et licences d'exportation de la part de collectionneurs soucieux de mettre leurs biens à l'abri »[135], par peur de cette hypothétique menace fiscale. Il est possible que cette instabilité fiscale ait conduit les collectionneurs à cacher leurs œuvres, plutôt qu'à les exposer. Cet obstacle potentiel à l'accès aux œuvres peut toutefois être contrebalancé par les propositions qui ont été faites en vue non pas d'exclure entièrement l'exonération mais de la conditionner à une présentation des œuvres concernées au public. Ainsi, plusieurs amendements ont été déposés en vue de refuser l'exonération d'ISF aux œuvres non mises à la disposition du public, de manière temporaire, sous la forme d'un prêt à certains musées[136]. En tout état de cause, l'adoption de l'IFI dans le cadre de la loi de finances pour 2018 a en principe ôté toute crainte aux collectionneurs, puisque le nouvel impôt ne vise que le patrimoine immobilier[137].

5. La « peur du fisc » se cristallise principalement à l'occasion de la transmission des œuvres, lors du calcul des droits de mutation qui en découlent. L'œuvre d'art étant « de nature discrète, parce que mobilière », le collectionneur peut être tenté de ne pas la déclarer. Or, « la non-déclaration successorale d'un patrimoine artistique implique le risque du contrôle, car l'administration fiscale peut avoir connaissance de l'existence des œuvres, notamment [...] à l'occasion de leurs prêts

---

[134] V. not. amendements n° 1497 rect. (AN, rejeté), 3 juin 2011, PLFR 2011 (n° 3406) ; n° I-665 Rect. (AN, Rejeté), 12 oct. 2012, PLF 2013 (n° 235) ; n°I-CF16 (AN, rejeté), 2 oct. 2013, PLF 2014 (n°1395) ; n°I-701 (AN, rejeté), 11 oct. 2013, PLF 2014 (n° 1395) ; n° I-238 (AN, rejeté), 9 oct. 2014, PLF 2015 (n° 2234) ; n° I-CF142 (AN, adopté), 3 oct. 2014, PLF 2015 (n° 2234) ; n° 505 (AN, rejeté), 1er déc. 2016, PLFR 2016 (n° 4235) ; ou encore n° I-1039 (AN, rejeté), 13 oct. 2017, PLF 2018 (n° 235).

[135] S. Travert, *Rapport* préc.

[136] Amendements n° 174 (AN, rejeté), 4 déc. 2007, PLFR 2007 (n° 421) ; n° 358 Rect. (AN rejeté), 1er juin 2011, PLFR 2011 (n°3406) ; n°1233 (AN, rejeté), 7 juin 2011, PLFR 2011 (n° 3406) ; n° I-242 (AN, rejeté), 14 oct. 2011, PLF 2012 (n° 3775) ; n° 229 Rect. (AN, rejeté), 25 nov. 2011, PLFR 2011 (n° 3952) ; n° 681 (AN, rejeté), 10 févr. 2012, PLFR 2012 (n° 4332) ; n° I-78 Rect. (AN, rejeté), 11 oct. 2012, PLF 2013 (n° 235). Dans ce dernier cas, l'obligation d'exposition était réservée aux œuvres valant plus de 50 000 euros. *Cf. supra*, l'intervention de M.-A. Reynolds.

[137] CGI, art. 964.

pour des expositions »[138]. Au-delà du risque de révélation de l'existence même de l'œuvre se pose la question de sa valeur. En effet, les règles d'évaluation des objets divergent selon qu'il s'agit de meubles meublants ou d'objets d'art ou de collection[139]. Aussi, l'on peut se demander si le prêt de ladite œuvre, en vue de son exposition au public, peut en modifier la nature (le meuble meublant devenant objet d'art), au point d'inverser la volonté initiale d'exposer du collectionneur. Il résulte du code général des impôts et de la doctrine administrative, qui renvoie au code civil et à la jurisprudence[140], que le critère de l'exposition du meuble au public n'est ni suffisant, ni nécessaire[141]. Un meuble pris isolément, dès lors qu'il n'intègre pas un ensemble, doit être considéré comme un meuble meublant. Ainsi, « ni [sa] valeur ni la circonstance qu'il ait occasionnellement fait partie d'une exposition ne sont de nature à écarter la qualification de meuble meublant »[142]. Contrairement à ce qui a été vu jusqu'à maintenant, c'est l'existence même d'une collection qui emporte la qualification d'objet d'art ou de collection[143]. Elle n'est pour autant pas vue comme une universalité

---

[138] B. Dauchez, « Appréhender une succession dont l'actif est composé d'œuvres d'art », *Droit & Patrimoine*, n° 176/2008. V. égal. la position de quatre praticiens défavorables au « culte du secret », S. Breuil, S. Aubert, E. Émile-Zola-Place, P. Cénac, « Patrimoine artistique et culturel : quelles opportunités juridiques et fiscales ? », *JCP N* 2014.1315.

[139] CGI, art. 764 ; v. C. Delory, « Point d'actualité sur l'évaluation du mobilier meublant et les droits de succession », *JCP N* 2001. 549. La valeur des meubles meublants est déterminée par le prix exprimé à l'occasion d'une vente publique dans les deux ans suivant le décès du collectionneur ; à défaut, elle résulte d'un inventaire dressé en application de l'article 789 du code civil ; et, enfin, faute d'un tel inventaire, elle est fixée selon la déclaration détaillée et estimative des parties, sans pouvoir être inférieure à un forfait fixé à 5 % de l'actif successoral, sauf preuve contraire. En ce qui concerne les œuvres d'art ou de collection, la loi dispose que « la valeur imposable ne peut [...] être inférieure à l'évaluation faite dans les contrats ou conventions d'assurances contre le vol ou contre l'incendie en cours au jour du décès et conclus par le défunt, son conjoint ou ses auteurs, moins de dix ans avant l'ouverture de la succession, sauf preuve contraire ».

[140] Com., 17 oct. 1995, n° 94-10196.

[141] Les textes se réfèrent aux tableaux et statues, mais cette interprétation semble pouvoir être étendue à tous les types de collections, v. not. A. Robert, « Que recouvre l'expression meubles meublants (article 534 du code civil) ? », *D.* 1996. 33.

[142] F. Zenati, « Meubles meublants », *RTD civ.* 1996. 650, à propos de Douai, 28 sept. 1965, *D.* 1966. Somm. 45.

[143] Comme le souligne B. Jadaud, « Ce n'est peut-être pas le nombre qui doit retenir l'attention. Deux tableaux ne font pas une collection, mais dix, quinze, vingt ? », *in* « Les "tableaux de maître" sont des meubles meublants (à propos de Cass. com.,

puisque, si chaque élément de la collection est susceptible de changer de nature du fait de son appartenance à un ensemble, cet ensemble n'est pas apprécié dans sa globalité.
Dans cette hypothèse, le fait que le public ait accès à l'œuvre est sans incidence. Qu'en est-il en présence d'une collection ? L'exposition de l'œuvre modifie-t-elle sa nature au regard des règles d'évaluation ? Oui, si l'on en croit la doctrine de l'administration fiscale, qui déduit du code civil[144], que les tableaux faisant partie d'une « collection du de cujus et exposés dans une galerie ou une pièce particulière d'un appartement »[145] sont des objets d'art et de collection. Ainsi, l'exposition apparaît comme un critère déterminant, mais il n'en reste pas moins qu'il n'est nullement question de « public ». Dès lors, « est-ce le regard du public, ou celui d'invités privés, ou l'aménagement d'un cabinet privé, qui donne à la pièce sa qualité de "pièce particulière" ? »[146]. L'aménagement est décisif[147]. En effet, « il ne suffit pas que la famille, des invités voit [l'œuvre]. Il faut une "mise en scène" : que l'œuvre d'art soit montrée, révélée, exposée en tant que telle »[148]. Pour autant, l'existence ou l'absence d'un public réel, même limité, est sans effet. La volonté du collectionneur de conserver à sa seule délectation les œuvres qu'il a accumulées n'exclut pas la qualification d'objet d'art ou de collection, dès lors qu'il les a exposées dans une « sorte de petit musée »[149]. Ce dernier n'est néanmoins pas une condition décisive puisque l'administration fiscale qualifie également d'objet d'art ou de collection les tableaux au sens du droit européen « et qui, non visés par l'article 534 du code civil, ne sont destinés ni à orner un appartement (meubles meublants) ni à être exposés (tableaux de collection). Entrent par exemple dans cette catégorie les tableaux conservés dans un coffre, ou simplement entreposés dans un appartement ou tout autre local »[150],

---

17 oct. 1995) », *JCP N* 1996. 451.
[144] C. civ., art. 534.
[145] BOI-ENR-DMTG-10-40-10-20, 30 mai 2016, § 20.
[146] B. Jadaud, « Les "tableaux de maître" sont des meubles meublants » préc.
[147] Les meubles meublants « ayant pour effet d'agrémenter les conditions d'existence, sont en quelque sorte au service du logement, et non le contraire » *in* A. Robert, « Que recouvre l'expression meubles meublants ? » préc. ; v. égal. F. Zenati, « Meubles meublants », *RTD civ.* 1996. 650
[148] B. Jadaud, « Les "tableaux de maître" sont des meubles meublants » préc.
[149] A. Robert, « Que recouvre l'expression meubles meublants ? » préc.
[150] BOI-ENR-DMTG-10-40-10-20, 30 mai 2016, § 20. Cette apparente extension, n'est peut-être qu'une façon de s'accorder à la lettre du Code civil, qui ne renvoie qu'à une exposition potentielle, C. civ., art. 534.

servant à l'habitation[151] ou encore un musée, au sein duquel l'œuvre serait laissée en dépôt par le collectionneur, qu'elle soit montrée ou non au public. Ainsi, si « l'exposition en public est une qualité essentielle de qualification de l'œuvre d'art »[152], elle n'est pas déterminante. Quoi qu'il en soit, conformément au code général des impôts, cette qualification ne lie pas l'administration fiscale pour l'évaluation de l'œuvre. En effet, si l'administration apporte « la preuve que la valeur des meubles meublants, y compris les tableaux, dépasse le chiffre du forfait de 5 % [méthode d'évaluation réservée aux meubles meublants], elle peut écarter ce dernier »[153], qui n'est en outre pas applicable en matière de donation[154].

L'étape de la qualification passée, il est possible de se demander si les règles d'évaluation fixées à l'article 764 du code général des impôts peuvent freiner l'accès du public aux œuvres. Notamment, la nécessité de souscrire une assurance pour garantir les œuvres prêtées pour une exposition, combinée aux règles d'évaluation des objets d'art ou de collection fixées à l'article 764 du code général des impôts, a-t-elle une incidence ? Si les évaluations résultant des contrats ou conventions d'assurance constituent un plancher des valeurs retenues pour la transmission des objets d'art ou de collection, elles ne peuvent être prises en compte que sous certaines conditions. Tout d'abord, le contrat doit être en « cours au jour du décès », ce qui implique un concours de circonstance malheureux, ou une exposition de longue durée (dépôt permanent par exemple). Il doit en outre être conclu par « le défunt, son conjoint ou ses auteurs », c'est-à-dire le plus souvent le prêteur, ce qui ne correspond pas aux pratiques courantes, les musées supportant généralement ce coût[155]. Dès lors, il serait erroné de considérer que

---

151 Selon la doctrine administrative, la notion d'appartement doit être entendue dans un sens large et « comprendre l'ensemble des immeubles servant à l'habitation y compris les maisons individuelles », *id.*, § 1.

152 B. Jadaud, « Les "tableaux de maître" sont des meubles meublants » préc.

153 BOI-ENR-DMTG-10-40-10-20, 30 mai 2016, à propos de Cass. com., arrêt du 3 mai 1995, n° 92-21836. Peuvent notamment être utilisés à titre de présomptions : les polices d'assurances ; les inventaires estimatifs, même irréguliers ; le prix d'acquisition à une date rapprochée de celle du décès ; la cote des œuvres les plus connues telle qu'elle ressort d'ouvrages ou de revues spécialisées (Gazette de l'Hôtel Drouot, etc.).

154 BOI-ENR-DMTG-20-30-10, 30 oct. 2014, § 50.

155 Dans l'hypothèse néanmoins possible où le collectionneur souscrit lui-même l'assurance, encore faut-il que l'évaluation des œuvres d'art ou de collection ne résulte pas d'un forfait global de l'ensemble du mobilier ou que le capital assuré fasse l'objet

l'accès aux œuvres se trouve freiné par les conséquences fiscales d'une souscription à une assurance en vue de l'exposition d'une œuvre[156]. De la même façon, d'un point de vue juridique, les catalogues d'exposition ne peuvent constituer des éléments de preuve susceptibles d'être invoqués par l'administration fiscale pour l'évaluation. En effet, ils ne répondent ni au formalisme de l'article 789 du code civil exigé pour l'évaluation des meubles meublants, ni même aux conditions des inventaires probatoires les conditions fixées à ce même article n'étant pas respectées, dès lors que les catalogues d'exposition ne sont pas des actes estimatifs. S'ils inventorient les œuvres, ils se contentent d'une description historique, artistique voire technique, sans apporter d'estimation, contrairement à des catalogues de ventes aux enchères publiques par exemple. En revanche, d'un point de vue économique, comme l'a démontré notamment Nathalie Moureau à propos de l'art contemporain, ces catalogues peuvent avoir une influence sur la valeur des œuvres. Ainsi, les événements consistant « en la rédaction de catalogues, en l'entrée d'œuvres dans des musées, fondations ou autres institutions, en l'organisation et la circulation d'expositions, en la publication d'articles [...] offrent autant de signaux durables, objectivés, qui accréditent la valeur artistique du travail des artistes, servent de repères aux acheteurs sur le marché et par ricochet accroissent la valeur économique »[157]. Faut-il pour autant en déduire que le collectionneur pourrait refuser d'exposer tout ou partie de sa collection de peur qu'elle prenne de la valeur ? Cela supposerait de considérer que le comportement du collectionneur n'est dicté que par cette « peur du fisc », alors que bien d'autres émotions l'animent[158].

---

d'une ventilation, BOI-ENR-DMTG-10-40-10-20, 30 mai 2016, § 160.

[156] V. égal. M. Ranouil, « L'assurance des objets d'art des personnes privées », *Dalloz IP/IT* 2018. 276.

[157] N. Moureau, « Valeur artistique et économique de la collection : un équilibre précaire », *JAC* n°18/2014, p. 31. V. dans le même sens, « exposer une pièce lui apporte de la valeur, et un simple bout de papier avec un dessin, s'il est accepté dans l'exposition monographique d'un grand peintre, peut passer d'une valeur zéro à une valeur phénoménale », P. Nitti, citée par A. Bavelier, « L'insolent succès des musées privés », *Le Figaro.fr*, 30 juin 2011.

[158] *Cf. supra*, l'intervention de Jean-Claude Gandur et d'Isabelle Tassignon ; v. égal. le cas de la collection Pinault, installé à Venise au lieu de l'Ile Seguin pour des raisons administratives, puis à Paris, sans recours au dispositif fiscal du mécénat, C. Sabbah, « Le projet du futur musée Pinault à la Bourse du commerce à Paris », 26 juin 2017, www.lesechos.fr.

Table des matières

Avant-propos 5
Sommaire 7

CONSTITUTION DES COLLECTIONS PRIVÉES
Sous la présidence de Jorge Sánchez Cordero

The private art collections. The challenges
Jorge Sánchez Cordero 11

I. Introduction 11
Section I. The Private Cultural Space 17
A. The Challenges of its Framing 17
B. Private and Public collections 20
Section II. The state and the private cultural collections 22
A. The legal issues 22
B. Private collections to public collections 25
C. Public access 31
II. Conclusions 33

Les collections privées en France au XVIIIe siècle : une approche méthodologique
Patrick Michel 35

I. Un siècle de collectionneurs : le XVIIIe siècle 36
Les sources textuelles et visuelles de l'histoire du collectionnisme au XVIIIe siècle 37
Les inventaires visuels : images de la collection (gravures, dessins, peintures) 41
Les différents types de questionnement autour de l'histoire des collections 42
Quelques questionnements ou axes forts de la recherche sur le collectionnisme 47
La formation d'une collection : les moyens de l'appropriation 47
Le cabinet du collectionneur : espace social et espace de savoir : sociabilité mondaine et pratiques savantes 48
Pratiques mondaines et savantes au sein de la collection 49
Les fins de la collection : enjeux des collections et motivations des collectionneurs 50
La collection comme tradition 51
La collection comme *status symbol* 52
La collection comme passion 52

Espace et dispositif de la collection : lieux et matérialité de la collection.... 53
La fin de la collection : transmission ou éclatement 56
Conclusion 58

Collectionnisme public et privé en comparaison
Antoinette Maget Dominicé.. 61

Qu'est-ce que le collectionnisme / Que comprend-on sous ce terme ?......... 61
De la frontière entre collectionnisme public et collectionnisme privé........ 62
1. Collectionnisme public – Caractéristiques principales 62
1.1. Le musée et ses collections comme outil de politique nationale 62
1.2. Enrichissement des collections 69
1.3 Collectionnisme public et temporalité 71
2. Collectionnisme public et objets.. 71
3. Collectionnisme privé 73
4. Rapprochements entre collectionnisme public et privé 73
Remarques conclusives.. 75

La collection source de savoir : les figures du collectionneur « scientifique » en histoire naturelle
Michel Van Praët 77

Le collectionneur scientifique une figure plurielle 77
Les collectionneurs figures fondatrices des sciences de la nature 78
Classer et ordonner la Nature conduit à organiser les collections 79
Collectionneurs institutionnels et collectionneurs privés, liens et ruptures .. 82
Les difficultés de conservation, élément discriminant pour les collections privées... 85
Collecteurs et collectionneurs, amateurs et scientifiques face à l'évolution des textes de protection de la nature 86
Bibliographie 91

National laws on private collections: problems and solutions
Elina N. Moustaira... 93

Introduction... 93
The opacity of the art collecting activity 93
Art Galleries – Contemporary Art 94
Art Market 95
Art dealers - Collectors.. 95
Authenticity of Artworks 96
Auction houses.. 97

Donations - Tax evasion 99
Immunity of collections from suit or seizure 100
Artists' rights 102
Collecting archaeological material 104

LA PROTECTION PUBLIQUE DES COLLECTIONS PRIVÉES

Sous la présidence de Marina Schneider

La notion de collection en droit français
Mathilde Roellinger 109

I. Caractérisation de la collection privée par ses liens avec le collectionneur 110
1. Une protection au titre de l'œuvre de l'homme 110
2. Une protection de la collection privée par le droit d'auteur 111
II. Figure autonome de la collection, indépendante de son créateur 113
1. La collection protégée par la législation sur la circulation des biens culturels 113
2. Le classement à titre de monument historique des ensembles et des collections 114

The notion of private collection and its protection from an Italian perspective
Manlio Frigo 119

1. The Italian legislator's approach to art collections and collectors 119
2. Protection and enhancement of art collections 120
3. International circulation 121
4. Art collections and the issue of generation transfer 122
5. The generation transfer options under Italian law 123
5.1 Trusts 123
5.2 Foundations 123
5.3 Benefit companies 124

La protection publique des collections privées
Marie Cornu 127

1. L'affectation au public des collections privées 127
1.1 Le label Musée de France 128
1.2 Le label FRAC 131
2. La protection d'ensembles remarquables 134
2.1. Les assises ponctuelles d'un droit des collections 134
2.2. La protection des ensembles au titre des monuments historiques 136

MISES EN VALEUR ET ACCESSIBILITÉ DES COLLECTIONS

Sous la présidence de Manlio Frigo

L'accessibilité publique des collections privées
Marc-André Renold 143

Introduction 143
I. Les différents modes d'accessibilité publique des collections privées 144
A. La fondation 144
B. Le trust 145
C. Autres mécanismes 146
II. L'encouragement à l'accessibilité publique 152
A. Par décision populaire (le cas du Canton de Bâle) 152
B. Par décret législatif (le cas de la Jordanie) 153
C. Par l'incitation fiscale 154
III. Les freins à l'accessibilité publique 155
A. Les exigences du collectionneur 155
B. Le trafic illicite 157
C. Les spoliations 158
Conclusion 159

Interactions entre collections privées et secteur privé. Approche de droit français, Géraldine Goffaux Callebaut 161

I. La variété des structures utilisées pour accueillir les collections 164
A. Le choix premier des fondations 164
B. Le choix récent des fonds de dotation 166
II. L'adaptation des règles aux spécificités des collections 168
A. L'adaptation de l'objet à l'intérêt général 168
B. L'adaptation de la gouvernance 170

L'enrichissement des collections publiques avec transfert de propriété : dons et legs des collectionneurs
Apolline Sans 173

Introduction 173
I. Remise en contexte historique et juridique de la pratique des libéralités 175
II. Dons et legs, entre geste de philanthropie et « générosité calculée »..... 178
III. La réception des collections privées par les musées : une entrée sélective 180
Conclusion 183
Éléments de bibliographie 184

Les archives privées
Stéphane Duroy 187

I. Les protections des archives privées. 189
A. Les protections assurées par les propriétaires successifs 189
B. Les protections assurées par la puissance publique 191
C. La protection résultant d'un contrat de dépôt 194
II. L'entrée dans les collections publiques 196
A. Les modes d'acquisition à l'amiable 196
B. Les modes d'acquisition selon des procédés de contrainte 197
C. Le cas particulier des actions en revendication d'archives publiques en mains privées. 199

Acquérir, documenter, intéresser, publier : les missions du conservateur à la Fondation Gandur pour l'Art
Jean-Claude Gandur & Isabelle Tassignon 203

I. Accroître les collections 204
A. Acquisition et bonne pratique archéologique 204
B. Acquisition et bonne pratique scientifique 206
II. Documenter et préserver. 208
III. Construire l'intérêt public 209
A. Exposer 209
B. Communiquer 210
IV. Publier 211
Conclusion 213

La fiscalité française favorise-t-elle l'accès aux collections privées ?
Armelle Verjat 215

Les incitations fiscales à l'accès aux collections en mains privées 217
Enrichissement des collections publiques : l'exposition garantie ? 217
Création et maintien des collections privées : l'exposition favorisée 224
Les freins fiscaux à l'accès aux collections privées 231
Les musées privés soumis à la pression fiscale ? 232
La « peur du fisc » 239

Table des matières 245

Structures éditoriales du groupe L'Harmattan

L'Harmattan Italie
Via degli Artisti, 15
10124 Torino
harmattan.italia@gmail.com

L'Harmattan Hongrie
Kossuth l. u. 14-16.
1053 Budapest
harmattan@harmattan.hu

L'Harmattan Sénégal
10 VDN en face Mermoz
BP 45034 Dakar-Fann
senharmattan@gmail.com

L'Harmattan Cameroun
TSINGA/FECAFOOT
BP 11486 Yaoundé
inkoukam@gmail.com

L'Harmattan Burkina Faso
Achille Somé – tengnule@hotmail.fr

L'Harmattan Guinée
Almamya, rue KA 028 OKB Agency
BP 3470 Conakry
harmattanguinee@yahoo.fr

L'Harmattan RDC
185, avenue Nyangwe
Commune de Lingwala – Kinshasa
matangilamusadila@yahoo.fr

L'Harmattan Congo
67, boulevard Denis-Sassou-N'Guesso
BP 2874 Brazzaville
harmattan.congo@yahoo.fr

L'Harmattan Mali
ACI 2000 - Immeuble Mgr Jean Marie Cisse
Bureau 10
BP 145 Bamako-Mali
mali@harmattan.fr

L'Harmattan Togo
Djidjole – Lomé
Maison Amela
face EPP BATOME
ddamela@aol.com

L'Harmattan Côte d'Ivoire
Résidence Karl – Cité des Arts
Abidjan-Cocody
03 BP 1588 Abidjan
espace_harmattan.ci@hotmail.fr

Nos librairies en France

Librairie internationale
16, rue des Écoles
75005 Paris
librairie.internationale@harmattan.fr
01 40 46 79 11
www.librairieharmattan.com

Librairie des savoirs
21, rue des Écoles
75005 Paris
librairie.sh@harmattan.fr
01 46 34 13 71
www.librairieharmattansh.com

Librairie Le Lucernaire
53, rue Notre-Dame-des-Champs
75006 Paris
librairie@lucernaire.fr
01 42 22 67 13

www.ingramcontent.com/pod-product-compliance
Lightning Source LLC
LaVergne TN
LVHW050653051026
849532LV00002B/621